Contents

EQUITY:
Theory and Research

ELAINE WALSTER
University of Wisconsin

G. WILLIAM WALSTER
University of Wisconsin

ELLEN BERSCHEID
University of Minnesota

in collaboration with
WILLIAM AUSTIN, JANE TRAUPMANN, MARY K. UTNE

Allyn and Bacon, Inc.
Boston   London   Sydney   Toronto

Library of Congress Cataloging in Publication Data

Walster, Elaine Hatfield, 1937–
    Equity : theory and research.

    Bibliography: p.
    Includes index.
    1. Social psychology. 2. Social justice.
3. Social interaction. I. Walster, G. William,
1941–   joint author. II. Berscheid, Ellen, 1936–
joint author. III. Title.
HM251.W2658   301.1'01   77–22877
ISBN 0–205–05929–5

Dedicated to
Charles Hatfield
Eileen Kalahar Hatfield

Preface

Social psychologists are painfully aware that social psychology needs a general theory of social behavior; one that can integrate the many specialized mini-theories that exist. Until recently, social psychologists felt that the times were not yet right to try to develop one. Recently, however, researchers have begun to make some efforts in that direction.

Equity theory offers us the beginnings of such a general theory. Essentially, Equity theory deals with two questions: (1) What do people think is fair and equitable? and (2) How do they respond when they feel they are getting far more or far less from their relationships than they deserve? How do they react when they see their fellows reaping undeserved benefits—or enduring undeserved suffering?

Equity theory has been applied to predict people's reactions in four major areas of human interaction: Exploiter/Victim relationships, Philanthropist/Recipient relationships, Business Relationships, and Intimate Relationships. In chapters 3–7, we will chronicle the insights Equity theory gives us in these areas.

The chapters are written for the casual reader. They are lively and easy to read, sprinkled with cartoons and illustrations. The endnotes are addressed to the specialist. They provide an encyclopedic review of the more than 400 existing Equity studies. (Until the publication of *Equity: Theory and Research* this research remained scattered in various specialized journals.) The endnotes also provide documentation of the chapter's conclusions.

Civilized people have always been concerned with the nature of justice. In the future, as the resources of our planet become increasingly unable to adequately sustain the lives of its inhabitants, civilized people will be forced to become even more concerned. In chapter 8, we consider the perplexing questions that people in the year 2000 may have to face—and speculate as to their answers.

This book was completed while the two senior authors were Guest Professors at the Sonderforschungsbereich 24 in Mannheim, West Germany. We would like to thank Dr. Martin Irle, Director of the SFB, for his personal kindnesses and William Austin, Mary Ann Pate, Suzanne Ishmael, Jane Traupmann, and Mary Utne for keeping Equity research alive in our absence. In addition, we would like to thank Stacy Adams, George Homans, Bibb Latané, Melvin Lerner, Gerald Leventhal, Jane Piliavin, and Lauren Wispé for their reviews of the early drafts of this manuscript.

Finally, we would like to thank Darcy Abrahams for her wonderfully whimsical illustrations.

This research was supported in part by National Science Foundation grant GS30822, National Institute of Mental Health grant MH 26681, and the Graduate School of the University of Wisconsin (to Elaine Walster), Russell Sage Foundation grant, "Evaluative Decision Making with Analysis of Variance" (to G. William Walster), and National Science Foundation grant GS35157X (to Ellen Berscheid).

CHAPTER

1

Introduction

Scientists, by inclination and by training, tend to be argumentative, compulsive, and stubborn. When eminent authorities and common sense both dictate that the sun must revolve around the earth, young Keplers are always around to point out that the ancients' theories are wrong—and, besides, they've made a few calculation errors. To make matters worse, usually the young critics then insist on explicating *their* half-baked theories in agonizing detail. There is one thing, however, that conscientious social scientists can agree on—psychology desperately needs a general theory of social behavior.

Currently, social psychology comprises a myriad of elegant little "mini-theories." For example, social psychologists have used a variety of reinforcement theories, cognitive consistency theories, psycho-analytic theories, and exchange models to predict how men react to their fellows. Empirical evidence supports each of these mini-theories, at least some of the time.

What we need now is a general theory that integrates the limited mini-theories. The need for such a general theory becomes painfully evident each time a practical man approaches and asks for practical advice. Theorists' answers are usually very unsettling. They can only report what each mini-theory predicts and advise the practical man to expect a variety of incompatible outcomes. Such advice is not very helpful.

Although social psychologists agree that we desperately *need* a general theory of social behavior, they have, until recently, assumed that it is far too early to try to develop one. Recently, however, a number of optimistic—or foolhardy—theorists and researchers have begun to challenge this assumption. We, too, would argue that scientists can afford to be a little more foolhardy. Although it probably is not yet possible to develop an all-encompassing general theory, we should at least begin this critical task.

What needs to be done is obvious. If a theorist is to construct a general theory of social behavior, he must: (1) rigorously define his terms, (2) specify a few precisely stated propositions, (3) deduce hypotheses from these principles, and (4) test these derivations. (5) Then he can use the general theory to make recommendations concerning critical social problems.

OVERVIEW

Equity theory was developed in the hope of providing the glimmerings of the general theory social psychologists so badly need. It attempts to integrate the insights of reinforcement theory, cognitive consistency theory, psychoanalytic theory, and exchange theory.

In chapter 2 ("The Heart of Equity Theory"), we will review Equity theory. We will (1) provide precise definitions of Equity terms, (2) explicate the theory's four core propositions, and (3) briefly sketch the empirical evidence that gives us confidence in these propositions.

Researchers have used the Equity framework to generate predictions concerning four major areas of human interaction: (a) exploiter/victim relationships, (b) philanthropist/recipient relationships, (c) business relationships, and (d) intimate relationships. In chapters 3–6, we will chronicle the insights Equity theory gives us in these areas. In chapter 7 ("Confronting Major Theoretical Issues"), we will enumerate some major theoretical issues that Equity theorists and researchers confront. Finally, in chapter 8 ("The Year 2000: The Future of Equity Theory and Research"), we will attempt to foresee what research questions will intrigue tomorrow's researchers.

WHY EQUITY THEORY?

"What's *fair* is *fair*!" "She *deserves* better." "It's just not *right*!" "He can't get away with that: It's *illegal.*" "It's *unethical*!" "It's *unjust*!"

Such statements pervade our lives. Each constitutes a judgment of what is fair or unfair, equitable or inequitable, in a particular situation. To arrive at such judgments, we spend, as individuals and as a nation, a good deal of our time, effort, and money.

Some observers think this is curious. Why are we so concerned about solving the question "What is fair?" each time it arises? After all, life is essentially "unfair."

It does seem true that the human condition is threaded through and through with injustice. Fate does not dole out her blessings and curses in an egalitarian way. At this moment, one child, the son of an unknown father and an impoverished mother, is being born into a harsh world of hunger, filth, disease, and death; another, the son of loving and prosperous parents, is entering a world of warmth and comfort. Nature's storehouse of assets and liabilities seems to be distributed in a haphazard lottery; a lottery in which some must bear the most emotionally and physically crushing burdens in order to barely sustain life, while others are endowed with fate's most precious gifts.

Given nature's monumental inequities, it has struck some observers as strange that we humans so vigorously undertake a task that the gods did not even attempt: to administer justice in human affairs— to give everyone their "just desserts," a "fair shake," and "square deal"—"equity," as best we mortals can define and deliver it.

But other observers (and in our society they are in a majority), do not find it at all curious that we are so determined in our quest for justice. They believe it is a proper, even a special, duty of civilized people to be concerned with the question, "What is fair?" They point out how vital the answer is to each of us. Perhaps more often than we like to think about, society's answer determines not just *how* each of us shall live, but even *whether* we shall live at all.

Questions of fairness are likely to become even more frequent in the future, as the resources of our planet become less and less adequate to sustain the lives of those who inhabit it. The lives of not just a few individuals, but of whole nations, will rest on the way a handful of men solve the equation, "What is fair?" Perhaps this is why even tentative answers to some of these questions are already of great interest and debate. How much profit is it fair for American farmers to make on a sale of wheat to the U.S.S.R.? Is it fair for the American people to lower their standard of living a little to try to feed starving millions in Pakistan, India, or South America? Is it fair for the Arab oil-producing countries to form a cartel to get higher prices from the western countries for their scarce and valuable resource? Should we form a cartel to get higher prices on our scarce products?

The answers to such questions, according to economist Robert Heilbroner (1974) may decide the fate of the human race:

> Is there hope for man? . . . The outlook for man, I believe, is painful, difficult, perhaps desperate, and the hope that can be held out for his future prospect seems to be very slim indeed. . . .
>
> The external challenges can be succinctly reviewed. We are entering a period in which rapid population growth, the presence of obliterative weapons, and dwindling resources will bring international tensions to dangerous levels for an extended period. . . . Indeed, there seems to be no reason for these levels of danger to subside unless population equilibrium is achieved and some rough measure of equity reached in the distribution of wealth among nations. . . .
>
> Whether such an equitable arrangement can be reached—at least within the next several generations—is open to serious doubt. (pp. 22, 127)

But what is "equitable?" How do people conceive of the principles of justice, which have life-and-death consequences for us all? Why does it so frequently happen that what is fair and equitable in the eyes of one person, or one nation, is unjust and exploitative in the eyes of another? Does each person, or each nation, follow different rules when deciding questions of fairness? Do they follow different rules when deciding different questions? If so, what does this mean for each of us and for the future of mankind?

What, for example, are the consequences of our American belief that poverty can be avoided—or, if not avoided, overcome? That rich people, and rich nations, deserve, somehow, to be rich? That the poor probably deserve their fate; they simply have not exerted the imagination, the dedication, and the energy necessary to pull themselves up out of their backwardness? Or the American belief that American "know-how" and hard work are two inputs that *anyone* should take into account when deciding what outcomes we "deserve" to have? What happens when other people and other nations challenge our rules of fairness?

We are finding out. We are learning, for example, that much of the rest of the world does not share our happy assumption that American know-how and hard work entitle us to the lion's share of the world's resources. We are discovering that other cultures and peoples insist that the inputs *they* possess are critically important, and that they "deserve" to take our valuable resources. For example (Maynes, 1974):

> Consider the current energy crisis. For years, the United States has told developing countries the way to advance economically is through hard work, prudent investment, and administrative discipline. Yet in a few short weeks, the oil-producing countries, which we now concede had a case for some price increase, gain more by changing the rules of the game than they could have expected in a life-time of hard work. (p. 1)

Charles Maynes, Secretary of the Carnegie Endowment for International Peace, goes on to point out that, "No action in international affairs in the post-war era has brought home more clearly the importance of the rules of the game." (And he further observes that, "Ironically, accompanying the breakdown in the international rules of the game has been a comparable breakdown in the domestic rules of the game.") (p. 10)

But what *are* the rules of the game, which is fast becoming the only one in town? How *do* we decide what is equitable or inequitable? And, once we decide, what do we do about it? These are issues that social scientists have begun to address.

CHAPTER
2

The Heart of Equity Theory

Equity theory is a strikingly simple theory; it comprises four interlocking propositions:

> **PROPOSITION I:** Individuals will try to maximize their outcomes (where outcomes equal rewards minus costs).
>
> **PROPOSITION IIA:** Groups can maximize collective reward by evolving accepted systems for equitably apportioning resources among members. Thus, groups will evolve such systems of equity, and will attempt to induce members to accept and adhere to these systems. **PROPOSITION IIB:** Groups will generally reward members who treat others equitably, and generally punish (increase the costs for) members who treat others inequitably.
>
> **PROPOSITION III:** When individuals find themselves participating in inequitable relationships, they will become distressed. The more inequitable the relationship, the more distress individuals will feel.
>
> **PROPOSITION IV:** Individuals who discover they are in an inequitable relationship will attempt to eliminate their distress by restoring equity. The greater the inequity that exists, the more distress they will feel, and the harder they will try to restore equity.

Let us now explicate these crucial propositions:

PROPOSITION I: Individuals will try to maximize their outcomes.

Even the most contentious scientist would find it difficult to challenge our first proposition. Theories in a wide variety of disciplines rest on

FIGURE 2.1. "Individuals Will Try to Maximize Their Outcomes."

the assumption that "Man is selfish." Psychologists believe that behavior can be shaped by the careful application of reinforcements. Economists assume that individuals will purchase desired products at the lowest available price. Moral philosophers conclude that the ideal society can only be one which insures the "greatest good for the greatest number." Politicians contend that "Every man has his price." Equity theory, too, rests on the simple, but eminently safe, assumption that man is selfish.

> **PROPOSITION IIA:** Groups can maximize collective reward by evolving accepted systems for equitably apportioning rewards and costs among members. Thus, groups will evolve such systems of equity and will attempt to induce members to accept and adhere to these systems.

In Proposition II, Equity theory pushes into new territory. Most psychological theories treat men as if they were in isolation. They are not. Men are social creatures; they congregate in societies, surrounded by their fellows. And, all the fellows are eager to attain the same goal—to acquire all the good things in life. If any one individual were totally unrestrained in his pursuit of material benefits, his fellows would suffer, and they are unlikely to suffer in silence. His rivals are more likely to band together, pool their strength, and wrench back community resources.

Thomas Hobbes (1588–1679) (reprinted 1881) was one of the first philosophers to point out that if individuals were unregulated in their attempts to gain their own ends, the result would be the "War of all against all."

> Nature hath made men so equall, in the faculties of body, and mind; as that though there bee found one man sometimes manifestly stronger in body, or of quicker mind then another; yet when all is reckoned together, the difference between man, and man, is not so considerable, as that one man can thereupon claim himselfe any benefit, to which another may not pretend, as well as he.
>
> From this equality of ability, ariseth equality of hope in the attaining of our Ends. And therefore, if any two men desire the same thing, which neverthelesse they cannot both enjoy, they become enemies; and in the way to their End . . . endeavour to destroy, or subdue one an other.
>
> Hereby it is manifest, that during the time men live without a common Power to keep them all in awe, they are in that condition which is called Warre.
>
> In such condition, there is no place for Industry; because the fruit thereof is uncertain: and consequently no Culture of the Earth; no Navigation, nor use of the commodities that may be imported by Sea; no commodious Building; no Instruments of moving, and removing such things as require much force; no Knowledge in the face of the Earth; no account of Time; no Arts; no Letters; no Society; and which is worst of all, continuall feare, and danger of violent death; And the life of man, solitary, poore, nasty, brutish, and short. (pp. 82–85)

As philosophers, sociologists, and economists have observed,[1] eventually, even the dullest collection of individuals comes to realize that the only way to avoid continual violent warfare and to maximize their collective outcomes is by compromising. Eventually, they work out some rough and ready rules for regulating the distribution of valuable resources. Proposition IIA simply states that societies will act in their own self-interest and will hammer out a set of rules for allocating community resources.

The individual members of society want to possess all of society's resources themselves (Proposition I). How can the group induce its members to accept its equity rules? There is one way to control human behavior.

> **PROPOSITION IIB:** Groups will generally reward members who treat others equitably, and generally punish (increase the costs for) members who treat others inequitably.

The group can only be effective in inducing its fellows to behave equitably if it makes it more profitable for them to behave equitably than inequitably (see Proposition I). This arrangement allows both the individual and the collectivity to maximize their outcomes. Thus, Proposition IIB proposes that groups will insure the profitability of equitable behavior by rewarding members who treat others equitably and by punishing those who do not.

What Constitutes an Equitable Relationship?

Although all societies must develop some system for equitably apportioning resources among members, they differ startlingly in *what* they think is equitable. Some societies, for example, contend that "All men are created equal," and thus each one is entitled to an equal share of community resources. Some societies assume a prominent family lineage entitles one to large rewards; in brief, "He who has, gets." Other socialistic societies assert "To each according to his needs." Capitalistic societies assume that the more capital or effort one invests in an enterprise, the more community resources one deserves.

In spite of the fact that different societies have established strikingly different rules for partitioning their resources, we have found a single general principle to be useful in characterizing these diverse conceptions as to what is fair and equitable.

Definition of an "Equitable" Relationship

For the professional social scientist and the student of mathematics, this principle may be best expressed *via* a single formula. The social scientist feels it is critical to have a formal definition of equity. In this book, we will usually talk about cases of equity/inequity that are so clear-cut that anyone—an outside observer or the participants themselves—could agree that the relationship was "fair" or "unfair." For the professional scientist, obviously, this isn't good enough. He needs some formal rule which, in borderline cases, will enable him to calculate

9

whether a relationship is equitable or not. In this section we will provide just such a formula.[2] (An elaboration of the assumptions and rationale underlying this equity definition appears in Appendixes I and II.)

For those students of human behavior who barely scraped through Algebra II, however, we hasten to offer some reassurance. If, from the subsequent discussion, you can get a general sense of what we mean by Equity, that will be enough. If you can get (1) a general sense of the way Equity theorists use such terms as *Scrutineer, Inputs, Outcomes, Net Gains,* and *Relative Gains,* and (2) a rough and ready idea of how Equity theorists have used the Equity formula, the rest of the book can be easily understood.

Definitional Formula

An equitable relationship exists if a person *scrutinizing* the relationship concludes that all participants are receiving equal *relative gains* from the relationship; i.e., where:

$$\frac{(O_A - I_A)}{(|I_A|)^{k_A}} = \frac{(O_B - I_B)}{(|I_B|)^{k_B}}$$

I_A and I_B designate a scrutineer's perception of Person A and B's *Inputs.*

[$|I_A|$ and $|I_B|$ designate the *absolute value* of their Inputs (i.e., the perceived value of their inputs, disregarding sign).][3]

O_A and O_B designate the scrutineer's perception of Person A and B's *Outcomes.*

The exponents k_A and k_B take on the value +1 or −1, depending on the sign of A and B's inputs and A and B's gains (Outcomes − Inputs). [k_A = sign $(I_A) \times$ sign $(O_A - I_A)$ and k_B = sign $(I_B) \times$ sign $(O_B - I_B)$.][4]

What does this mean?

Definition of Terms

Scrutineer: The *scrutineer* is simply the person who is examining any given relationship, in order to determine if it is fair or unfair. The scrutineer may be an outside observer or either of the participants. As we observed earlier, scrutineers commonly disagree about what constitutes equity or inequity.

Inputs (I_A or I_B) are defined as "the participant's contributions

FIGURE 2.2. *"Definitional Formula*: An Equitable Relationship Exists
if a Person *Scrutinizing* the Relationship Concludes that All Participants
Are Receiving Equal *Relative Gains* from the Relationship."

to the exchange, which are seen (by a scrutineer) as entitling him to reward *or* cost." The inputs that a participant contributes to a relationship can be either assets, which entitle him to rewards, or liabilities, which entitle him to suffer costs (or punishments).

In different settings, people consider different inputs to be relevant. For example in industrial settings, businessmen assume that such hard assets as "capital" or "manual labor" entitle a man to reward. Liabilities such as "incompetence" or "disloyalty" entitle him to costs. In social settings, friends assume that social assets such as beauty or kindness entitle one to reward. Social liabilities, such as drunkenness or cruelty, entitle one to costs.

Once a scrutineer senses what participants have put *into* their relationship, he can gauge whether or not they are getting the outcomes they deserve from the relationship.

Outcomes (O_A or O_B) are defined as "the positive *and* negative consequences that a scrutineer perceives a participant has received in the course of his relationship with another." The participant's outcomes, then, are equal to the *rewards* he obtains from the relationship minus the *costs* that he incurs.

Net Gains: Participants net gains (or losses) are simply their outcomes from the relationship minus their inputs to the relationship. Person A's net gain is thus ($O_A - I_A$); Person B's net gain is ($O_B - I_B$). A participant's net gain will be positive if he is reaping a profit from the relationship (i.e., if $O > I$). (The more O exceeds I, the greater the profit.) His net gain will be zero if he is breaking even (i.e., if $O = I$). His net gain will be negative if he is suffering a loss from the relationship $O < I$). (The more O falls short of I, the greater his loss.)

Net Gain gives us some critical information. From the sign and the magnitude of this measure, we can tell how "profitable" a relationship is to each of the participants.

Now that we've defined inputs, outcomes, and net gain, it is easy to understand the statement that "an equitable relationship exists if the person scrutinizing the relationship concludes that:

$$\frac{(O_A - I_A)}{(|I_A|)^{k_A}} = \frac{(O_B - I_B)}{(|I_B|)^{k_B}} \text{,,5}$$

If we were asked to say, in a nutshell, what principles the equity formula expresses, what would we say? Actually, the formula is based on two fundamental principles:

The Nature of the Person. It seems fair that the more a person contributes to a relationship, the more he should profit from it (i.e., the greater his Inputs into the relationship, the greater his Net Gain, i.e., Outcomes minus Inputs, should be).

The Nature of the Situation.   One must recognize that what a person can get out of *any* relationship varies. Sometimes times are good; a person makes the most minimal of contributions to a relationship and reaps an enormous profit. Sometimes things are so-so; one gets out of a relationship exactly what one puts into it—no more and no less. Sometimes times are bad; a person gives and gives to a relationship and reaps only losses.

Under these varying conditions, the following things seem equitable:

1. *Times are good:*   If Person *A* is reaping a profit from a relationship, it seems only fair that his partner should reap some profit, too. (Of course, the participants may deserve very different amounts of profit.) For example, in good times, if Person *A,* who has contributed a slightly positive Input, reaps a huge reward, his partner, who has contributed a large negative Input, should reap only the most minimal of profits.

2. *Times are so-so:*   Each person should get out of the relationship just about what he puts into it. Neither partner should reap a profit nor suffer a loss.

3. *Times are hard:*   If one person is suffering a loss from the relationship, it seems only fair that his partner should suffer some loss, too. (Of course, participants may deserve very different amounts of loss.) For example, in hard times, if Person *A,* who has contributed a slightly positive Input, suffers a large loss, his partner, who has contributed a large negative Input, should suffer the most horrendous of losses.

Let's see how this Equity formula would operate in practice. Suppose the Department of the Interior hired two students, Art Goodman and Bob Ramsey, to study the Menominee Indians' economic aspirations. The men agreed to spend forty hours apiece contacting and interviewing the Menominees. Art's contacts were a disaster. He was arrogant and tactless. The Indians complained about his rudeness to the Tribal Council and to the Department of the Interior. The Council declared Art *persona non grata,* and threw him off the reservation. Bob's interviews went enormously well. The Indiana treated him warmly and answered all of his questions. In the end, the Department of the Interior concluded that, all in all, Art contributed less than nothing to the project (his Inputs were evaluated at $I_A = -2$). Bob

contributed a great deal (I_B = +5). Both men agreed with this evaluation.

The Menominee Indian study was published. The Society for the Study of Social Issues (SSSI) was so impressed by the students' work that they awarded each of them a $1,000 prize. This award was valued at +20 units by both Art and Bob (O_A = +20; O_B = +20).

According to Equity theory, since Art's work was far inferior to Bob's, and yet both men received identical outcomes, Art should feel "overbenefited" while Bob should feel "exploited."

$$\frac{(O_{Art} - I_{Art})}{(|I_{Art}|)^{k_A}} = \frac{20 - (-2)}{(|-2|)^{(-1)(+1)}} = 22 \times 2 = 44.00$$

[k_{Art} = (−1)(+1), since the sign I_A = (−) and the sign ($O_A - I_A$) = (+).]

$$\frac{(O_{Bob} - I_{Bob})}{(|I_{Bob}|)^{k_B}} = \frac{20 - (5)}{(|5|)^{(+1)(+1)}} = \frac{15}{5} = 3.00$$

[k_{Bob} = (+1) since the sign I_B = (+) and the sign ($O_B - I_B$) = (+).]

From these calculations, it is clear that Art's relative gain (his net gain relative to his inputs) is greater than Bob's relative gain (his net gain relative to his inputs). It is the equality or inequality in relative gains that determines whether or not a relationship is equitable.

According to Equity theory, the Department of Interior and the men should feel things were "fair," only if the collaborators (who made markedly different contributions to the project) received mark-edly different net gains. For example, everyone might feel things were fair if Art had received less reward for his efforts (say a miserly −.5 units of reward), while Bob received the standard 20 units of reward.

$$\frac{(O_{Art} - I_{Art})}{(|I_{Art}|)^{k_A}} = \frac{-.5 - (-2)}{(|-2|)^{(-1)(+1)}} = 1.5 \times 2 = 3.00$$

$$\frac{(O_{Bob} - I_{Bob})}{(|I_{Bob}|)^{k_B}} = \frac{20 - (5)}{(|5|)^{(+1)(+1)}} = 3.00$$

Alternatively, they might also have felt things were fair if Art had received the standard 20 units of reward for his efforts, but Bob had received more (say a generous +225 units of reward).

$$\frac{(O_A - I_A)}{(|I_A|)^{k_A}} = \frac{20 - (-2)}{(|-2|)^{(-1)(+1)}} = 22 \times 2 = 44.00$$

$$\frac{(O_B - I_B)}{(|I_B|)^{k_B}} = \frac{225 - (5)}{(|5|)^{(+1)(+1)}} = \frac{220}{5} = 44.00$$

Thus, Art's relative gains = Bob's relative gains.

Who Decides Whether a Relationship Is Equitable?

In Propositions IIA and IIB, we argued that societies develop norms of equity and teach these systems to their members. Thus, in any society there will be a *general* consensus as to what constitutes an "equitable relationship." In the end, however, equity is in the eye of the beholder. Ultimately, the scrutineer's perception of how equitable Art and Bob's relationship is will depend upon the *scrutineer's* assessment of the value and relevance of the students' inputs and outcomes. For example, it is likely that the Menominee Indians, the Department of the Interior, SSSI, Art, and Bob, even after prolonged negotiation with one another, might not always agree completely as to the value and relevance of various inputs and outcomes. For example, when the Department of the Interior scrutinized Art/Bob's relationship, they considered Art's "boorishness" to be a negative input (−1). Art may well see things quite differently. Art might insist that his "frankness" with the Indians is a positive input (+1) entitling him to reward.

If scrutineers assess participants' inputs and outcomes differently, and it is likely that they will, inevitably they will show some disagreements as to whether or not a given relationship is equitable.

THE CONSEQUENCES OF EQUITABLE/INEQUITABLE BEHAVIOR

Some critics of Equity theory have scoffed at the proposal that society induces its members to behave equitably—voluntarily. These critics insist that people will grab everything they can get. We agree. We acknowledge (Proposition I) that man is motivated by self-interest. We agree that each of us would monopolize resources if we knew we would not be caught and punished. But the point is that we *do* know; society has taught all of us, albeit painfully, that if we behave equitably we will be rewarded; if we consistently try to snatch more benefits than we deserve we will get caught and punished. We soon learn that the most profitable way to be selfish is to be "fair."

> Witness the reasoning of Thrasymachus and Glaucon on the nature of justice in the Platonic Dialogues. "Men revile injustice, not because they fear to do it, but because they fear to suffer it," states Thrasymachus. And Glaucon drives the point home in the famous parable of Gyges' ring. The moral is plain. Only fear of reprisal stands between every man and the gratification of his lust and appetite for power. Is it seriously suggested, Glaucon asks Socrates, that any man who could steal with impunity, ravish his neighbours' womenfolk, kill or set free his neighbours at will, would refrain from doing so

through a love of justice! When men act justly, either they have not been put in the way of temptation, or they do so under compulsion out of fear of the consequences of acting otherwise, never willingly.* (p. 147)

For some reason, Equity critics have often become confused on this point. They forget that Proposition I stressed the fact that individuals try to maximize their own rewards—*period.* For some reason, readers have assumed that the laboriously learned principle that one must behave equitably, or suffer, somehow gains a life of its own. They assume we are arguing that if the world were to change drastically tomorrow, and it became a more profitable strategy to be totally selfish at all times, people would tend to plod along, behaving equitably, in violation of their own self-interest. This is not our belief. Hobbes (1588–1679) (reprinted 1958) aptly phrased the necessity for societies to reinforce their norms, including their norms of equity, with sanctions: "Covenants without the sword are but words and no strength to secure a man at all." (p. 128) It is only because individuals can maximize their outcomes by behaving equitably (and usually they can) that they do so.[6]

There is some evidence that individuals evidently do generally feel that it is in their best interest to act fairly, for they generally do so. Individuals who secure more reward than they know they deserve, voluntarily surrender their unearned benefits to their deprived partners. Individuals who secure less reward than they deserve, quickly demand additional benefits.[7]

In spite of the evidence that people generally do behave equitably, we must remember that, on occasion, people should perceive that it is far more profitable to be selfish than to be equitable. And, *on those occasions,* they should behave selfishly.[8] If one wished to explicitly recognize this fact, he might wish to rephrase Proposition I ("Individuals will try to maximize their outcomes") as follows:

PROPOSITION I: COROLLARY 1: So long as individuals perceive they can maximize their outcomes by behaving equitably, they will do so. Should they perceive that they can maximize their outcomes by behaving inequitably, they will do so.

Occasionally, then, an individual should decide that he can maximize his outcomes by violating the laws of equity. On these occasions, how

*From *The Psychology of Power,* by Ronald V. Sampson. Copyright © 1965 by Ronald V. Sampson. Reprinted by permission of Pantheon Books, a Division of Random House, Inc.

would Equity theory expect the socialized individual to react? Equity theorists would expect the person to behave inequitably, but to feel badly about it. These predictions follow from Proposition I (men will try to maximize their outcomes) and Proposition II. Proposition II points out that society punishes those who are caught behaving inequitably. Children and adults learn, again and again, that the man who dares to take too much, and gets caught, can expect venomous retaliation; the man who accepts too little is not only deprived of material benefits, but he may reap derision as well.[9]

 Proposition III explicitly recognizes that as a consequence of inevitable and repeated socialization experiences, individuals who find themselves in inequitable relationships come to experience distress.

> **PROPOSITION III:** When individuals find themselves participating in inequitable relationships, they become distressed. The more inequitable the relationship, the more distress individuals feel.

Compelling experimental evidence supports Proposition III's contention that individuals participating in inequitable relationships do feel distress. And, they feel distress regardless of whether they are the *victims* or the *beneficiaries* of inequity.

 For example, Austin and Walster (1974) conducted an experiment to determine how students would react when they were over-rewarded, equitably treated, or deprived of the salary that they deserved. Students entered the experiment expecting to be paid two dollars an hour. During the experiment they proofread materials for their supervisor; they read diverse material and circled all the spelling errors they encountered. After they had finished their task, their supervisor told them they had done a good job; they had caught almost all the spelling errors. Their supervisor confirmed the fact that he planned to give them two dollars. However, when students received their pay envelopes, they learned that the supervisor had overpaid them (given them three dollars), equitably paid them (given them two dollars), or had underpaid them (given them only one dollar).

 Students then filled out a variety of questionnaires. Among these questionnaires was the *Mood Adjective Check List*. The *MACL* consists of thirty adjectives that describe six moods. This scale enables one to determine how contented or distressed students were by their equitable or inequitable treatment.

 The results provide firm support for Proposition III. Equitably treated students were far more content than were either unrewarded or overrewarded subjects. This last finding is an especially convincing answer to critics who have agreed that inequity would be disturbing to underrewarded people, but have stoutly insisted that inequity would not be disturbing to overrewarded people.

Evidence also exists to support the contention that the greater the inequity, the more distress participants will feel.[10]

The final proposition of Equity theory simply asserts that when people feel distress, they are likely to try to alleviate it.

> **PROPOSITION IV:** Individuals who discover they are in an inequitable relationship attempt to eliminate their distress by restoring equity. The greater the inequity that exists, the more distress they feel, and the harder they try to restore equity.

Proposition IV proposes that individuals who are distressed by their inequitable relations will try to restore equity to their relationship in order to eliminate their distress.

There are only two ways that a person can restore equity to a relationship: (1) he can restore *actual* equity to the relationship, or (2) he can restore *psychological* equity to the relationship.

Restoring Actual Equity. A person can restore *actual equity* by actually altering his own or his partner's relative gains in appropriate ways. For example, imagine that an unskilled laborer discovers that the contractor has been paying him less than the minimum wage. Theoretically he can reestablish actual equity in four different ways: (1) he can lower his own inputs (e.g., he can start to "fool around" on the job); (2) he can raise his own outcomes (e.g., he can start to steal equipment from the company); (3) he can raise his employer's inputs (e.g., he can make mistakes so that the contractor will have to work far into the night undoing what he has done); or (4) he can lower his employer's outcomes (e.g., he can damage company equipment).[11]

Restoring Psychological Equity. A person can restore *psychological equity* to a relationship by distorting reality in appropriate ways. He can try to convince himself that the inequitable relationship is, in fact, equitable. Suppose once again, for example, that the unskilled laborer becomes uncomfortably aware that he is being underpaid, but is also aware that there is nothing he can do about it. The underpaid and overworked laborer could try to convince himself that his relationship with his employer is equitable. He can restore psychological equity to their relationship in four different ways: (1) he can minimize his inputs ("After all, I don't have very much social polish, education, or get-up-

and-go"); (2) he can exaggerate his outcomes ("This kind of work gives me a chance to see my family, and in the end, the family is what really matters"); (3) he can exaggerate his employer's inputs ("Without my boss's know-how, the company would fall apart and I would have no job"); or (4) he can minimize his employer's outcomes ("The tension on his job is probably giving him an ulcer").

Summary

Equity theorists concur that men try to maximize their outcomes (Proposition I). A group of individuals can maximize their total outcomes by devising an equitable system for sharing resources. Thus groups try to induce members to behave equitably, i.e., they try to insure that all participants receive equal relative gains:

$$\frac{(O_A - I_A)}{(|I_A|)^{k_A}} = \frac{(O_B - I_B)}{(|I_B|)^{k_B}}$$

They can do this in only one way: by making it more profitable to be "fair" than to be greedy. They reward members who behave equitably and punish members who behave inequitably (Proposition II). When socialized individuals find themselves enmeshed in an inequitable relationship, they experience distress (Proposition III). They can, and do, reduce their distress either by restoring actual equity or by restoring psychological equity to their relationship (Proposition IV).

ENDNOTES

1. See, for example, Blau (1964), Chavannes (reported in Knox, 1963), de Jong (1952), Hobbes (1588–1679, reprinted 1881), Homans (1958, 1961), Levi-Strauss (1949), Locke (1632–1704, reprinted 1821), Novicow (1917), Simmel (1900), and Smith (1723–1790, reprinted 1892).

2. In Appendix 1, we list several features that we think *any* Equity formula should possess. There may be other "Equity" formulae that could satisfy these constraints. Currently, we think that the definitional formula we have chosen makes the most sense. However, we hope that subsequent researchers will revise and refine this formula.

3. There is one restriction on inputs: the smallest absolute input must be $\geqslant 1$, i.e., $|I_A|$ and $|I_B|$ must both be $\geqslant 1$.

4. The exponent's effect is simply to change the way relative gains are computed: if $k = +1$ then we have $(O - I)/|I|$, but if $k = -1$ then we have $|I| \cdot (O - I)$. Without the exponent k, the formula would yield meaningless results when $I < O$ and $O - I > 0$, or $I > O$ and $O - I < 0$. Mathematically sophisticated students may find the detailed description of the logic underlying the Equity formula (which is printed in Appendix 1) helpful.

5. There is only one restriction on this formula: $|I|$ must be > 1.

6. For evidence in support of the contention that Proposition I supersedes all others, see Burgess and Gregory (1971).

7. See, for example, Leventhal, Allen, and Kemelgor (1969) or Marwell, Ratcliffe, and Schmitt (1969).

8. There are two reasons why we would expect a participant in a relationship to behave in a way that he acknowledges is inequitable. First, an individual should behave inequitably whenever he is confident that in a given instance he can maximize his outcomes by doing so. Second, it is to the individual's long-range benefit to behave inequitably now and then. Only by varying the equitableness of his behavior can a participant ascertain whether or not sanctions against inequity are still operating. (Only by occasionally testing limits can one discover if the world has changed.) Thus, an individual can maximize his total outcomes if he tests equity norms now and then.

9. Data from Brown (1968) indicate that victims do experience "retaliation" distress." Brown found that when subjects were informed that others thought they had been "suckered," they were more likely to show face-saving behaviors. Brown interpreted his data as evidence of subjects' desire to bolster their self-esteem *and* to avoid future exploitation.

10. See Leventhal, Allen, and Kemelgor (1969), Leventhal and Bergman (1969), and Austin, McGinn, and Traupmann (submitted).

11. The ingenious ways individuals contrive to bring equity to inequitable relationships are documented by Adams (1963a).

CHAPTER
3

Equity Theory and Exploiter/ Victim Relationships

Researchers have applied the Equity framework to four major areas of human interaction: (a) exploiter/victim relationships, (b) philanthropist/recipient relationships, (c) business relationships, and (d) intimate relationships. Let us review this voluminous research.

APPLICATIONS OF EQUITY THEORY TO EXPLOITER/VICTIM RELATIONSHIPS

People have always been concerned with promoting perfect justice. It is not surprising, then, that early Equity theorists, who *could* have begun by investigating any of the Equity propositions, in fact, focused on a single question: "How do people respond when they treat, and are treated, fairly versus unfairly?" It may be that most people, most of the time, behave equitably. What they wanted to know was: "What happens when they *don't*?"

Equity theorists began by attempting to determine whether or not Equity theory could predict reactions in "exploitative" exchanges; exchanges in which one participant takes far more than he deserves while his hapless partner gets far less.

Theorists found that it is easy to analyze exploitative relations within the Equity framework.

First, they defined terms. They defined an *exploiter* or *harm-doer* as "a person who commits an act that causes his relative gains to exceed his partners's." The *exploited* or the *victim* is "a person whose relative gains fall short of his partner's."

Let us now consider how exploiters, the exploited, and outside agencies might be expected to react to inequity.

REACTIONS OF THE EXPLOITER

Distress

According to Equity theory (Proposition III), any time an individual takes more than he deserves, he should feel distress. Compelling evidence exists to support the contention that an individual does feel intense distress after exploiting others. Different theorists label this distress in different ways: some theorists label it "guilt"; others call it "fear of retaliation"; still others label it "dissonance," "empathy," or "conditioned anxiety." Basically, however, such distress is presumed to arise from two sources: fear of retaliation and threatened self-esteem. Presumably, both retaliation distress and self-concept distress have their roots in the socialization process.

Retaliation Distress. Children are often punished if they are caught injuring others. Soon they come to experience conditioned anxiety when they harm another, or even contemplate doing so. (Aronfreed, 1961, 1964, provides a description of the development of conditioned anxiety in children.) By the time the normal person reaches adulthood, we experience some conditioned anxiety whenever we harm another. *How much* anxiety we experience in a given situation will depend, in part, on how similar the stimuli associated with our exploitative act are to those stimuli associated with previous punishments, and on the magnitude and timing of those previous punishments.

When we perform an exploitative act, we often experience vague distress even though we have no realistic basis for doing so. In spite of the fact that we performed our deed in complete secrecy, we have a vague fear that "somehow" someone will find out. This phenomenon is not really so surprising. As children, when we were certain that our harmdoing was not observed by anyone, we were often startled to find that our sophisticated parents "somehow" discerned even our best concealed acts. And, even if they didn't, God did. As children, most of us received religious training which convinced us that an omniscient

God observes and records each wickedly inequitable act. Presumably, we'd pay for them in the end.

It is no wonder, then, that even when we adults commit trangressions in complete privacy, we uneasily fear that "somehow" someone will detect and publicize our misdeeds.

Exploiters may label the conditioned anxiety that they experience after harming others as fear that the victim, the victim's sympathizers, legal agencies, or even God, will restore equity to the exploiter/victim relationship by punishing the exploiter.

Self-concept Distress. Harmdoing often generates a second kind of discomfort: self-concept distress. In all societies, nearly everyone accepts the ethical principle that "One should be fair and equitable in his dealings with others."[1] Exploiting another violates the normal person's ethical principles and conflicts with his self-expectations. Thus, when the normal individual violates his own standards he experiences self-concept distress.

In arguing that the "normal" individual accepts norms of "fairness," we are *not* arguing that everyone internalizes exactly the same code, internalizes it to the same extent, and follows that code without deviation. Juvenile delinquents and confidence men, for example, often *seem* to behave as if the exploitation of others was completely consonant with their self-expectations. Evidence suggests, however, that even deviants do internalize society's standards of fairness, at least to some extent. They may repeatedly violate such standards for financial or social gain, but such violations do seem to cause at least minimal distress. Exploitation evidently causes deviants enough discomfort that they spend time and effort trying to convince others that their behavior is "fair." Anecdotal evidence on these points comes from interviews with confidence men[2] and delinquents.[3]

The distress that arises when one performs unethical or dissonant acts has been discussed in great detail by guilt theorists and by cognitive dissonance theorists.[4]

Experimental Evidence for Propositions III and IV. According to Equity theory: (1) A person should feel distinctly uncomfortable when he is overbenefited. (2) The *more* he is overbenefited, the more uncomfortable he should be. (3) The more distressed he is, the harder he should work to restore equity.

A person will feel distress when he is overbenefited. There is some evidence that individuals feel uneasy when they receive more than they deserve. Austin and Walster (1974) recruited students to participate in a psychological study of decision making. One student (who was actually an experimental confederate) was assigned to be the decision maker; the two real students were assigned to be workers. The workers worked at identical tasks, and performed identically well. The decision maker was then asked to decide how much each worker deserved. Since they performed equally well, the workers naturally assumed they would each be paid two dollars. For some "unknown" reason, however, the decision maker overpaid some of the students (i.e., gave them three dollars) while paying the others equitably (i.e., gave them two dollars). The authors predicted, and found, that overpaid individuals were more distressed cognitively and emotionally than their equitably paid counterparts.

The more a person is overbenefited, the more uncomfortable he will be, and thus, *the harder he will try to restore equity.* There is some indirect evidence to support the notion that the more one exploits another, the more distressed the overbenefited will be. Brock and Buss (1964) asked students if they were willing to assist them in a learning experiment. The researchers made it clear that students were certainly not obligated to help. It was the student's job to shock a fellow student, either mildly or painfully, each time he made a learning error. Needless to say, the more the student assistant was required to shock his fellow students, the more guilty he felt. Paradoxically, the more he shocked his partner, and the more guilty he felt, the more likely he was to insist the supervisor "made him do it."

Lerner and Simmons (1966) found that the more one allows another to suffer, the more one will denigrate the hapless victim. Lerner and Matthews (1967) concluded that the more responsible subjects feel for another's suffering, the more they will denigrate the victim. If we assume that a harmdoer will be especially distressed when he is obviously responsible for another's suffering, or when his victim suffers a great deal, these findings are consistent with Propositions III and IV.

Restoration of Equity

Theoretically, an anxious person could be taught to perform *any* given action that reduces his anxiety. Aronfreed (1961) has demonstrated that, indeed, in practice, harmdoers have learned to reduce their anxiety in a wide variety of ways: uneasy transgressors may find relief by confessing their sins, in self-criticism, by apologizing and making reparation to their victim, or in promising to modify their future behavior. Two classes of responses seem to occur most commonly, however (perhaps because they reduce the exploiter's anxiety most effectively). There is compelling evidence to support the contention (Proposition IV) that participants involved in inequitable relations try to eliminate their distress by restoring either actual or psychological equity to their relationship.

Restoration of Actual Equity

Compensation. Exploiters can restore actual equity to the exploiter/ victim relationship in a straightforward way: they can *compensate* their victims. When we think of "compensation" we usually envision acts designed to increase the victim's outcomes. However, one can also "compensate" a victim by allowing him to lower his inputs. The underpaid and overworked secretary, for example, may be encouraged to "take Monday off" by her uneasy boss.

Cynics such as Junius have acidly observed that even "a death bed repentence seldom reaches to restitution." Such pessimism is not always warranted. Recent studies verify the fact that harmdoers often do voluntarily compensate their victims.[5]

One unusually realistic experiment was conducted by Brock and Buss (1966). The experimenter asked students to perform "a simple motor learning test." He told them to light ten lights by pressing a series of buttons, in the right order, and then turn them off. (He cautioned them to press the buttons carefully, since the apparatus was rather fragile, and he had all his research money tied up in it.) The subject dutifully began pressing the buttons but "somehow" broke the machine. (Actually, of course, the experimenter had designed the machine so that it would break when a crucial button was pushed.) How much the student's "carelessness" damaged the machine (and presumably the experimenter's project) was randomly varied. Half of the time (in the Low Damage condition) when the student pressed the button, a loud "pop" occurred. In the High Damage condition, the critical button press set off a loud, startling "band," a whistle began to wail, and swirling clouds of thick, white smoke began to pour out through vents in the side of the apparatus. This smoke soon filled the air. Inevitably, the distraught students apologized.

As the distressed student packed up to leave the experiment, the experimenter asked if he would do him a favor. (This request was really designed to see how eager subjects in the various conditions would be to make restitution.) The experimenter said that he was circulating a petition stating: "The tuition at Ohio State University should be doubled to $250 in order to improve the quality of the faculty and the physical condition of the university." He asked the student if he would sign. Now, under normal conditions, no student in his right mind advocates raising tuition. So, not surprisingly, when students believed they had done only slight damage to the experimenter's machine, they were reluctant or totally unwilling to sign. However, when students believed they had done extensive damage, more than 50 percent of them were willing to sign the experimenter's petition.

Self-Deprivation. Theoretically, an exploiter can restore actual equity to the exploiter/victim relationship by using a second strategy: *self-deprivation.* The exploiter could voluntarily reduce his own relative gains.

The anecdotal and clinical literature provide support for the notion that individuals sometimes do react to the commission of harmful acts by administering punishment to themselves or by seeking punishment from others. Indeed, Sarnoff (1962, p. 351) has suggested that "punishment is the only kind of response that is sufficient to reduce the tension of guilt."

However, only one of several attempts to demonstrate self-punishment in the laboratory has been successful.

Wallington (1973) asked: How will a transgressor handle his feelings of distress and guilt when he finds it is not possible either to make actual restitution or to justify his own behavior? She proposed that: "when these responses are not available, the wrongdoer may even punish himself."

Wallington tested her hypothesis in an ingenious experiment. In the Transgression condition, a student was kept waiting for a test. While he was waiting around, a "fellow student" who had just finished the test dropped by. He began describing the test and reviewing the questions he thought he had gotten right or wrong. In the No-transgression condition, the "fellow student" dropped in, but did not discuss the test. Shortly thereafter, the experimenter picked up the student, took him to the testing room and started to explain the test. She asked the boys in both the Transgression and No-transgression conditions if they had heard anything about the test. Without exception, the students insisted they had not. The experimenter then administered the test. Clearly, the Non-transgressors, who were never tempted to cheat, had nothing to feel guilty about. The Transgressors did. Wallington asked: Will the Transgressors, suffering from guilt, be unusually masochistic? Wallington assessed Transgressing versus Non-transgressing boys' eagerness to injure themselves in a straightforward way: The boys were allowed to "try" a few electric shocks to see how they felt. Presumably no one would· ever know how much shock the boys took. As predicted, Transgressing boys exhibited far greater self-aggression than did Non-transgressing boys.

We have assumed that individuals prefer to maximize their rewards whenever possible (Proposition I). In view of this, the finding that self-deprivation is not a popular strategy for equalizing relations with others is not surprising.

Retaliation. Of course, a victim may take matters into his own hands and "get even" with his exploiter.

Cultural common law is inconsistent as to whether or not a victim *should* retaliate against his tormentor. On one hand, tradition encourages victims to take appropriate revenge. The *Code of Hammurabi* (codified in 2250 B.C.) sanctioned "An eye for an eye and a tooth for a tooth" as the code of justice. (In Harper, 1904, p. 73)

> If a man destroy the eye of another man, they shall destroy his eye.
>
> If one break a man's bone, they shall break his bone.

On the other hand, a variety of religious codes reject the notion that revenging man is ever justified. For example, Matthew 5:38–41 says:

> You have heard that it was said, "An eye for an eye and a tooth for a tooth." But I say to you, Do not resist one who is evil. But if anyone strikes you on the right cheek, turn to him the other also; and if anyone would sue you and take your coat, let him have your cloak as well; and if anyone forces you to go one mile, go with him two miles.

Although moralists cannot agree as to whether or not men should seek revenge, it is obvious that men often do "retaliate." We have in recent years witnessed several ways in which groups of society's victims have responded: rioting, sniping at police and firemen, looting, burning, destroying. Their intent is clear in Equity terms: if I can't get more, you'll have less.

What happens when the exploited seek revenge? Theorists and the existing data suggest that the wrongdoer's interpretation of the retaliatory act will be a crucial determinant of his response.

Legant and Mettee (1973) point out that exploiters are often uncertain as to whether or not they have treated another person unfairly. They argue that a person's perception of whether or not he has done any harm may be dramatically influenced by the victim's

FIGURE 3.1. (Copyright © 1976 King Features Syndicate. Reprinted by permission.)

response. Consider, for example, the case of the student who is hired to serve as an experimenter and to shock a fellow subject each time he makes a mistake. Should the student-experimenter feel guilty? Proud of contributing to science? Confident that any student would have done what he did? Legant and Mettee argue that the student-experimenter's perception of the situation is bound to be influenced by the learner's response. If the learner is enraged and attempts to retaliate, he makes it clear that *he* thinks the student-experimenter is responsible for his suffering, and that he suffered intensely. Under these conditions, the student-experimenter may agree. On the other hand, the harmdoer might reasonably interpret the situation in quite a different way if the learner stoically volunteers to continue suffering. Under these conditions, the student-experimenter may refuse to accept responsibility for the victim's suffering, feel that the suffering was trivial, or conclude that the victim has forgiven him. Thus, the authors argue, a harmdoer's perception of a given interaction may be markedly influenced by whether the victim "takes it" or tries to retaliate.

Other researchers suggest that once the harmdoer decides that he *is* responsible for an injustice, the *timing* and *magnitude* of the victim's retaliation should be crucial determinants of how the exploiter reacts to revenge.

Magnitude: An exploiter may perceive the victim's retaliation as inadequate, adequate, or excessive. We would expect an exploiter to be more willing to accept retaliation when he acknowledges that "the punishment fits the crime" than when he does not. Excessive retaliation does not right a wrong; it merely transforms the exploiter into the victim. The original exploiter thus has every reason to feel that he has been treated unjustly; that the original victim owes *him* apology and restitution. If the victim retaliates inadequately, the exploiter must act to restore equity to the relationship; either actual or psychological equity.

Timing: The victim's retaliatory *timing* should also be important.

Bersheid, Boye, and Walster (1968) argued that a victim could restore equity to the harmdoer/victim relationship by retaliation. They argued that if an exploiter discovers immediately after exploiting another that his victim will inexorably even the score, he will concede that their relationship is equitable, albeit unprofitable. He should have no need to restore additional actual or psychological equity. Of course, if the exploiter discovers that the victim will be unable to retaliate, he should be motivated to completely restore actual or psychological equity to their relationship.

The authors found support for their derivations by a simple experiment. The authors hired high school boys to work as experimenters. Their job was to severely shock a fellow student, presumably to find out how he would respond to stress. Some of the student experimenters knew at the time they shocked the victim that he would not be allowed to retaliate. Other students knew at the time they shocked the victim that he would soon have an opportunity to shock them in return. As predicted, only when the experimenters knew the victim could not retaliate were they motivated to denigrate him. When students knew from the start that the victim could, and probably would, retaliate, they did not find it necessary to derogate him. Legant and Mettee (1973) corroborated these findings.

But what would have happened if the victim's timing had been different? What would happen if all the while the students were shocking the victim, they were under the illusion that he would never have the power to retaliate? We might expect that each time the experimenters delivered a shock, they would be eagerly trying to rationalize their behavior. We might expect that by the end of the experiment they would have managed to convince themselves that the "helpless" victim was an irritating idiot who deserved to suffer. What should happen if, after they had come to thoroughly dislike the victim, the "powerless" victim turned out not to be so helpless after all? What would happen if the victim reacted to their "perfectly reasonable" behavior with anger and retaliation?

We might expect that in such circumstances, retaliation might *not* "set things right." The harmdoer (who already feels that his relationship with the victim is equitable) may well conclude that the victim's retaliation has destroyed the equitableness of their relationship rather than reinstated it. Now, the original harmdoer might well feel entitled to apology and restitution.

The timing of retaliation, then, may be an important determinant of a harmdoer's reaction to it.

Restoration of Psychological Equity

As we noted earlier, one can restore psychological equity to a relationship by distorting reality. If an exploiter can aggrandize the victim's relative gains or minimize his own, he can convince himself that his inequitable relationship is, in fact, equitable. Some distortions that harmdoers use include blaming the victim, minimization of the victim's suffering, or denial of responsibility for the victim's suffering.

Blaming the Victim.   A well-publicized incident that took place during the 1976 Republican convention was reported in *Rolling Stone* magazine by John Dean, former counsel to Richard Nixon. Dean, entertainer Pat Boone, and former Secretary of Agriculture Earl Butz were talking together at the end of the convention. Boone asked Butz why the Republican Party, which was the party of Abraham Lincoln, now has so little support among members of the Black community. Butz, a loyal Republican, replied by telling an obscene and racially discriminatory joke. He said, in effect, that the inability of the Republican Party to appeal to Black people was a result of racial limitations rather than a result of limitations within the Republican Party. In terms of wealth and political power, the general relationship between the Republican Party and Blacks is an exploiter/victim relationship. Butz reacted to the inequity by blaming the victim, thereby restoring psychological equity to his situation for the time being.

Injury to another is not inequitable if the other deserves to be harmed. Thus, an obvious way by which a person who has harmed another can persuade himself that his act was equitable is by devaluing the victim's inputs.

That harmdoers will often derogate their victims has been demonstrated by a number of researchers.[6] In a typical experiment, Davis and Jones (1960) found that students who were recruited to insult other students (as part of a research project) generally ended up convincing themselves that the student deserved to be ridiculed. Sykes and Matza (1957) found that juvenile delinquents often defend their victimization of others by arguing that their victims are really homosexuals, bums, or possess other traits that make them deserving of punishment. In tormenting others, then, the delinquents can claim to be the restorers of justice rather than harmdoers.

Minimization of the Victim's Suffering. If a harmdoer can deny that the victim was harmed, he can convince himself that his relationship with the victim is an equitable one. Sykes and Matza (1957) and Brock and Buss (1962) demonstrate that harmdoers will consistently underestimate how much harm they have done to another. Brock and Buss, for example, found that college students who administer electric shock to other students soon come to markedly underestimate the painfulness of the shock.

Denial of Responsibility for the Act. If the harmdoer can convince himself that it was not his own behavior, but rather the action of someone else (e.g., the experimenter or fate) that caused the victim's suffering, then *his* relationship with the victim becomes an equitable one. (The person who is unjustly assigned responsibility for reducing the victim's outcomes will now be perceived as the harmdoer, and it will be this third party's relationship with the victim, not the original harmdoer's relationship, that is perceived as inequitable.)

That harmdoers will often deny their responsibility for harmdoing has been documented by Sykes and Matza (1957) and by Brock and Buss (1962; 1964). In daily life, the denial of responsibility seems to be a favorite strategy of those who are made to feel guilty about exploiting others. War criminals protest vehemently that they were "only following orders."

Apology: A Mixed Case. Anyone who observes and attempts to catalog exploiters' responses is forced to recognize how frequently exploiters reduce their anxiety by apologizing to their victims.

Upon examining apologies, however, we soon see that an "apology" is not a single strategy for restoring equity, but comprises several quite different strategies.

1. An apology may restore actual equity to the exploiter/victim relationship. During an effusive apology, the harmdoer may humble himself and exalt the victim. This redistribution of esteem may be a valuable reward for the victim and, thus, even the score.
2. An apology may be designed to inform the victim that the relationship is an equitable one. For example, a harmdoer may explain how much personal suffering and guilt he has endured as a consequence of his unjust treatment of the victim. If the description is suffi-

ciently heart-rending, the victim may become convinced that their score is settled.

The notion that a harmdoer's description of his remorse and suffering, if convincing, will, in fact, attenuate the victim's wrath and relatiatory intentions is supported by Bramel, Taub, and Blum (1968).

3. An apology may be a persuasive communication designed to convince the victim that the harmdoer's behavior was justified. (For example, a harmdoer may say, "You hit me first," "I didn't mean it. It was just an accident," or "He made me do it.") If the victim agrees that these justifications are plausible, the exploiter/victim relationship becomes psychologically equitable. (Scott and Lyman, 1968, provide a devastating description of how one goes about devising a compelling excuse.)

4. Sometimes an exploiter can find no satisfactory way to restore actual or psychological equity to a relationship. In such cases, an apology is often simply a way by which an exploiter can acknowledge that he was wrong, but suggest that since nothing can be done to remedy the injustice, the victim should "forgive and forget" so that their relationship can begin anew. The preceding analysis makes more explicable the common television scenario of the careless driver rushing to the hospital room of his dying victim to express his remorse. An observer not familiar with the common, "I'm sorry"–"You're forgiven" sequence might wonder what wrongs are righted by such emotional demonstrations. The answer is none. The act is performed for the harmdoer's benefit; not for the victim's. To say "I'm sorry" is to express remorse in the hope of being forgiven.

When observing an "apology," then, we may not be able to guess exactly what function it is serving. There is some evidence, however, that an exploiter feels less distress when he believes he will be able to apologize and "explain things" to the victim than when he believes he cannot.

In a simple experiment, Davis and Jones (1960) invited psychology students to assist them in a study on "first impressions." The assistant's job was as follows: the assistant was to pretend to be just another student. During the experiment, the experimenter would interview a fellow student. The student would describe his family, background, current interests, etc. Then, the experimenter would ask the student-assistant how *he* felt about the interviewee. In a secret conversation, the experimenter told the assistant *not* to say what he really thought; instead he was to claim that his first impression was devastatingly critical. Presumably the assistant was delivering the bogus evaluation so that the experimenter could see how students responded to favorable versus unfavorable evaluations. The student-assistant's "brutally frank" evaluation was as follows:

> As I understand it, my job is to tell you in all honesty what my first impression of you is. So here goes: I hope that what I say won't cause any hard feelings but I'll have to say right away that my overall impression was not too favorable. To put it simply, I wouldn't go out of my way to get to know you. Maybe I'd change my mind if we could talk together in a more natural surrounding, but from the way you spoke—not so much what you said but how you said it—I'd guess that you have some personal problems that would make it hard for us to get along very well. Your general interests and so on just strike me as those of a pretty shallow person.
>
> To be more specific: *Frankly, I just wouldn't know how much I could trust you as a friend after hearing your answers to those moral questions. You took the easy way out every time.* I guess that I should point out some of the things that you said that made a good impression on me, but that would be kind of a waste of time since the general impression that I have is not too good. That's all that I have to say. (p. 405)

The assistants read the negative evaluation, but needless to say, they didn't feel comfortable about it. (As one assistant said, "I hope he's not a big guy.")

As you might have guessed, in this topsy-turvy experiment the experimenter was studying the *assistant's* reactions, not the insulted student's reactions. While giving instructions, the experimenter casually mentioned to half of the assistants that they would have a chance to meet the insulted student later, so that things could be explained to him. The remaining assistants were led to believe that such a meeting was impossible. Davis and Jones predicted that when the assistants knew they would not have a chance to meet the other person, apologize, and rescind their critical remarks, they would respond as harmdoers usually do—they would denigrate the student; they would convince themselves that he deserved all the mean things they said about him. On the other hand, when the assistants knew they would have a chance to explain things to their partner, they should have little need to denigrate him. These predictions were borne out.

Prediction of a Harmdoer's Response

The research results enumerated in this section document the eagerness with which exploiters restore equity after injuring others. Equity theory provides an orderly framework for cataloging the possible reactions of exploiters. But this is not enough. Researchers are more interested in prediction and control than in description.

In an effort to predict which of my potential techniques harmdoers will use, researchers adopted a simple strategy. They tried to: (1) condense the multitude of potentially equity-restoring responses into a few sensible categories; (2) isolate variables that determine which class of responses harmdoers will choose.

Condensation of Reactions into a Few Categories. Prediction was facilitated when researchers realized that exploiters' responses generally fall into two distinct categories: exploiters tend either to compensate their victims (and to restore actual equity) *or* to justify the victim's deprivation (and to restore psychological equity).

Of course, exploiters could conceivably use both techniques to restore equity, either in sequence or simultaneously. For example, an exploiter could try one technique, fail, and switch to another. A harmdoer could offer to compensate his victim, be rebuffed, and decide that further compensatory attempts are not worthwhile; then he might resort to justification (i.e., "I don't know what he's so huffy about. The whole fiasco was really *his* fault anyway."). Or, the exploiter may attempt to justify his victimizing behavior, discover everyone thinks his rationalizations are laughable, and then shamefacedly accede to demands for compensation.

Exploiters might even try to use both techniques simultaneously. A reckless driver might sideswipe a neighbor's car and do $200 worth of damage to the fender. He could then volunteer to make a deal with the neighbor—he'll give him $100 in cash, but no more. If the neighbor accepts the offer, perhaps on the grounds that some restitution is better than none, the driver may justify depriving the victim of the remaining $100 by arguing that the victim deserves to bear part of the cost ("If he hadn't parked so far from the curb, I never would have hit him. He probably won't even get the fender bumped out; he'll simply pocket the money.").

Although all things are possible, observation suggests that in fact exploiters usually use only one equity-restoring technique at a time. Logically, the simultaneous use of compensation and justification techniques is difficult. To do this, the harmdoer may have to: (1) acknowledge that he is at fault for the victim's undeserved suffering and exert himself in an attempt to assist the victim, *and,* simultaneously, (2) insist that his victim deserves to suffer, that he is not really suffering, and that in any case, he is not responsible for the victim's suffering.

There is empirical evidence that individuals generally do not use compensation and justification in concert.[7] Walster and Prestholdt (1966) led social work trainees to inadvertently harm their clients. Subsequently, trainees were asked to evaluate the clients and asked to volunteer their free time to help them. Compensation and justification responses were found to be negatively related; the more time trainees volunteered to help their clients, the less they derogated them.

Lincoln and Levinger (1972) found that observers either helped or derogated a victim. The authors described an episode in which a policeman wantonly attacked an innocent black man. If observers knew they could lodge a complaint against the assaulting officer, they evaluated the victim fairly objectively. If, however, they believed there was no way to rectify the injustice, they found reason to condemn the victim.

Thus, Equity theorists conclude:

CONCLUSION I: Exploiters tend to use *either* justification techniques or compensation techniques to restore equity.

Isolating Variables that Influence an Exploiter's Response. Once researchers discovered (1) that a hodge-podge of equity-restoring techniques could be classified into two distinct categories, compensation or justification, and (2) that compensation and justification tend to be mutually exclusive techniques for restoring equity, their task was vastly simplified. Detecting the antecedents of two alternative responses, compensation or justification, is easier than ferreting out the antecedents of a multitude of disorganized responses.

In addition, the minute one recognizes that exploiters will either compensate their victim or justify their act, the theoretical and practical importance of discovering what will motivate harmdoers to make one or the other response becomes evident.

All societies have a vested interest in encouraging harmdoers to voluntarily compensate their victims. If a harmdoer does not make restitution, the victim is left in sad straits. He is deprived of the material benefits he deserves. Even worse, he must endure the indignity of derogation and the disheartening realization that the exploiter will probably continue to treat him unjustly in the future.[8] Society would naturally prefer that its citizens restore actual equity after committing injustices, rather than engage in a series of justifications that end in shared bitterness and possible future harmdoing. For theoretical and practical reasons, then, we are interested in identifying those variables that encourage exploiters to make voluntary compensation or that encourage justification.

A cost-benefit analysis: Theoretically, two situational variables should be crucial determinants of an exploiter's response: (1) the *adequacy* of the possible techniques for restoring equity, and (2) the *cost* of the possible techniques for restoring equity. We would expect people to prefer techniques that completely restore equity to techniques that only partially restore equity, and to prefer techniques with little material or psychological cost to techniques with greater cost. More precisely we would expect:

> **PROPOSITION IV: COROLLARY 1:** Other things being equal, the more adequate an exploiter perceives an available equity-restoring technique to be, the more likely he is to use this technique to restore equity.

> **PROPOSITION I: COROLLARY 2:** Other things being equal, the less costly an exploiter perceives an available equity-restoring technique to be, the more likely he is to use this technique to restore equity.

Adequacy of equity-restoring techniques: The *adequacy* of a technique is defined as the extent to which that technique will *exactly* restore equity to the exploiter/victim relationship. As we pointed out in Proposition III, participants in inequitable relations feel uncomfortable. The more inequitable the relationship, the more uncomfortable they feel. Thus participants have a vested interest in reestablishing as equitable a relationship as possible. Data support the contention (Proposition IV: Corollary 1) that exploiters are more likely to compensate their victims if adequate compensation is available than if it is not.

Adequacy of compensation: By definition, an *adequate compensation* is one that can exactly balance the harm done. Both *insufficient* compensations and *excessive* compensations lack adequacy; thus, harmdoers should be reluctant to make such compensations.

Why should an exploiter be reluctant to make an insufficient compensation? (Certainly his victim would prefer insufficient compensation to no compensation at all.) If insufficient compensation were the only way by which an exploiter could reduce his distress, rather than do nothing, he would probably choose to restore at least partial equity to his relationship with the victim. But insufficient compensation is not the only equity-restoring technique open to the exploiter. A technique incompatible with compensation is available to him. He can always completely eliminate his distress by completely *justifying* the victim's suffering. Thus, as available compensations become increasingly insufficient, justification techniques should become increasingly appealing to the harmdoer.

Making an excessive compensation is also an unsatisfactory way to restore equity. An excessive compensation eliminates one kind of

FIGURE 3.2. "... His Victim Would Prefer Insufficient Compensation to No Compensation at All."

inequity by producing another. The exploiter who compensates his victim excessively does not restore equity; he simply becomes a victim instead of a harmdoer—a most undesirable transformation.

Berscheid and Walster (1967) tested the hypothesis that a harmdoer's tendency to compensate his victim will be an increasing function of the adequacy of the compensations available to him. Their results provide support for Proposition IV: Corollary 1. In this experiment women from various church groups were led to cheat fellow parishioners out of trading stamps, in a vain attempt to win additional stamps for themselves. When the women were subsequently given an opportunity to compensate the victim (at no cost to themselves), the adequacy of compensation was found to be a crucial determinant of whether or not the women chose to compensate. Women who could compensate with an adequate compensation (exactly restoring the number of books her partner had lost) were much more likely to make restitution than were women limited to insufficient compensation (a few stamps) or to excessive compensation (a great many stamp books).[9]

The hypothesis that individuals are predisposed to make adequate compensation and to resist making inadequate or excessive compensation has some interesting implications. In life, exploited individuals sometimes try to impress on those in a position to make restitution how much they have suffered. They naturally assume that the better a case one makes, the more likely he is to be compensated. The preceding research, however, indicates that in some instances the victim might do better by minimizing his suffering than by aggrandizing it.

The greater the inequity a victim documents, the more restitution the harmdoer should be willing to make—up to a point. However, at some point, the described inequity will become so large that the harmdoer will despair of ever being able to make complete restitution. Once this point is reached, the victim will not profit by exaggerating his suffering. Further exaggeration will *not* elicit increased restitution because the harmdoer has already reached his limit. In fact, the more additional suffering the victim describes, the more inadequate the compensations available to the harmdoer become, and thus the more reluctant he should be to provide any compensation at all.

The preceding reasoning may provide some insight into the public reactions in the 1960s to James Farmer's demands that American churches make financial "reparation" to blacks for "300 years of exploitation." Probably most Americans realized that there was no possibility of ever adequately compensating blacks for their centuries of exploitation; many of the most deprived blacks had died long ago. Black leaders argued that citizens should at least take some token steps toward restoring equity. However, the idea of making a small compensation is not very attractive to many citizens. It is easy to see why this might be so. The effort to make a partial compensation mocks their rationalizations that blacks deserved their treatment. If one cannot compensate enough to reduce his own distress, he is perhaps happier with his rationalizations.

If we generalize shamelessly from the preceding findings, we might speculate that a more effective strategy for the blacks might have been to *minimize* their description of their suffering, and to make it clear that if available compensations were extended it would completely *eliminate* the debt owed to them. While this is not true, it may have been a profitable strategy, since it would have insured that the blacks would have at least received minimal compensation.

Adequacy of justifications: If he is to restore complete psychological equity to his relationship with a victim, an exploiter must be able to conceive of justifications that: (1) adequately justify the exploitation, and (2) are plausible to himself, the victim, and to others. (Only if the exploiter believes his own distortions will he be able to eliminate self-concept distress. Only if he imagines that the victim accepts his justifications will he be able to eliminate fear of retaliation.)

The *adequacy of a justification* can be defined as the extent to which an explanation restores psychological equity to the relationship. Consider the following example:

A small boy trips a teammate during a ball game; he claims he did it because the boy spit at him. Regardless of whether or not we approve of his behavior, we would probably all think that his excuse sounds "reasonable." If, on the other hand, the boy brutally stabs the teammate and claims he did it for the same reason, we are appalled. Alternative answers such as, "My mother likes my sister more than she likes me" or "The sun was shining in my eyes" sound equally bizarre.

Unfortunately, scientists know little about what determines whether or not an excuse will be seen as adequate justification for a harmful act.

Credibility of a justification: Once a harmdoer conceives of an adequate justification, however, scientists know a great deal about the factors that determine how plausible or *credible* a given justification is.[10] For a delightful and extensive account of excuses that work, see Scott and Lyman (1968).

Let us review just one factor that influences how plausible various justifications will be.

An exploiter will perceive a potential justification to be more credible when it requires little distortion of reality than when it requires a great deal of reality distortion.

The more serious or extensive a distortion of reality required by a justification, the less credible these justifications should be to the victim, the exploiter, and others. A justification that no one believes is not very effective in restoring equity. Some tangential support for this argument comes from Rosenberg and Abelson (1960), who provide evidence that individuals prefer to distort reality as little as possible.

On the basis of the preceding logic, one might also expect that: *The more contact the exploiter has had (or anticipates having) with the victim or the victim's sympathizers, the less likely he will be to justify his harmdoing.*

There are two compelling reasons why an exploiter should be more reluctant to distort an intimate's relative gains than those of a stranger. First, the more intimate we are with someone, the more likely we are to have voluminous information about that person. Thus, if an exploiter tries to distort an intimate's characteristics, he will soon find himself in trouble. The exploiter's fine rationalizations will keep bumping up against recalcitrant facts. However, his fantasies about a stranger can easily proliferate.

Virtually all the cognitive consistency theorists[11] acknowledge that isolated beliefs are easier to change. Walster, Berscheid, and Barclay (1967) demonstrated that one is more likely to avoid distortions when future objective evidence will be unavailable. Both these observations are consistent with the expectation that it is harder to distort the familiar than the unknown.

There is a second reason why an exploiter should be more reluctant to distort an intimate's relative gains than those of a stranger. One should expect more difficulty *maintaining* an adequate distortion when the distortion involves an intimate than when it involves a stranger. If one engages in a massive distortion of an intimate's character, he must anticipate that his friend will have more opportunities (than a stranger would) to confront him, challenge his rationalizations, and perhaps retaliate.

For two reasons, then, familiarity with the victim should breed accuracy and discourage justification as a distress-reducing technique. Data are available to support this hypothesis. We recall that Davis and Jones (1960) found that students who ridicule another person (victim), will derogate him more when they do not expect to see him again than when a meeting is expected. Davis and Jones assumed that they secured this result because students who anticipate future contact plan to "neutralize" their harmdoing by explaining that their negative evaluation does not represent their true feelings. However, since the victim has already suffered by the time neutralization occurs, this explanation is not totally satisfactory. An equally plausible interpretation is that students were more comfortable about distorting the other's characteristics when they knew they would not soon be forced to confront their victim.

Ross (1966) conducted an experiment in which students were led to choose to give their partner electric shock to avoid painful shock themselves. In some situations, students believed they would work with their partner only once. In other cases, they believed they would work with him on many tasks. Ross discovered that when the students allowed their partners to be injured, derogation occurred more often when subsequent contact was *not* anticipated. This finding is, of course, satisfactorily explained by the hypothesis that we only distort the characteristics of those individuals who can be kept "out of sight and out of mind."

Pannen (1976) directly tested the hypothesis that the anticipation of future interaction with another breeds accuracy of perception of our relationship with him and inhibits distortion. The women who participated in his experiment engaged in a nonverbal bargaining task; the only way they could communicate with their partner (another college woman) was *via* a series of tickets, each of which represented a varying number of points. The object of the task was for each woman to accumulate as many points as she possibly could, since those who ended up with the most points could possibly win one of several twenty-five dollar prizes. The women's partners were actually confederates of the experimenter, and they delivered tickets representing a random distribution of points to the women. Some women expected to interact in a second bargaining session with the same partner, some expected future interaction with a different partner, and some expected to be engaged in only one bargaining session (and thus did not anticipate any future interaction with anyone). Pannen found that women who expected to interact with the same person in the future were more accurate in their assessments, both of the number of points they had sent and of the number of points they had received, than were women in either of the other two conditions.

This conclusion suggests that it may be a mistake for the exploited to be stoic and patient; rather, the exploited might do well to harass their exploiters. For example, so long as exploited minorities are geographically and socially segregated, an exploiter can conveniently reduce whatever vague feelings of guilt he might have by justifying his exploitation. The harmdoer can easily maintain that minority members deserve their exploitation ("The poor are shiftless and lazy and don't want a steady job.") or that they are not really suffering ("A Chicano can live better on one dollar than a white man can on five dollars."). We might expect that integrated housing and forced association will make such rationalizations more difficult. Until such integration occurs, however, minority members could arrange "symbolic integration." Welfare mothers who feel that suburban whites reinforce one another's "preposterous rationalizations," could arrange to expose the taxpayers to reality. They might, for example, travel to the suburbs, talk to suburbanites about their plight, confront shoppers, or speak up in suburban PTA's.

We stated that two variables should be crucial determinants of an exploiter's choice of equity-restoring techniques: the *adequacy* of the techniques and the *cost* of the techniques for restoring equity. In the last section we reviewed evidence that adequate compensations and justifications are preferred to inadequate ones. In the next section, we present evidence that the greater the cost of an equity-restoring technique, the less likely an exploiter is to use it.

Cost of equity-restoring techniques. Central to Equity theory is the proposition that individuals try to maximize their outcomes. Proposition I: Corollary 2 ("the less costly an exploiter perceives an available equity-restoring technique to be, the more likely he is to use it") simply rephrases this principle.

This proposition is identical to Adams' hypothesis that a person "will reduce inequity, insofar as possible, in a manner that will yield him the largest outcomes" (1965, p. 284). Adams presents evidence supporting the validity of his hypothesis.[12] This hypothesis is also supported by the results of an experiment concerning preferences among forms of equity resolution in fictitious work situations.[13]

Proposition I: Corollary 2 is also consistent with the observation that self-punishment seems to be an unpopular way for exploiters to restore equity to a relationship. Theoretically, both compensation to the victim and self-punishment are equally adequate techniques for restoring actual equity to a relationship. In practice, however, one rarely finds exploiters restoring equity by self-punishment. Corollary 2 reminds us of the reason for the aversion to this equity-restoring technique; exploiters resist lowering their outcomes unnecessarily.

Anecdotal evidence supports the proposition that subjects in laboratory experiments energetically resist restoring equity by self-punishment.[14] A very few experiments have demonstrated that individuals are more willing to perform unpleasant altruistic acts following the committing of harmful acts.[15] However, in these experiments the experimenters made compensating the victim difficult or impossible for the harmdoer. In addition, the guilt-inducing procedures used in these experiments were such that justification (denial of responsibility for the harm, denial that the harm was done, or perception that the act was just) was difficult, if not impossible. Thus, evidence of self-punishment following harmdoing is restricted to situations in which compensation and justification techniques are almost totally unavailable.

REACTIONS OF THE EXPLOITED

When one reviews existing Equity research, a curious anomaly appears. Equity theory presumably deals with the relations of *two* participants in an exploiter/victim relationship—the exploiter and his victim. Yet, virtually all research has focused on the reactions of the exploiter. We know a great deal about exploiters; we know very little about the exploited. Why have psychologists been so disinterested in victims? We do not know. In any case, let us review what we *do* know about how victims react to inequity.

Distress

I'd rather be a hammer than a nail. *

"El Condor Pasa," Simon (1970)

If an inequitable relationship is distressing to the exploiter, it is doubly distressing for the exploited. Although both the exploiter and the victim must endure the discomfort of knowing they are involved in an inequitable relationship, the exploiter at least has the consolation that he is benefiting materially from his discomfort. The victim has no such comfort; he is losing in every way from the inequity. He is deprived of desired outcomes and must face the unsettling realization that unless he can elicit restitution, his colleagues are likely to justify his exploitation by derogating him.

Propositions I, II, and III lead to the following derivation:

DERIVATION I: A participant will be more distressed by inequity when he is a victim than when he is a harmdoer.

Several theorists have noticed that those who materially benefit from inequity are more tolerant of injustice than those who are deprived.[16]

Austin and Walster (1974) directly investigated individuals' cognitive, affective, and physiological reactions to equity and inequity. They tested the dual predictions that (1) participants will be more content (and less distressed) when they are equitably rewarded than when they are either overrewarded or underrewarded. Further, (2) participants will be less distressed when they are overrewarded than when they are underrewarded.

Austin invited college students to participate in a psychological study of decision making. Each student was assigned to work on a task with a partner (actually an experimental accomplice.) A third student

---

*From the song "El Condor Pasa," Paul Simon (1970). Copyright © 1933, 1963, 1970 Edward B. Marks Music Corp. and Jorge Milchberg. English Lyric © 1970 Charing Cross Music, Inc. Used with the permission of the publisher.

(also an experimental accomplice) was designated "decision maker" and told to pay the two students on the basis of their task performance. Since both students performed equally well, the "decision" was a simple one—each student should receive two dollars. Sometimes, the decision maker did pay the student an equitable two dollars. However, sometimes, by prearrangement, he did the unexpected: sometimes he overpaid her (i.e., gave her three dollars; a dollar more than she deserved); other times he underpaid her (i.e., gave her one dollar; a dollar less than she deserved). The student was then quizzed about how she felt about the way she had been treated. As predicted, equitably paid students *were* more cognitively and emotionally content than either overpaid or underpaid individuals. Also as predicted, overbenefited students were more content than underbenefited ones. The women who received a dollar more than they deserved were slightly upset; those who received a dollar less than they deserved were extremely upset.

Physiological data tend to substantiate the women's reports of how they felt about the decision. *Galvanic Skin Response* measures revealed that equitably treated students were the most tranquil. Deprived students were more intensely distressed than were overbenefited individuals.

Researchers have also documented that those who materially suffer from inequity are quicker to demand a fair distribution of resources than those who do not.[17]

> Aristotle argued that the desire to secure equitable treatment was the universal cause of revolution. He notes: "The universal and chief cause of this revolutionary feeling has already been mentioned; viz. the desire of equality; when men think that they are equal to others who have more than themselves; or, again, the desire of inequality and superiority, when conceiving themselves to be Superior, they think that they have not more but the same or less than their inferiors; pretentions which may or may not be just." (Paynton and Blackey, 1971, p. 11)

Restoration of Actual Equity

Demands for Compensation. Undoubtedly the victim's first response to exploitation is to seek restitution.[18] If the victim secures compensation, he restores the relationship to equity, and benefits materially. It is easy to see why this is a popular response.

In an ingenious experiment, Stephenson and White (1968) tested the hypothesis that victimized boys would be so eager to "right" things that they would perform delinquent acts in order to do so. The authors invited ten-year-old school boys to play a model racing car game. In the equitably treated condition, the boys spent half of their time racing cars and half of their time retrieving their partner's cars. In the relatively deprived group, the boys spent most of their time retrieving their partner's cars. In the absolutely deprived group, the boys were never given a chance to race the cars; they spent all of their time retrieving cars for another group of boys.

The authors then attempted to determine whether or not the boys in the various groups were willing to cheat in order to win a prize. The boys were told that if they performed well on a "motor racing quiz" they could win a prize. Actually, the quiz was so hard that no ten-year-old boy could answer the questions; they could only win a prize if they cheated. And, they were soon presented with an opportunity to cheat. The experimenter gave them the correct answers and told them to correct their own papers. As predicted, the equitably treated boys were least likely to cheat (and thus the least likely to win a prize). The relatively deprived boys were somewhat more likely to cheat. The absolutely deprived boys were the biggest cheaters (and the biggest illicit prize winners) of all.

Retaliation. A *Newsweek* article about a Hell's Angels' massacre dramatically illustrates how a victim can also restore equity to the exploiter/victim relationship by retaliating against his exploiter.

> Before that bloody Sunday was out, the bodies of three more drug pushers were found in the Oakland hills—and bullets taken from them matched up with a slug taken from Agero's body. After state's witness quoted Barger as telling him: "If someone does something wrong to you, then it's not for you to judge—kill him first, then God will do the judging."*

Victims are not hesitant to "get even" with those who treat them unjustly by retaliating against them.[19] And, as we pointed out in the preceding section, a victim can indeed restore equity through such retaliation.

Berscheid, Boye, and Walster (1968) conducted an experiment designed to assess the effect of a victim's retaliation on the exploiter's tendency to justify the victim's suffering by derogation. The results of this study indicate that a victim can indeed restore equity through retaliation against the exploiter. In this experiment, individuals were hired to administer severe electric shocks to another person. If the victim could not retaliate against the harmdoer, the harmdoer subse-

---

*From "Fallen Angels," *Newsweek* (January 8, 1973): 25. Copyright © 1973 by Newsweek, Inc. All rights reserved. Reprinted by permission.

quently derogated the victim. However, when the exploiter expected retaliation for his harmful act, the derogation process was arrested; the harmdoer did not derogate the victim.

The insight that a victim can restore equity to the exploiter/ victim relationship simply by retaliating has interesting implications: a victim would naturally prefer that equity be restored by receiving compensation. Frequently, however, it becomes obvious to the victim that compensation is unlikely to be forthcoming. In such circumstances the victim must realize that the exploiter is likely to justify the victim's suffering. This is not a pleasant prospect. The exploiter's justifications are potentially dangerous. The exploiter who justifies his actions will end up with a distorted and unreal assessment of his own actions. If he distorts the extent to which the victim deserved to be hurt, for example, or minimizes the victim's suffering as a consequence of the act, he may commit further acts based on these distortions.[20] Thus, speculating from the little we know, one could argue that once a victim becomes certain that his harmdoer is not about to compensate him, he might well consider retaliating.

Civil rights leaders have arrived at a similar conclusion. James Baldwin (1963), in a statement concerning the blacks' struggle for minority rights in the United States, argues: "Neither civilized reason nor Christian love would cause any of those people to treat you as they presumably wanted to be treated; only fear of your power to retaliate would cause them to do that, or to seem to do it, which was (and is) good enough." (p. 35) Black militants have taken an even stronger position. They have argued that widespread black violence is necessary to restore blacks to full citizenship. The variables they discuss sound much like those we have considered. They talk of the "white devil," his guilt, his denial of racial injustices, and the equity-establishing effects of violence.

However, if extrapolation from the Berscheid, Boye, and Walster (1968) and Legant and Mettee (1973) findings is relevant, we might suggest that threats of retaliation will be beneficial *only* if the recipient of the violence feels that he is responsible for blacks' suffering. Retaliation against those who feel themselves to be innocent observers of injustices would seem to be a disastrous strategy.

Slaves are expected to sing as well as to work.

Frederick Douglass

Justification of the Inequity. Sometimes a victim finds that it is impossible either to elicit restitution or to retaliate against the harmdoer. The impotent victim is then left with only two options: he can acknowledge the exploitation and his inability to do anything about it, or, he can justify his exploitation. Often, victimized individuals find it less upsetting to distort reality and justify their victimization than to acknowledge that the world is unjust and that they are too impotent to elicit fair treatment.[21]

Victimized individuals have been found to restore psychological equity to the exploiter/victim relationship in several ways:

Sometimes victims console themselves by imagining that they were not really exploited, or by insisting that exploitation has brought compensating benefits. For example, there is evidence that when things are arranged so that a person cannot win, he often convinces himself that he does not want to win. Solomon (1957) set up an experimental game.[22] A favored player treated some players benevolently (benefitting them whenever he could) and others malevolently (depriving them whenever he could). As we would expect, the benefited players were more content than the frustrated ones. More interestingly, the players who were treated benevolently attached far more importance to doing well in the game than did the malevolently treated ones.

Sometimes victims console themselves by concluding that in the long run the exploiter will be punished as he deserves ("The mill of the Lord grinds slowly, but it grinds exceedingly fine.").

Or, victims may convince themselves that their exploiter actually deserved the enormous benefits he received. Recent data demonstrate that the exploited are inclined to justify their exploiter's excessive benefits. Jecker and Landy (1969), Walster and Prestholdt (1966), and Hastorf and Regan (personal communication, 1962) pressured individuals into performing a difficult favor for an unworthy recipient. They found that the abashed favordoers tried to justify the inequity by convincing themselves that the recipient was especially needy or worthy.

Reformers who work to alleviate social injustice are often enraged to discover that the exploited themselves are sometimes vehement defenders of the status quo. Black militants encounter "Uncle Toms" who defend white supremacy. Women's liberation groups lobbying for the Equal Rights Amendment must face angry housewives who threaten to defend to death the inferior status of women. Reformers might have more sympathy for such "Uncle Toms" and "Aunt Tomasinas" if they understood the psychological underpinnings of such reactions. When one is treated inequitably, but has no hope of altering the situation, denying reality is often less degrading than facing up to one's humiliating position.

Prediction of a Victim's Response

It is the peculiar triumph of society—and its loss—that it is able to convince those people to whom it has given inferior status of the reality of this decree; it has the force and the weapons to translate its dictum into fact, so that the allegedly inferior are actually made so, insofar as the societal realities are concerned. (Baldwin, 1955, p. 19)

The Making of an Uncle Tom. According to Equity theory, when a victim perceives that he is being exploited, he has two options: (1) he can become angry and demand justice, or (2) he can suppress his anger and justify his own deprivation—he can become an "Uncle Tom."

Several researchers have examined the factors that determine how a victim will respond to inequity. They have found that two variables seem to have an important influence on whether a victim seeks justice or justifies his situation. These variables are: (a) the victim's original expectations and (b) his hope for change.

Expectations. Austin[23] hypothesized that if an individual is warned to expect injustice, he will be less outraged when he encounters it than he normally would be. He reasoned that when a person expects something, he "gets set" for it. Thus, when a person learns that he will be involved in unjust dealings with another, he begins to rehearse for the stressful event. By the time he finally encounters the injustice, he will be able to react calmly to it.

Austin tested his hypothesis in a simple experiment: he hired college students to participate in a study of decision making, presumably in return for two dollars. Two of the students were assigned to be workers; their job was to proofread some material and to circle any spelling errors. A third student was designated the decision maker; his job was to decide how much the two workers should be paid.

As soon as the workers finished their task, the decision maker evaluated their work. At this point, the student's expectation as to whether or not he would be treated justly was varied. The decision maker reported that both the student and his partner had discovered 94 percent of the errors. (According to the implicit rules, each should have been paid two dollars.) However, the decision maker indicated that he had made a *tentative* decision to pay the student ___ dollars (one, two, or three) and the student's partner ___ dollars (the remaining three, two, or one). By this report then, the decision maker led some students to expect that for some inexplicable reason they would be underpaid, others to believe they would be equitably paid, and still others to believe that they would be overpaid.

Five minutes elapsed while students had a chance to think about this turn of affairs. Then the decision maker sent a second message. He indicated that he had thought things through and settled on a final decision. He had decided to give the student one, two, or three dollars. (The amount he cited was randomly determined.) Then he paid him.

Austin predicted that individuals who received far more (or far less) than they deserved would be most comfortable about their unfair treatment if they had expected it.

Austin's hypotheses received strong support. (See Figure 3.3.) Austin measured the student's "comfort" in two ways:

1. At the end of the experiment he asked them to assess their feelings via the *Mood Adjective Check List (MACL)*. The *MACL* measures individuals' feelings of elation, activation, social affection, aggression, anxiety, and depression. In essence, the more positive the student's *MACL* score, the more contented he was. As predicted, students who expected to be paid equitably (two dollars) and were, were the most contented group of all. Also, as predicted, both overpaid students (three dollars) and underpaid students (one dollar) were more content when they had been forewarned that they would be treated unjustly than when it came as a surprise.
2. Austin also collected physiological data which seem to substantiate students' reports. The *Galvanic Skin Response* has long served as a measure of physiological arousal and as an indirect indicant of anxiety.[24] The students' self-reports were mirrored by the *GSR* data. (This time, however, the predicted differences were not statistically significant.)

These findings are intriguing. The data imply that whether or not an individual realizes he will be involved in an exploitative relationship should profoundly affect his reactions to it. A warning seems to dampen one's affective and physiological response to injustice. Perhaps it also depresses one's motivation to resist the injustice.

Austin suggests that such data might explain the frequent observation that elderly women, blacks, and Mexican-Americans tend to react less violently to discrimination than their youthful counterparts. Since many of the elderly have come to expect and accept the discrimination they have encountered in their lifetime, not surprisingly they often become less aroused and angry when they encounter injustice than do their younger counterparts.

Who is "right," of course, is unclear. Whether resignation or resistance to injustice is the most profitable strategy depends, of course,

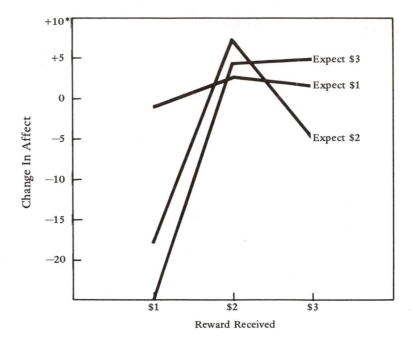

* The more positive the number, the more contented the student is.

FIGURE 3.3. The Effect of Equitableness of Expectancy and Equitableness of Reward on Student's Mood.

on whether a group has a realistic prospect of securing equitable treatment.

Hope. According to Equity theory, how an individual responds to inequity should depend upon the probable benefits and costs of possible reactions. Not surprisingly then, on the basis of cost-benefit considerations, theorists have speculated that the victim's *hope* that he can benefit from rebellion vs. his terror that he might not, should be a potent determinant of whether he demands justice or accepts justification.

If a citizen has learned through crushing experience that "You can't fight City Hall," he should assume that passivity is the most profitable strategy. He should suppress his rage and try to accommodate to the inevitable. However, if he has learned that his fellow citizens will insist that equity be restored, he will benefit by expressing his righteous anger and demanding compensation.

There is some evidence that hope vs. despair does determine whether individuals freely express their feelings or deny them. Thibaut (1950) invited boys from settlement houses and summer camps in the

Boston area to form teams and play some games. The games were arranged so that one team performed all the exciting tasks while their competitors performed all the servile tasks. For example, the deprived team members were told to stand side by side in a line, and then to bend over to form an arch or "wicket." The overbenefited team was supposed to squirm through the wickets and back again, race back to touch the second team member of the relay team, and so on. The experimenter timed the race. In game after game, the overbenefited boys got to do the things that were fun; the underbenefited boys were forced to assist them. Things got so bad that during recess a bystander urged the boys to complain and to insist that the experimenter allow them to at least try the good games. By design, the experimenter sometimes went along with the boys' request (i.e., he allowed the boys to toss bean bags and required the previously overbenefited boys to hold them). Sometimes, the experimenter rejected the boys' reasonable request (i.e., he claimed he wanted to see if the overbenefited boys could better their earlier performance).

Thibaut found that a group's effectiveness or ineffectiveness in altering their fate markedly influenced how much aggression they were willing to express toward their overbenefited rivals. When boys were successful in securing some compensation, they suddenly began to freely express their pent-up hostility. They began to taunt their rivals and to strike them with open hands or fists. When the boys were totally unsuccessful in altering their fate, however, they withdrew, and became even less aggressive than they had been.

Social theorists[25] agree that hope is a potent determinant of whether or not exploited individuals rebel or passively accept their fate. Let us review these theorists' somewhat poetic arguments:

de Tocqueville (1856) observed:

> Nations that have endured patiently and almost unconsciously the most overwhelming oppression often burst into rebellion against the yoke the moment it begins to grow lighter . . . Evils which are patiently endured when they seem inevitable become intolerable when once the idea of escape from them is suggested. (p. 214)

Similarly, Soule (1935) concluded:

> When the people are in their most desperate and miserable condition, they are often least inclined to revolt, for then they are hopeless . . . Only after their position is somewhat improved and they have sensed the possibility of change do they revolt effectively against oppression and injustice. What touches off insurrection is hope, not lack of it, rising confidence, not bleak suffering. (p. 20)

51

Trotsky (1932) agreed:

> The mere existence of privations is not enough to cause an insurrection: if it were, the masses would be always in revolt. It is necessary that the bankruptcy of the social regime, being conclusively revealed, should make these privations intolerable, and that new conditions and new ideas should open the prospect of a revolutionary way out. (Cited in Gurr, 1970, p. 104)

Davies (1962) offered a more specific proposal. He insisted that both rising expectations *and* subsequent frustration are crucial precursors of revolution. He pointed out that if individuals have an unimpeded opportunity to satisfy their ever-escalating needs, revolution should be an utter improbability. Similarly, if individuals have no hope that their needs will be met, revolution is also improbable. Davies contended that only if men have consistently learned that their reasonable expectations *will* be met, if not this year, then certainly next year, and then, for some reason, they are not—only then will they become angry enough to revolt. (Davies' model is diagrammed in Figure 3.4.)

Davies examined Dorr's Rebellion in 1842, the Russian Revolution in 1917, the Egyptian Revolution in 1950, and a variety of civil disturbances, and concluded that each of these cases fits his *J-Curve* model.

Ross, Thibaut, and Evenbeck (1971) provide some support for Davies' proposal. The authors were interested in illuminating the conditions under which groups will respond to social inequities. They pre-

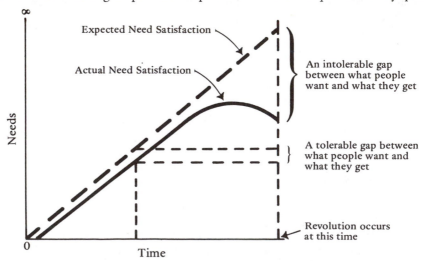

FIGURE 3.4. Need Satisfaction and Revolution. (From J. C. Davies, "Toward a Theory of Revolution," *American Sociological Review*, 27, 1963, p. 6. Reprinted by permission.)

dicted that the more competent exploited individuals believe they are, the more readily they will retaliate against an exploitative elite.

Ross et al. tested this hypothesis in a laboratory experiment. They invited teams of fifth and sixth grade boys to compete in a rope pulling contest. Each team of boys was told to try to pull a rope with a specific amount of pressure. Half of the boys were led to believe they were highly competent at rope pulling. Half were led to believe they were hopelessly poor.

Two boys (actually experimental confederates) were designated as managers. The managers' job was to divide up points among themselves and the team members. By prearrangement, the managers distributed points unfairly. During the first fourteen rope pulls, the managers gave the workers an ever-increasing percentage of the available points. Suddenly, for no reason, on the fourteenth trial they began ceding fewer and fewer points to the workers.

As expected, the "competent" boys were most indignant about their unfair treatment than were their incompetent peers. They were also more likely to retaliate. When the boys were given a chance to "buzz" the unfair manager with "unpleasant, painful, white noise," the competent boys retaliated more severely than their peers. When they were given a chance to choose a bonus prize for the managers, the competent boys chose worse prizes for the managers than did the incompetent boys.

The expectations aroused by the great judicial and legislative victories of the Civil Rights movement have led to frustration, hostility and cynicism in the face of the persistent gap between promise and fulfillment.

The National Advisory Commission on Civil Disorders (1968)

Gurr (1970) provides an even more comprehensive analysis of the relationship between relative deprivation, frustration, and revolution. He argues that any time individuals feel they deserve more than they are getting, they are primed for rebellion. Like other Equity theorists, Gurr assumes that there is a direct relationship between the magnitude of a group's relative deprivation and its impetus to violence.

Gurr argues that *three* types of relative deprivation, rather than the single type Davies describes, can spark revolution.

1. *Decremental deprivation:* (See Figure 3.5.) (Individuals feel they deserve the benefits they have traditionally received. Their benefits, however, continue to decline.)

Gurr cites several instances in which decremental deprivation sparked rebellion. He notes, for example, that when stable medieval

53

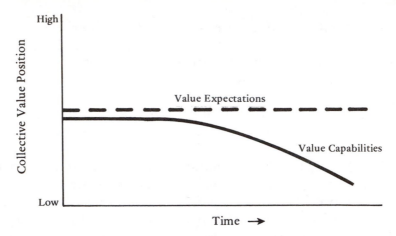

FIGURE 3.5. Decremental Deprivation. (From T. R. Gurr, *Why Men Rebel.* Copyright © 1970 by Princeton University Press; Princeton Paperback, 1971, p. 47. Reprinted by permission of Princeton University Press.)

European societies were confronted by natural disaster, plagues (such as the Black Death), and famine, they reacted with collective violence, embarking, for example, on the First Crusade and the flagellant movements of 1260, 1348–1349, and 1400.

  2. *Aspirational deprivation:* (See Figure 3.6.) (Although individuals feel they deserve more and more, their outcomes remain the same.)

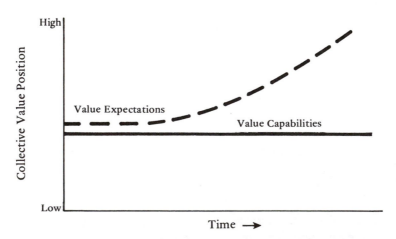

FIGURE 3.6. Aspirational Deprivation. (From Gurr, *Why Men Rebel,* p. 51.)

Gurr observes that the Industrial Revolution made a few businessmen rich and convinced most intellectuals that they should be rich. They weren't. He observes that the gap between their rising expectations and stable attainments soon impelled the intellectuals to revolutionary fervor.

3. *Progressive deprivation:* (See Figure 3.7.) (In spite of the fact that men feel deserve more and more, their benefits continue to decline.)

This is the paradigm discussed by Davies.

Gurr argues that relative deprivation can arise in a variety of ways. Regardless of how it arises, however, it provokes rebellious anger. According to Gurr, whether or not this deprivation leads to rebellion depends on two factors: the benefits the citizen expects from a successful revolution versus the costs of successful, or even worse, unsuccessful revolutionary activity. Gurr observes:

> This disposition to violence, discontent, can be tempered by socially implanted attitudes that condemn violence, facilitated and focused on the political system by similarly derived doctrines and experience that suggest its justifiability and utility. (p. 317)

Given the evidence, then, that cost-benefit considerations shape a discontented group's receptivity to revolutionary ideas, to find that revolutionary leaders often cannot resist the temptation to lie to their fellows is not surprising. They cannot resist exaggerating the likelihood of revolutionary success while minimizing the oftentimes terrifying costs of defeat.

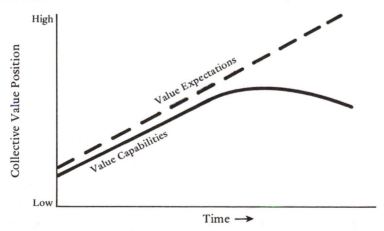

FIGURE 3.7. Progressive Deprivation. (From Gurr, *Why Men Rebel*, p. 53.)

REACTIONS OF OUTSIDE AGENCIES

The preceding discussion has focused upon the techniques participants use to restore an unjust relationship to equity. The exploiter and the exploited are not the only possible agents of equity restoration, however. The participant's friends, social workers, the courts, etc., may all observe the inequity, become distressed by it, and intervene to right existing wrongs. What effects do such interventions have on the harmdoer, the victim, and the "impartial" observer himself?

Intervention by Outside Agencies

The Impact of Intervention on the Harmdoer. Outside agencies often intervene when relationships become disturbingly inequitable.[26] Religious and legal agencies prod their clients to make restitution to their victims. Social welfare agencies and insurance companies compensate the disadvantaged. What are the effects of such interventions? Probably they depend on whether the intervening agency prods the exploiter to compensate, preempts his plans to compensate, punishes him, or simply provides backup compensation to his neglected victim.

Prodding the harmdoer to make restitution: Society's first intervention attempts are usually directed toward persuading harmdoers to voluntarily compensate their victims. This is a wise policy. If individuals can be induced to voluntarily compensate those they have injured, everyone benefits. The repentant harmdoer should become a stauncher adherent of the equity norm.[27] He should also serve as a behavioral model for others; when observers find themselves in similar situations, they should tend to imitate the models they have; in this case, an equitable model.[28]

Forcing the harmdoer to make restitution: Once it becomes evident that a social agency is not going to be able to persuade the harmdoer to make restitution, other agencies may intervene and force him to make restitution. There is some wisdom in this strategy. The harmdoer who is forced to compensate at least is dissuaded from justifying his inequitable behavior and is prevented from serving as a negative model for others.

Throughout time, societies have tried a variety of techniques to force individuals to make restitution. For example, Schafer (1960) observes that the ancient Germanic laws (*leges barbarorum*) consisted of an intricate tariff system, which stipulated how much a harmdoer must compensate various victims for various crimes. For example, a freeborn man was worth more than a slave, an adult more than a child, a man more than a woman, and a person of rank more than a freeman. Every kind of blow or wound given to every kind of person also had its price. The stipulated amount of compensation varied according to the nature of the crime and the age, rank, sex, and prestige of the injured party. Part of the "composition" was paid to the victim (*Wergeld, Busse, emenda, lendis*) and part to the community or king (*Frienden-geld, fredus, gewedde*). The Germanic tribes exerted intense pressure on the wrongdoer to make restitution. If the wrongdoer redeemed himself, he was protected from retaliation; if he was reluctant to pay, or could not raise the necessary sum, he was declared as *friedlos* or outlaw. He was regarded as ostracized and anyone might kill him with impunity.[29]

Today, in almost every country, legal agencies have hammered out procedures for forcing harmdoers to make restitution to their victims. For example, in most countries, a victim can sue a harmdoer for material exploitation, loss of potential income, and for physical or psychic damage, as well. (In Holland one can sue an insulting person for damage to one's honor and reputation. In the German Federal Republic one can recover a *solatium* for his injured feelings.)

These same systems have worked out complementary procedures for making sure the harmdoer pays the damages he owes. (For example, in Finland, Italy, Turkey, Canada, and Cuba, the state may turn a portion of the prisoner's earnings over to his victim.) The Danish, Hungarian, and Norwegian legal systems take the harmdoer's willingness to make restitution into account when determining sentences or granting paroles. When a prisoner's freedom is contingent on his eagerness to make restitution, restitution is obviously not voluntary. In these countries, however, the courts consider it better from a rehabilitative point of view to elicit involuntary restitution than to allow the prisoner to make none at all.

Macaulay and Walster (1971) surveyed the American legal system with two questions in mind: To what extent do existing laws and informal legal procedures encourage restitution and reconciliation? To what extent do existing legal procedures foster self-justification; i.e., derogation, denial, and minimization of the victim's suffering? They concluded that:

> On its face, American law is consistent with the goal of supporting compensation ... For example, the common law of torts consists of rules which say that a wrongdoer must compensate his victim. In addition, the legal system in operation provides more avenues to restitution than are available in its formal rules. A wide variety of informal procedures encourage compensation. For example, criminal sanctions are sometimes used as leverage to induce restitu-

tion. A police officer may decide not to arrest a shoplifter if the wrongdoer is not a professional thief and if the stolen items are returned; a district attorney may decide not to prosecute if the amount embezzled is returned. (p. 179)

The authors also acknowledge, however, that other legal rules and procedures exist that dilute a harmdoer's incentive to restore equity. The legal necessity of determining who is at fault, the inevitable delays in securing judgments, the costs of litigation, and impersonal insurance systems all tend to emphasize bargaining and to de-emphasize exact equity restoration. They conclude:

The tendency in the law, then, is not to support the ideal of having the wrongdoer make good the harm he has done, but to support the best balance of self-interest possible between harmdoer and victim, in light of bargaining skill and position. Rather than develop the harmdoer's best motives, the system tends to guard against his worst since the potential of litigation forces him to try to strike some bargain rather than to ignore totally the victim's claim (Friedman & Macaulay, 1969). (p. 182)

The American legal system then, exerts modest pressure on wrongdoers to behave fairly.

The psychological literature[30] and the observations of penal theorists[31] provide some support for the contention that if one can induce fair behavior, fair attitudes will follow.

Punishing the harmdoer: If outside agencies are completely thwarted in their attempts to persuade—or to force—the harmdoer to make voluntary restitution, there is one final avenue of equity restoration open to them: they can see to it that the harmdoer "pays his debt to society."

Legal philosophers have never been able to agree on *why* society should punish wrongdoers. Should we punish men to restore equity? To protect society by isolating them? To set a harsh example for other potential harmdoers? To rehabilitate them? They cannot agree. In spite of philosophers' disagreements, however, many observers feel that, at least in part, wrongdoers should expiate their crimes by suffering. Historically, retaliation and punishment were inextricably intertwined. For example, the *Code of Hammurabi* (about 2250 B.C.) is evidently based on the philosophy that things should be "set right" via *exact* punishment: "If one break a man's bone, they shall break his bone." (In Harper, 1904, p. 73) Today, in spite of the admonitions of penologists, many people still feel the punishment should fit the crime.[32]

For example, Durkheim (1933) observes:

And in truth, punishment has remained, at least in part, a work of vengeance. It is said that we do not make the culpable suffer in order to make him suffer;

it is none the less true that we find it just that he suffer . . . In supposing that punishment can really serve to protect us in the future, we think that it ought to be above all an *expiation* of the past. The proof of this lies in the minute precautions we take to proportion punishment as exactly as possible to the severity of the crime; they would be inexplicable if we did not believe that the culpable ought to suffer because he has done evil and in the same degree. (pp. 88–89)

In spite of the fact that citizens have debated whether the aim of imprisonment should be vengeance, isolation of the criminal, punishment, and/or rehabilitation, no one really knows the effect of various kinds of punishments on the harmdoer.

Providing compensation to the victim: Sometimes an agency must admit defeat. There is no way they can elicit restitution. (For example, harmdoers are often unknown or indigent.) Some theorists argue that in such cases, the community should reconcile itself to the fact that an injustice has occurred and simply intervene to alleviate the victim's suffering. Such intervention is consistent with our notions of fairness (the innocent victim is recompensed) and is expedient (society affirms the legitimacy of equity norms).

Some legal theorists have even proposed that, in the interests of justice and efficiency, the state should *routinely* assume responsibility for compensating victims of criminal violence.[33] They argue that the state could save time and money if, instead of tracking down harmdoers and prodding them into making restitution, the state simply provided automatic compensation to the disadvantaged.

Equity theorists would warn that society should be wary of eroding an individual's feeling of responsibility for restoring equity. If the harmdoer knows that an outside agency will reestablish equity, he should have little motivation to initiate a program of his own. Even worse, it is probable that an agency set up to "right all wrongs" would soon be unable to fulfill its mandate. Funds for social justice are always meager. Although citizens may be unanimous in their agreement that social justice is desirable, they seldom agree that society ought to pursue this goal at all costs. Inevitably, agencies are forced to do the best they can with meager funds. Social welfare agencies thus soon evolve from agencies of perfect "social justice" into agencies of "social compromise."[34] For these reasons, most policy makers view public compensation as a source of residual restitution, to be resorted to only when agencies have totally failed to induce the exploiter to make restitution.

The Impact of Intervention on the Victim. As yet, Equity theorists have not investigated the impact that outside agencies' intervention has on the victim.

FIGURE 3.8. "Funds for Social Justice Are Always Meager."

The Impact of Intervention and Nonintervention on the Outside Observers Themselves. Thus far, we have spoken as if outside agencies are, somehow, capable of objectively evaluating a relationship and objectively deciding how its wrongs can best be righted. This characterization is not an honest one, however. According to Equity theory, a "scrutineer" is a "scrutineer." For all men, outside agencies, supposedly impartial observers, as well as participants themselves, equity is in the eye of the beholder. And, all men's eyes are clouded by bias.

The evidence suggests that when impartial observers perceive injustice, they generally react in precisely the same ways that participants do, with one qualification: observers respond far less passionately than do participants. The discovery that observers faintly echo participants' fiery reactions should come as no surprise. Human beings are able to empathize with others. An observer who empathizes with a harmdoer may well share his embarrassment and rationalizations; the observer who empathizes with a victim may well share his anger and indignation.[35] If, as seems likely, the feelings we empathize with are less intense than the ones we experience, we can understand why observers react to injustice less intensely than do actual participants.

Evidence that impartial observers react to injustice in much the same was as do participants comes from a wide variety of sources:

Restoration of actual equity: When participants are unable or refuse to restore equity, impartial observers often intervene and attempt to set things right. Indeed, social welfare and legal structures are primarily designed to prod harmdoers into "paying their debt" to their victims and to society.[36] Individuals often take it upon themselves to do the same kind of balancing.

Berkowitz and Daniels (1963) and Berkowitz and Connor (1966) found that college students will work hard to help a fellow student get the rewards he deserves. More impressively, they found that students will expend such effort even when there is little chance that anyone will ever realize that *they* were the ones who volunteered to help.

Baker (1974) also demonstrates that third parties will sacrifice themselves in order to insure that others are treated equitably. Baker points out that unless individuals can rely on the continuing cooperation of other group members, they will be unable to secure many of the things they need. As a consequence, third parties have a vested interest in encouraging everyone to behave fairly, and in stepping in to set things right when they don't. Thus, Baker argues, it is not surprising to find that third parties will sometimes behave irrationally (uneconomically) to make sure that all's right with the world.

Baker tested his notions in a two-part gaming experiment. In the first game, the payoff structure was rigged. The third party watched two equally competent players earn markedly different payoffs: one player received far more than he deserved; the other received far less. In the second game, the third party was given a chance to allocate points to the participants.

Baker's results are interesting. Most of the observers (seventy-three percent) played in a way designed to allow the initially disadvantaged person to catch up with the favored one. A minority of the observers (twelve percent) maintained equity between the players in quite a different way. These players ignored the first session injustice and either allocated points on the basis of participants' performance in the *second* game or split points evenly. In any case, the vast majority of third parties *were* sensitive to equity considerations in allocating rewards.

One of Baker's most intriguing observations is that in his experiment, observers had quite different ideas as to how far back in time one should go in assessing the equitableness of a relationship. Some observers thought they should restore equity in the total "social segment" ("first game *plus* second game"). Others thought that "what was done in game number 1 was done," and that they should focus simply on distributing rewards fairly in the second session.

Baker (1973) argued that usually individuals will agree concerning the length of a "social segment" and that in most casual relationships social segments will be fairly short. He notes:

> What really overwhelms the memory capacity is the problem of remembering each *I* (Input). For example, consider two men in a bar. Man One asks who buys? We do not expect the other to calculate the answer by saying "Well, on July 3, 1933 I bought one and you bought two. On July 5, 1933 etc., etc." Not only would an accurate calculation of whose turn it was to buy be beyond their memory capacity, it would also be a great waste of time to figure it out. Instead, they are much better served if they have some simple rule defining a drinking social segment. No problems will arise if they stay in the bar long enough to consume an even number of drinks and if "you bought the last one, I'll get this one" prevails. Any reasonable excuse may be used for deciding who buys the first drink. Thus, the social segment facilitates one's social life as well as keeping the mind from getting bogged down trying to remember everything that happened in the past. (pp. 5-6)

Thus, Baker argues individuals try to maintain equity within a single social segment.

Sometimes, however, (as in Baker's experiment) the boundaries of the social segment are ambiguous. For example, one man might think that the round he bought last week should count in this week's exchange; his drinking buddy may disagree.

Individuals may also disagree as to the boundaries of the social segment because they are motivated to do so by self-interest. For example, recently James Farmer asked the churches to pay reparation for 300 years of the social degradation of black Americans. Farmer wished to define the social segment as spanning three centuries and an infinity of separate interactions. Most whites insisted that they were only responsible for harm they had done personally to specific blacks.

Restoration of psychological equity:

One nightfall a man travelling on horseback toward the sea reached an inn by the roadside. He dismounted, and confident in man and night like all riders toward the sea, he tied his horse to a tree beside the door and entered into the inn.

At midnight when all were asleep, a thief came and stole the traveler's horse.

In the morning the man awoke, and discovered that his horse was stolen. And he grieved for his horse. . .

Then his fellow-lodgers came and stood around him and began to talk.

And the first man said, "How foolish of you to tie your horse outside the stable."

And the second said, "Still more foolish, without even hobbling the horse!"

And the third man said, "It is stupid at best to travel to the sea on horseback."

And the fourth said, "Only the indolent and the slow of foot own horses."

Then the traveller was much astonished. At last he cried, "My friends, because my horse is stolen, you have hastened one and all to tell me my faults and my shortcomings. But strange, not one word of reproach have you uttered about the man who stole my horse." (Gibran, 1963, pp. 33–34)

Gibran's anecdote suggests that when "impartial" observers of injustice cannot reestablish actual equity, they tend to settle for restoring psychological equity.

Lerner (1971*b*) would agree. Lerner argues that even the most impartial of observers possesses an intense desire to believe in a just world. In an impressive body of research, he documents observers' eagerness to convince themselves that people get what they deserve and deserve what they get.

For example, Lerner (1965*a*) found that if one worker in a team of workers was *arbitrarily* given a large bonus, observers would soon manage to convince themselves that he was entitled to it. Although they knew a coin flip determined who won and who lost, they couldn't help but believe that the winner's work must have been superior to the loser's—somehow.

Other studies provide evidence that observers do tend to blame innocent victims for their suffering.[37] In Lerner and Simmons (1966) and Lerner (1969), for example, students observed a fellow student trying to learn a list of paired-associates. Each time she missed a word, she was painfully shocked. When observers knew that in spite of their best efforts, the girl would continue to be shocked in a subsequent session, the observers devalued her. Observers have been found to react in essentially the same condemnatory way, whether they're males or females, Berkeley high school students, college students from Kentucky or Pennsylvania, or graduate students in the helping professions.

Chaiken and Darley (1973) provide impressive evidence that a bystander's reaction to an event will depend on whether he identifies with the perpetrator or the victim of an inequity. The authors asked college students to watch a videotaped "accident." The students carefully observed a supervisor guide a worker in performing a task. When the worker finally finished his task, the supervisor stood up, remarking, "I guess that's it." As he pushed away from the table, it began to wobble. The worker's carefully completed project toppled over and was destroyed. As a consequence of this accident, the worker lost the bonus he had expected. The authors predicted that when students expected to become supervisors themselves, their sympathies would be with the supervisor, and they would be motivated to perceive the event as an accident. Conversely, when they expected to be workers themselves, their sympathies would be with the worker, and they should condemn the supervisor for his carelessness. These predictions were confirmed.[38]

The preceding speculations and evidence lead us to conclude that although "impartial" observers can certainly evaluate the fairness of an interaction more objectively than can participants, we must remember that even the most aloof of judges is personally motivated to believe the world is a fair and equitable place. He is personally motivated to right existing wrongs, and, failing that, to at least convince himself that this is a just world; a place where exploiters are, somehow, entitled to their excessive benefits and the deprived, somehow, deserve to suffer.

Equity and the Law

There is no social psychological theory in existence that will give us a complete understanding of the American legal system, or even a complete understanding of even a tiny part of the legal system. Yet, even a superficial glance at Equity theory makes it evident that the theory must have *some* relevance to the legal process. Equity theory deals with men's perceptions of fairness and justice. Not surprisingly then, legal theorists quickly realized that the theory might provide some insights into the reaction of impartial observers, such as judges, jurors, and courtroom spectators, to the legal process.

For example, Austin, Walster, and Utne (1976) argued that if Equity theory is correct, judges, jurors, and spectators should have profoundly different reactions to the harmdoer who has suffered than to the harmdoer who has not.

Austin et al.'s argument goes as follows. Presumably, society punishes wrongdoers, *at least in part,* "to set things right"; to balance the crime against appropriate punishment. If this is so, it raises a fascinating possibility. It should be possible for a defendant to "pay for" his crime, or convince the jury he has, before he ever comes to trial. If the defendant

reveals he suffered from intense remorse;
was accidentally injured while committing the crime;
volunteered financial restitution;
was held in lengthy pretrial detention;
suffered in ways unconnected with his crime

judges and jurors may well conclude that he has paid for his crime. This perception may affect both their liking and sympathy for him *and* the sentence they assign him.

Many legal scholars have remarked that a criminal's suffering weighs heavily on the minds of judges and juries. The bank robber who is crippled when making a getaway may get an unusually light sentence. The mother whose child is killed when she runs a stop sign may be treated with similar leniency.

Equity theory makes some intriguing predictions as to the effect that a defendant's suffering might have on a judge's and juror's eagerness to punish him and their liking for him.

Harmdoer's Suffering and Sentencing. Let us consider a typical case. A trusted accountant embezzles $10 thousand from his employer. The employer catches him. He is so enraged at his accountant's exploitative behavior that he complains to their mutual friends, clients, and, finally, to the police. Then the accountant's troubles begin. His outside clients abandon him in droves, he suffers business losses, his wife divorces him, and he faces the threat of imprisonment.

How will such information affect jurors? How will they react if the accountant's losses are described as negligible compared to his crime (i.e., say $10)? If they balance out his crime (say $10 thousand)? If they far exceed his crime (say $100 thousand)?

Equity theorists would predict that jurors will take information concerning the embezzler's suffering into account when deciding how much restitution he owes the victim and society. When the embezzler has lost only $10 as a consequence of his crime, he has made only the most token of atonements. When he has lost $10 thousand or $100 thousand as a result of his $10 thousand embezzlement, however, he has, in a sense, completely paid for his theft. Thus, we would expect jurors to feel he had a more severe punishment "coming to him" when he has lost only $10 than when he's lost $10 thousand or $100 thousand.

Contingency of Suffering. According to Equity theory, "an equitable relationship exists when all participants are receiving equal relative outcomes *from the relationship.*" This statement suggests that the *context* in which a harmdoer suffers should be an important determinant of whether his suffering "counts" as atonement or whether it is judged to be irrelevant to his relationship with the victim. For example, if the jurors know that the irate employer ruined the embezzler's outside business in order to punish him for his theft, the embezzler's suffering is clearly a "consequence of his relationship with the victim." Under these conditions, the embezzler's suffering may well be considered partial atonement for his theft. If, on the other hand, the jurors learn that a playmate accidentally shot the embezzler when he was a child, his early suffering will probably not be considered to be partial atonement for his theft. It should not "count."

On the basis of this reasoning, we would predict that how relevant to the harmdoer/victim relationship the harmdoer's suffering is will determine whether or not the exploiter's suffering counts against the debt he owes the victim and society.

Harmdoer's Suffering and Liking. Clarence Darrow declared in 1933 that:

> Jurymen seldom convict a person they like, or acquit one they dislike. The main work of the trial lawyer is to make a jury like his client, or at least to feel sympathy for him; facts regarding the crime are relatively unimportant. (In Sutherland, 1966, p. 442)

Kalven and Zeisel (1966) point out that jurors' liking and sympathy for the defendant and plaintiff have a dramatic impact on the way they evaluate evidence. The first thing Equity theorists might ask, then, is: Does a harmdoer's suffering affect the jurors' liking and sympathy for the defendant?

According to Equity theorists, a person will evaluate another person differently depending on the *function* that he thinks his expressions of liking will have. They note that expressions of liking can serve to (1) compensate or punish another, (2) mirror one's justifications, or (3) simply reflect one's mood.

Expression of Liking as Compensation: Sometimes people are keenly aware that their expressions of regard for someone will have actual consequences for that person's life. We know that if we report that an acquaintance is a "dislikable, repulsive, filthy crook," our listeners will probably not be eager to invite him to dinner—or to offer him a job. If we say he is "likable, charming, and conscientious," he may well reap those social benefits.

In any case, if, when courtroom spectators, character witnesses, or jurors discuss the defendant's personality or character, they know that their answer may have practical consequences for the defendant, they can't help but equate "expressions of liking" with "conferring reward or punishment."

Under conditions that make connections between "expressed liking" and "reward vs. punishment" salient, Equity theorists would expect a positive relationship between the harmdoer's suffering and the witnesses' expressed liking for him. When an embezzler has not paid sufficiently for his crime, spectators, witnesses, and jurors should be motivated to express disapproval and disliking, in the hope that he will be punished. When the harmdoer has already suffered overmuch, they should express approval and liking in an effort to compensate him for his suffering. (See Figure 3.9.)

Previous research has documented the eagerness of impartial observers to reward the deprived with public praise and to punish the overbenefited with public condemnation.[39]

Expressions of Liking as Justification. Sometimes, individuals know that they are powerless to right social wrongs. Nothing they can do will have any conceivable effect on their fate. The lawbreaker may be so poor he can never make restitution to his victim; he may be so old he could never serve out an appropriate sentence. Or, it may be clear to the juror that a guilty defendant will be released on a technicality.

In such cases, observers are left with only two options: they can acknowledge the irremediable inequity or they can justify its existence. They can convince themselves that the participant deserved his excessively lenient or excessively harsh treatment. In such cases, observers' "expressions of liking" may simply reflect their consoling justification of the *status quo*. For example, if the courtroom spectator or juror learns that the ubiquitous embezzler has gotten away with an exces-

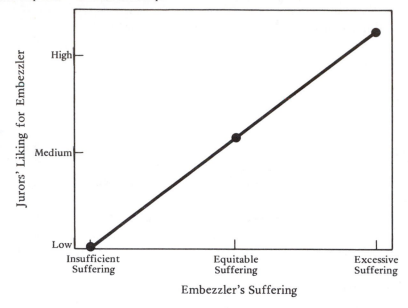

FIGURE 3.9. The Predicted Relationship between the Embezzler's Suffering and Jurors' Liking for Him: Liking as Compensation. (From M. K. Utne, "Functions of Expressions of Liking in Response to Inequity," in L. Berkowitz and E. Walster, eds., *Advances in Experimental Social Psychology*, vol. 9. New York: Academic Press, 1976, p. 175. Reprinted by permission.)

sively lenient punishment ($10), and he can do nothing to right this injustice, he might be motivated to convince himself that extenuating circumstances were such that the defendant only deserved that little punishment; that the defendant is a likable fellow who really didn't deserve to suffer. On the other hand, when he learns that the embezzler has received an excessively harsh penalty ($100 thousand worth), the observer might be motivated to convince himself that in fact the embezzler is a despicable fellow who deserved what he got. ("Probably this wasn't the first time he embezzled from his firm; only the first time he'd been *caught*.") (See Figure 3.10.)

Previous theorists have documented that impartial observers' "expressions of liking" often reflect their intense desire to derogate or aggrandize another.[40]

Expressions of Liking as Emotion. Sometimes individuals have reactions to others that have nothing to do with equity restoration; they simply feel what they feel even though it doesn't do them or anyone else a bit of good. As Homans (1961) points out, one tends to

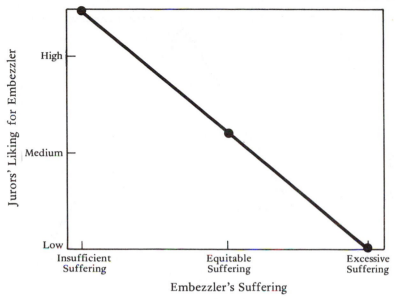

FIGURE 3.10. The Predicted Relationship between the Embezzler's Suffering and Jurors' Liking for Him: Liking as Justification. (From Utne, in *Advances in Experimental Social Psychology*, p. 176.)

feel contented when he and his acquaintances are being treated equitably and to feel distressed when they are being treated inequitably. Since people have a strong tendency to dislike those who are associated with unpleasantness and injustice,[41] we might expect people to have a positive reaction to the defendant who has paid in full for his crime and a negative one to the defendant who has either escaped punishment or been punished overmuch.

We can easily acknowledge our tendencies to dislike wrongdoers, in part because they confront us with the unsettling realization that injustice exists. It is harder to admit that one might feel some anger at the excessively tormented person because he reminds us of the same thing. Yet, psychologists have observed that we do feel some resentment toward anyone, harmdoer *or* victim, who threatens our comfortable world. To the extent that spectators' and jurors' expressions of "liking" simply reflect their "mood," we would expect the defendant's suffering and liking to be related as shown in Figure 3.11.

It is apparent, then, that the expected relationship between a harmdoer's suffering and an observer's liking for him is a complicated one. An inquirer may get quite different replies if the observer believes his expressions of liking (1) can facilitate restitution or retaliation,

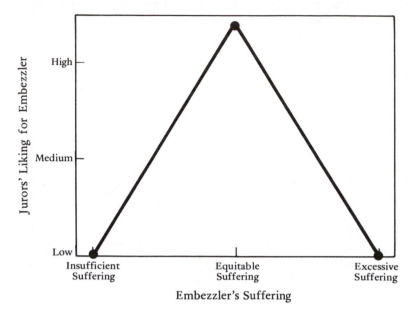

FIGURE 3.11. The Predicted Relationship between the Embezzler's Suffering and Jurors' Liking for Him: Liking as Emotion. (From Utne, in *Advances in Experimental Social Psychology*, p. 177.)

(2) can only support his justifications, or (3) simply reflect his mood.

Suffering and Liking: The Evidence. Some theorists have long been aware that liking might serve as a compensation; others were aware that liking might serve as a justification; still others were aware that liking could reflect emotionality. Unfortunately, no one ever put these ob-servations together before. No one realized "liking" might serve three distinct functions.

Thus, there is little information as to the conditions that moti-vate individuals to use expressions of liking in one or another way. For this reason, Utne (1974) attempted to determine whether or not, under appropriate circumstances, courtroom spectators may respond to the simple question: "How much do you like Defendant X?" in the three ways we've proposed.

Utne asked college students to act in the role of courtroom spectators. The criminal case she gave them was a completely fictional account of the circumstances surrounding an embezzlement. She explained:

Facts of the Case

The defendant, Robert Brown, is a 32-year-old white male. He is a practicing accountant in Oakdale, a midwest city of approximately 250,000.

Plaintiffs are Smith, owner of a drycleaning store, and Jones, owner of a carry-out food outlet. Plaintiffs also work and reside in Oakdale.

In June of 1962, Smith and Jones opened their businesses. Defendant Brown, a certified public accountant, was retained at this time to manage their books and in general act as financial overseer for the businesses.

Although initially in debt, by January 1, 1964, the businesses were prospering. The successful working association of Brown, Smith and Jones continued.

Two years later, winter of 1966, plaintiffs realized that although daily cash receipts had increased tremendously, their total profits had not increased accordingly. Both Smith and Jones were earning a modest, comfortable yearly income, but relative to the great expansion of their businesses, net income was too low.

Aware that something was amiss, Smith and Jones hired another accountant to privately review their books and find the source of the discrepancies. After a careful and extensive investigation, this accountant reported gross irregularities in the books.

Smith and Jones went immediately to their attorney for counsel, and on February 15, 1966, brought suit against Robert Brown for embezzlement under grounds as set forth in Ill. Stat. 277.04.

During the trial Brown admitted embezzling almost $100,000 of Smith's and Jones' money over a two-year period." (pp. 13–14)

Varying the defendant's sentence: Immediately following this case description, mock spectators were told of the sentence given the defendant. All were told of the *possible* range of punishment:

"THE SENTENCE. The possible range of punishments Brown could have received according to the law varied from a minimum of $10,000 fine (no repayment of embezzled money) with a suspended sentence, to a maximum of $200,000 repayment plus fine, and 40 years in prison." (p. 14)

The students were told that Brown had received an excessive, an equitable, or an insufficient punishment.

"*Excessive Punishment condition.* Robert Brown was given the especially severe punishment of $100,000 repayment to Smith and Jones, plus $100,000 fine, and 40 years in prison without consideration for parole until 20 years had been served.

Equitable Punishment condition. Robert Brown was given the moderate punishment of paying back all the money he had taken from Smith and Jones ($100,000), plus paying their expenses for trying to get their money back (legal, court costs). In addition, a deterrent punishment was given—2 years in prison with a chance for parole after 6 months.

Insufficient Punishment condition. Robert Brown was given the especially light punishment of paying a $10,000 fine. He was not required to repay Smith and Jones. Brown was given no deterrent punishment such as a prison term, but rather received a suspended sentence." (p. 15)

71

After reading these facts of the case, students were asked about *their* reactions to the *Brown* vs. *Smith and Jones* controversy. (At this point, Utne tried to lead "jurors" to think of their expressions of liking/disliking in quite different terms.)

Jurors in the *Compensation* condition were led to believe their responses would have actual consequences for the defendant:

> "A current legal trend is to consider community standards in the assignment of criminal penalties. . . . Your town is partaking in this trend by conducting an experimental court procedure. After a case has been tried and sentence determined, courtroom spectators from the community are asked to anonymously complete questionnaires asking about their feelings regarding the trial, the people involved, the verdict and the sentence. *The responses are read by the presiding judge, and he uses them to the primary factor in determining a new sentence when the defendant appeals his sentence.* This procedure worked extremely well in two recent appeals, where one sentence was made lighter, another heavier, on the basis of community responses to the original case." (p. 16)

Jurors in the *Justification* condition were told their responses would have no effect on the defendant's legal situation. Utne tried to stimulate justification by presenting possible rationales for the defendant's sentence. Jurors were expected to "pick up" on the one more appropriate to their particular punishment level.

> "Carefully and thoughtfully consider the details of the case and the decision of the court when you answer the questions. For example, you may feel like the jurors who commented that Robert Brown was a contemptible criminal, willing to take advantage of the trust placed in him by his friends. He was a man with no regard for morals or principles, these jurors said, and they felt he showed no remorse for his actions.
>
> Or you might feel as some of the jurors did that Robert Brown was a good, hardworking man who'd helped his friends and community for years, and unfortunately gave in to a very human temptation. In their view, the carelessness of his partners in ignoring their own financial matters made it especially easy for this basically good man to make a mistake. . . . Whatever your feelings are about the case, please consider the facts carefully when answering the questions." (pp. 17–18)

Finally subjects in the *Emotion* condition were encouraged to give a purely emotional expression of liking for the defendant.

> "A rational, analytical response is *not* what is wanted here. *Of primary importance in answering these questions is that you be in touch with your feelings, unafraid to say whatever comes into your mind.* There may be features of the case that just 'ticked off' a response in you. For example, one of the jurors commented that any person in Robert Brown's position, a

defendant in a criminal proceeding, just naturally aroused feelings of warmth and sympathy which couldn't help but influence his decision. Another juror noted the opposite response in himself, that anyone on trial for lawbreaking like Robert Brown was made him experience feelings of disgust and contempt, feelings which also influenced his decision.

No matter what your feelings about Robert Brown and his case are, don't be afraid to express them. Give your first, immediate 'gut response' to the embezzler Robert Brown, and his trial."*

Finally the jurors were asked about their reactions to the case. Included in the questions was the critical question: "How much do you like the defendant?"

Utne's data provide compelling support for Equity theorists' contention that: (1) expressions of liking *can* serve at least two different functions, and (2) the amount of punishment given a defendant ("too much," "just right," "not enough") does interact with the subject's motivation ("compensation," "justification," "emotional expressions") in determining his expressed liking for the defendant. (See Figure 3.12.)

In the *Compensation* condition, spectators knew that any expressions of liking/disliking could have practical consequences for the defendant. As predicted, under these conditions, observers expressed moderate dislike for the insufficiently punished defendant, slight dislike for the equitably punished defendant, and moderate liking for the excessively punished one.

In the *Justification* condition, spectators knew that they were powerless to alter the defendant's prison sentence. Their expressions of liking were expected to reflect their acceptance of the *status quo*. As predicted, under these conditions observers slightly liked the insufficiently punished defendant, slightly disliked the equitably punished defendant, and moderately disliked the excessively punished one.

In the *Emotion* condition, spectators were encouraged to simply express their mood. They were expected to like the equitably treated defendant most and the inequitably treated defendants—i.e., the insufficiently *and* excessively punished defendants—least. This prediction was *not* confirmed. Regardless of whether the defendant had been insufficiently punished, equitably punished, or excessively punished, spectators slightly disliked him.

---

*From M.K. Utne, "Functions of Expressions of Liking in Response to Inequity," in L. Berkowitz and E. Walster, eds., *Advances in Experimental Social Psychology*, vol. 9 (New York: Academic Press, 1976), pp. 177–181. Reprinted with permission.

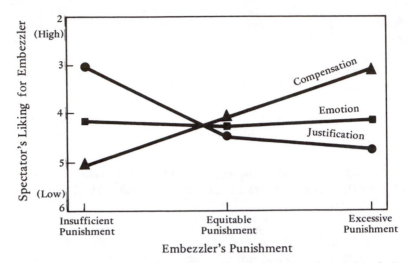

FIGURE 3.12. The Relationship Secured between the Embezzler's Punishment and the Spectator's Liking for Him as a Person. (From Utne, in *Advances in Experimental Social Psychology*, p. 181.)

We opened this section with Clarence Darrow's statement emphasizing the importance of liking for the legal process. Undoubtedly, Darrow's, and Kalven and Zeisel's, observations are correct; jurors' liking for the defendant and the plaintiff must have *some* impact on the way they process information and on their ultimate decisions. However, Utne's data suggest that the link between "liking" and the "processing of information" and "sentencing behavior" is not as simple as theorists have supposed. The legal process is just that—a process. Courtroom interactions are ongoing, dynamic processes. Jurors constantly receive new information about their own roles as jurors, about the defendant and the plaintiff, and about their ability to affect the situation; e.g., the freedom to set penalties. Nor is liking static. The opinions one forms of others are constantly being altered by the input of new information. One's affective orientations, in turn, filter incoming information, and shape one's critical decisions. For example, jurors might enter the courtroom, naively assuming that they will have the power to set things right. They will have the power to decide the defendant's guilt or innocence, and in a few instances, to give him an appropriate sentence.

During the course of the trial, the testimony might yield new information which arouses a strong emotional response in the jurors; their liking for the defendant might then be colored by those feelings.

When the judge issues his instructions, however, the jurors may discover that they have far less power than they had thought. The jury deliberation may further reinforce their feeling of powerlessness. They may discover that all the other jurors want to let the "guilty" defendant go, or they may discover that the defendant will be let off on a legal technicality in spite of the jury's unanimous decision that he is guilty. Under these conditions, the disenchanted jurors might resign themselves to the *status quo*.

Each of the preceding events should affect the jurors' liking for the defendant and the victim, and their liking, in turn, should color their reaction to new information and affect their sentencing behavior. It is clear that the link between "liking" and sentencing behavior is, at best, a complex one.

Suffering and Sentencing: The Evidence. Initially, we proposed that there would be a link between the juror's perception of the defendant's suffering and his liking for him. Utne (1974) demonstrated that this suffering and liking are linked. Liking, in turn, presumably affects the juror's evaluation of evidence and his sentencing. This relationship has not been empirically tested, but it has been noted by legal scholars.

Secondly, we proposed that there would be a link between the juror's perception of the defendant's suffering and his sentencing behavior. Since the liking/sentencing relationship may be so complex, and since we do not yet know how much of an impact liking has on sentencing, we might do well to turn directly to our second question and ask: What impact does a defendant's suffering have on the spectators' and jurors' desire to punish him further?

Many theorists and lawyers believe that jurors will be sympathetic toward defendants who claim they have endured great remorse or great personal and financial losses. In two recent and highly publicized legal cases, the Watergate burglaries of the Democratic party headquarters and the resignation and conviction of ex-Vice President Spiro Agnew, the defendants used appeals to sympathy with varying success.

E. Howard Hunt was convicted of breaking into the Democratic party national headquarters during the 1972 presidential election campaign. He was convicted of burglary and given a preliminary sentence of six to twenty years in prison. In his testimony during his trial, before a grand jury, and before a Senate special investigation, Mr. Hunt pleaded for leniency on the basis of his suffering from the crimes he committed. During the Senate hearings he noted:

> Now I find myself confined under a sentence which may keep me in prison for the rest of my life. I have been incarcerated for six months. For a time I was in solitary confinement. I have been physically attacked and robbed in jail. I have suffered a stroke. I have been transferred from place to place, manacled and chained, hand and foot. I am isolated from my motherless

FIGURE 3.13. "Your Honor, Can We Just Take the Pardon and Go?...We've Suffered Enough Already!" (Editorial cartoon by Pat Oliphant. Copyright © The Denver Post. Reprinted with permission of Los Angeles Times Syndicate.)

children. The funds provided me and others who participated in the break-in have long since been exhausted. I am faced with an enormous financial burden in defending myself against criminal charges and numerous civil suits. (As reported by UPI, 1973)

Hunt's attempt to win sympathy and leniency has thus far failed to either reduce his prison sentence or to increase public support for his predicament.

In ex-Vice President Agnew's case, Elliot Richardson, the United States Attorney General in the government investigation and prosecution of charges of bribery and tax fraud, called for leniency on the grounds that the Vice President had suffered substantially. Richardson stated:

> I am firmly convinced that in all the circumstances leniency is justified. I am keenly aware, first, of the historic magnitude of the penalties inherent in the vice president's resignation from his high office and his acceptance of a judgment of conviction for a felony.
>
> To propose that a man who has suffered these penalties should, in addition, be incarcerated in a penal institution, however briefly, is more than I as head of the government's prosecuting arm, can recommend or wish. (As reported by AP, *Milwaukee Journal,* 1973)

Agnew was fined only $10 thousand and put on three years probation on only one charge of tax evasion. The prosecutors dropped all other charges.

In their classic survey of jury trials, Kalven and Zeisel (1971) found evidence that jurors do take a harmdoer's suffering into account when deciding on a penalty. These authors found that when a defendant reports great remorse, suffers in the commission of the crime, endures lengthy pretrial detention, or even when he has suffered misfortunes unconnected to the crime, jurors tend to be lenient. Consider, for example, the presiding judges' descriptions of why jurors, in a potpourri of cases, were more lenient than they should have been:

Defendant Suffers as a Consequence of Crime.
> While the Court sitting without a jury would have found him guilty, there was no difficulty for the Court to understand why a jury of laymen would find the defendant not guilty. The police chief and his witnesses were six-foot, one-inch men, weighing over 200 pounds, and the defendant was about five-foot seven, weighing about 118 pounds. . . . The police . . . beat the defendant up before they got him into the car. (p. 237)

Defendant Suffers Remorse. The authors report two cases in which judges mention the "defendant's remorse" as an explanation of the jurors' leniency.

Defendant Suffers Pretrial Detention.

The jury felt sorry for the defendant because he had been in jail for over two months and the lumber allegedly stolen was worth $2.50. I think the jury had a Jean Valjean complex. (p. 264)

It is customary for the judge in sentencing to give the defendant credit for the time he has already spent in jail; the jury, however, would at times not only give him credit, but would set him free. (p. 303)

The defendant is charged with the rape of his ten-year-old daughter and at the first trial of his case is found guilty and sentenced to life imprisonment. On appeal, a new trial is granted with a change of venue. At the second trial the jury hangs. The case is tried a third time, and it is for this third trial that we have the judge-jury report. At this trial it is disclosed that the defendant has at that point been in jail for thirteen months. The extraordinary reaction of this third and last jury, which acquits, is set forth by the judge as follows: They were out just 30 minutes. The jury took up a collection of $68 and gave it to the defendant after the case was over. (p. 304)

Defendant Suffers—Suffering Unrelated to Crime.

Defendant did not testify but the evidence shows that, during the years in question, his home burned, he was seriously injured, and his son was killed. Later he lost his leg, his wife gave birth to a premature child which was born blind and spastic. These, however, are only a portion of the calamities the defendant suffered during the years he failed to file his income tax return. The jury cannot bring itself to add to the misfortune of the defendant. The judge gives full recognition to the point, adding: "This is a typical case of the jury exercising the power of pardon."* (p. 305)

Kalven and Zeisel conclude, on the basis of these reports, that jurors' decisions are markedly influenced by whether or not the defendant has suffered, even if his suffering is unrelated to his crime.

Recently, Austin and his colleagues have amassed voluminous evidence that jurors do take a criminal's suffering into account when settling on an appropriate sentence.

In these early studies, Austin and his colleagues studied how observers respond to harmdoers when they believe they have or have not suffered as a direct consequence of their wrongdoing.

In a study with grade school children, Austin, Walster, and Pate (1973) tested the notion that children will assign harmdoers who have not suffered more punishment than they assign harmdoers who have already suffered as a consequence of their acts. Austin et al. asked the

---

*See H. Kalven, Jr. and H. Zeisel, *The American Jury* (Boston: Little, Brown & Company, Inc., 1966). Reprinted by permission.

children to read a story describing two boys, Steve and Bob. Steve was described as the harmdoer; Bob was the victim. During recess, while the two boys were playing baseball, Steve deliberately tripped Bob. Bob fell down and sprained his ankle and cut his lip. Steve lost his balance and fell down *in the act of tripping Bob.* Steve's suffering was then systematically varied: in the Insufficient Suffering condition his suffering was described as slight (he received "a few scratches on his hands"). In the Moderate Suffering condition he received "some painful cuts on his hands and knees." In the Excessive Suffering condition he "broke his arm and leg."

The story then reported that the school principal had appointed a student panel to decide how much punishment Steve should receive. "The principal tells the panel to decide how many hours Steve should have to stay after school. You are on the panel. How many hours would you say Steve should have to stay after school?" Students were asked to indicate their opinion on a "punishment scale," which ranged from zero to seven hours. Austin et al. found that students *did* assign Steve a harsher penalty when he had suffered insufficiently than when he suffered moderately or excessively.

Austin, Walster, and Utne (1976) found that college students take a criminal's suffering/non-suffering *in the act* into account when settling on his sentence.

In Studies 1 and 2, Austin et al. asked college students to read a synopsis of the proceedings of an actual trial. First, they read an eye-witness account of a crime. In Study 1, the defendant's crime was the relatively minor one of purse snatching. In Study 2, the defendant's crime was a far more serious one—he had not only snatched a purse, but he had severely beaten his female victim, causing her to be hospitalized for ten days.

After committing his crime, the defendant attempted to escape from the scene (and from the police). In the process, the purse-snatcher suffered not at all, or suffered moderately, or suffered excessively. In Study 1, the defendant was said to have suffered not at all, moderately (i.e., receiving cuts and bruises and a broken arm), or excessively (paralyzed from the neck down). In Study 2, the defendant was said to have suffered not at all, moderately (i.e., suffering cracked ribs and a broken leg), or excessively (paralyzed from the neck down).

Then, students were told that after deliberating for only ten minutes, the jury had convicted the defendant.

Students were asked to play the role of presiding judge. They were asked to carefully study the synopsis and then to recommend an "appropriate" sentence (within the minimum-maximum set by law).

In both studies, Austin and his colleagues found strong support for the "Suffering in the Act" hypothesis. The more the defendant was said to have suffered in the "getaway," the smaller the prison sentence mock judges gave him.

Finally, in an as yet unpublished series of studies, Austin and Utne (1975) tested an intriguing hypothesis. They proposed that jurors will be less impressed by a criminal's suffering if it is unrelated to his criminal activity than if it is a direct consequence of his criminal behavior.

Austin and Utne's experimental design was much like that used by Austin in the two studies described earlier. Mock jurors read an eye-witness account of a crime. They learned that after committing his crime, the defendant had been injured not at all, moderately, or excessively. In this study, however, Austin and Utne attempted to determine whether it made any difference if the defendant's suffering was totally unrelated to his crime or a direct consequence of it. In the Irrelevant Suffering condition, students read that while out on bail, the defendant accidentally fell down some stairs at his home and suffered moderately (receiving painful cuts, cracked ribs, and a broken leg) or excessively (becoming permanently paralyzed from the waist down). In the Relevant Suffering condition, the trial report claimed that the defendant was injured not at all, moderately, or excessively while attempting to escape police capture.

In this study, the authors found that jurors gave more lenient sentences when the defendant had "paid" for his crime—*regardless of whether his suffering was "relevant" or "irrelevant."*[42] (See Table 3.1.)

It appears, then, that observational data, survey data, and experimental data combine to provide support for the contention that

TABLE 3.1. The Effect of Magnitude and Relevance of a Criminal's Suffering on the Length of the Prison Sentence Jurors Assign to Him (in Months).*

		Magnitude of Offender's Suffering		
		None	*Moderate*	*Excessive*
Relevance of	Irrelevant Suffering		101.1	47.8
Offender's Suffering	Relevant Suffering	101.2	102.8	40.4

*By law, jurors *could* assign the defendant a prison sentence ranging from zero to eighteen months.

jurors will take the harmdoer's suffering into account when calculating how severely he should be punished.

Summary

In this chapter on exploiter/victim relationships, we considered the alternative ways that exploiters, their victims, and outside observers may respond to injustice. We found that regardless of whether the "scrutineer" is a participant in an inequity or merely an observer, injustice is disturbing, and the scrutineer is motivated to do "something" about it. That something, of course, may consist of actually setting things right—or of merely convincing oneself that things are right and that nothing needs to be done. Finally, the impact that equity considerations may have on shaping judges', jurors', courtroom spectators', as well as plaintiffs' and defendants' behavior was discussed.

ENDNOTES

1. See, for example, Fromm (1956) and Whiting and Child (1953) for an interesting discussion of the pervasiveness of the "fairness" principle.

2. See Goffman (1952).

3. See Sykes and Matza (1957).

4. See, for example, Allensmith (1960), Arnold (1960), Bramel (1969), Brock and Buss (1964), Freud (1936), Henry and Short (1954), and Maher (1966).

5. See, for example, Berscheid and Walster (1967), Berscheid, Walster, and Barclay (1969), Brock and Becker (1966), Carlsmith and Gross (1969), Freedman, Wallington, and Bless (1967), Walster and Prestholdt (1966), and Walster, Walster, Abrahams, and Brown (1966).

6. See Berkowitz (1962), Davidson (1964), Davis and Jones (1960), Glass (1964), Katz, Glass, and Cohen (1973), Sykes and Matza (1957), and Walster and Prestholdt (1966).

7. See Lerner (1968), Lerner and Simmons (1966), Lincoln and Levinger (1972), Ross (1966), and Walster and Prestholdt (1966).

8. See Berscheid, Boye, and Darley (1968).

9. This finding was replicated by Berscheid, Walster, and Barclay (1969).

10. See McGuire in Lindsey and Aronson (1968).

11. See Abelson and Rosenberg (1958), Cartwright and Harary (1956), Festinger (1957), Rosenberg (1960), and Zajonc (1960).

12. See Adams and Rosenbaum (1962) and Adams (1963).

13. See Weick and Nesset (1968).

14. Jon Freedman (personal communication).

15. For example, Darlington and Macker (1966), and Freedman, Wallington, and Bless (1967).

16. See Adams (1965), Blumstein and Weinstein (1969), Homans (1961), Lawler (1968*b*), Leventhal, Weiss, and Long (1969), Weick and Nesset (1968), or Wicker and Bushweiler (1970).

17. See, for example, Andrews (1967), Leventhal and Anderson (1970), Leventhal and Lane (1970), Leventhal, Weiss, and Long (1969). Blumstein and Weinstein (1969) are the only researchers to secure inconsistent findings.

18. See Leventhal and Bergman (1969) and Marwell, Schmitt, and Shotola (1971).

19. See Brown (1968), Thibaut (1950), and Ross et al. (1971).

20. See Berscheid, Boye, and Darley (1968).

21. See Lerner and Matthews (1967).

22. As reported in Thibaut and Kelley (1959).

23. In Austin and Walster (1974).

24. See Forrest and Dimond (1967), Geer (1966), and Sternbach (1966).

25. See Davies (1962), de Tocqueville (1856), Gurr (1970), Soule (1935), and Trotsky (1957).

26. See Baker (1974).

27. See Mills (1958).

28. See Bandura (1965).

29. See Pollock and Maitland (1898).

30. For example, see Brehm and Cohen (1962).

31. For example, see Del Vecchio (1959), Schafer (1960), and Spencer (1874).

32. See Fry (1956), Rose and Prell (1955), or Sharp and Otto (1910).

33. For example, see Fry (1956).

34. See Macaulay and Walster (1971) for a lengthy discussion of this problem.

35. See Aderman et al. (1974).

36. See Schafer (1960).

37. See Lerner (1968, 1970, 1971*a*, 1971*b*), Lerner and Matthews (1967), and Lerner and Simmons (1966).

38. Additional support for Chaiken and Darley's contention that *whom* we empathize with determines how we respond to an inequity comes from Aderman et al. (1974).

39. See Lincoln and Levinger (1972), and Walster et al. (1966).

40. See Berkowitz (1962), Davidson (1964), Davis and Jones (1960), Glass (1964), Katz et al. (1973), Lincoln and Levinger (1972), Sykes and Matza (1957), and Walster and Prestholdt (1966).

41. See Berscheid and Walster (1967).

42. Only one researcher, Legant (1973), found that jurors seem to be unimpressed by a wrongdoer's suffering. In an ingenious set of laboratory experi-

ments, Legant tested the hypothesis that jurors will decide what sentence a defendant deserves—and then tidily "deduct" from the sentence the amount of time the defendant was detained between arrest and trial. (She expected that a defendant who had been held in pretrial detention only a few days would get a fairly heavy sentence; a defendant who had been held in jail for a year without trial would get a fairly light sentence.) She found no evidence for this proposition.

CHAPTER
4

Equity Theory
and Philanthropist/Recipient
Relationships

People routinely volunteer to help one another. Parents care for their children, public assistance agencies support welfare recipients, Boy Scouts help elderly ladies across the street, Congress aids underdeveloped nations, and eager suitors urge gifts on overdeveloped maidens.

Can Equity theory give us any insight into philanthropist/recipient relationships? We think so.

Equity theorists would begin an Equity analysis of philanthropist/recipient relationships by classifying the relationship between the giver and the receiver of help into one of three categories: (1) exploitative and excessively profitable relationships, (2) reciprocal relationships, (3) truly altruistic relationships. Although in day-to-day conversation all three are commonly labeled "helping relationships," they are, in fact, strikingly different.

1. *Exploitative and Excessively Profitable Relationships:* Professional "philanthropists" are often fully aware that the best way to help themselves is to "help" others. For example, the foundation president may know that his charitable donations will, via tax write-offs, increase his relative outcomes far more than the recipient's. The professional fund raiser may know that his charitable solicitations will benefit him. (In such situations, both the philanthropist and his ostensible recipients may correctly perceive that the philanthropist is using

the recipients.) A philanthropist/recipient relationship of this type is probably best labeled an *exploitative relationship*.

Sometimes a person becomes aware that in the past he has received far more, and his fellow man has received far less, than he deserves from the relationship. The person helps in an effort to partially remedy the inequity; his recipient accepts it as such. In such situations, the philanthropist is not a helper in the usual sense; a philanthropist/recipient relationship of this type is probably best labeled an *excessively profitable relationship*.

$$\frac{(O_A - I_A)}{(|I_A|)^{k_A}} > \frac{(O_B - I_B)}{(|I_B|)^{k_B}} \qquad \begin{array}{l} A = \text{The Philanthropist} \\ B = \text{The Recipient} \end{array}$$

2. *Reciprocal Relationships.* Sometimes a participant alternates between being the philanthropist and the recipient. Philanthropist/recipient relationships of this type are best labeled *reciprocal relationships*.

$$\frac{(O_A - I_A)}{(|I_A|)^{k_A}} = \frac{(O_B - I_B)}{(|I_B|)^{k_B}}$$

3. *Altruistic Relationships.* Sometimes the philanthropist is truly a philanthropist. He offers the recipient greater benefits than the recipient could ever return. For the moment, we will label relationships of this type *altruistic relationships*.

$$\frac{(O_A - I_A)}{(|I_A|)^{k_A}} < \frac{(O_B - I_B)}{(|I_B|)^{k_B}}$$

THE PHILANTHROPIST/RECIPIENT'S RESPONSE TO EXPLOITATIVE AND EXCESSIVELY PROFITABLE RELATIONSHIPS, RECIPROCAL RELATIONSHIPS, AND ALTRUISTIC RELATIONSHIPS

From the preceding discussion, it should be clear that if Equity theorists are to predict how a potential philanthropist/recipient will respond to a helping opportunity, they must know two facts: (1) Does the potential philanthropist/recipient perceive that he is in a relationship with the other? (2) *At the start* of the philanthropist/recipient interaction does the philanthropist/recipient feel that the philanthropist is overbenefited, equitably benefited, or underbenefited, relative to the recipient?

Does the philanthropist/recipient perceive that he is in a relationship with the other? Equity theory deals with the behavior of individuals enmeshed in equitable or inequitable relationships. To calculate equity, we must know what inputs participants perceive they and their partners are contributing to their relationship, and how much profit they are deriving from it. Unfortunately, in much of the research that is available, researchers did not ascertain whether or not participants perceived themselves to be in a relationship. (This problem is especially acute in the research on innocent bystanders and victims. We simply do not know if, when a bystander observes someone in a burning building, he gradually comes to think he is in a relationship with the victim. It is probable that he does *not.*) However, for purposes of this discussion, let us assume that the participants in the helping situations we will consider did feel that they and their fellow man were in a relationship. Otherwise this discussion can proceed no further.

Does the philanthropist/recipient perceive that the philanthropist is overbenefited, equitably treated, or underbenefited? Most of the time when we consider others' research, we will feel fairly confident that we can guess whether the philanthropist/recipient relationship should be classified as an exploitative (or excessively profitable), a reciprocal, or an altruistic relationship.[1]

Let us now consider these three different types of relationships in greater detail.

The Philanthropist/Recipient's Response to Exploitative and Excessively Profitable Relationships

The Philanthropist's Response:

$$\frac{(O_A - I_A)}{(|I_A|)^{k_A}} > \frac{(O_B - I_B)}{(|I_B|)^{k_B}}$$

Exploitative Relationships. Earlier we pointed out that although the public may label a relationship philanthropic, the participants in the relationship may see things quite differently. In some relationships, both the philanthropist and his ostensible recipient may correctly perceive that the philanthropist is using the recipient. Since such exploiter/victim relationships were fully discussed in chapter 3, we will not consider them further in this section.

Excessively Profitable Relationships. In some settings, potential helpers are uncomfortably aware that, by design or accident, they are partially responsible for the victim's suffering. They may feel partially responsible for his initial suffering, or, by their action or inaction, they may feel that they are contributing to its continuation. An example: the night watchman who snuck out for an unauthorized smoke may feel he is at least partially responsible for the theft of equipment from his employer's factory. A second example: in March, 1964, a tragic event horrified and puzzled the nation. Rosenthal (1966) reports:

> For more than half an hour thirty-eight respectable, law-abiding citizens in Queens watched a killer stalk and stab a women in three separate attacks in Kew Gardens. . . . Twice the sound of their voices and the sudden glow of their bedroom lights interrupted him and frightened him off. Each time he returned, sought her out and stabbed her again. Not one person telephoned the police during the assault; one witness called after the woman was dead. (pp. 29–30)

Rosenthal attributed bystanders' perplexing reluctance to help Kitty Genovese to man's callous indifference to the suffering of other men:

> What happened in the apartments and houses on Austin Street was a symptom of a terrible reality in the human condition—that only under certain situations and only in response to certain reflexes or certain beliefs—will a man step out of his shell toward his brother. (p. 81)

In recent interviews, a number of the Kew Gardens residents who neglected to call the police while Kitty Genovese was stabbed again and again, admitted that, to this day, they are responsible for her death.

What does Equity theory have to say about such relationships? Probably the best way to demonstrate how Equity theorists would analyze the whole potpourri of excessively profitable relationships is to focus on one sample relationship—the relationship between the "not-so-innocent" bystander and his victim.

The Not-So-Innocent Bystander. Perhaps the best way to analyze the bystander/victim relationship is to organize our discussion chronologically, in the way an emergency unfolds. First we will discuss variables that seem to determine how aroused the bystander will become by the emergency. Then we will discuss the determinants of how the bystander responds to the emergency; by helping, by derogating the victim, or by fleeing.

Sources of a bystander's distress on observing an emergency: The bystander who observes a victim's suffering may feel physiologically aroused for two entirely different reasons: equity reasons and empathy reasons. *Equity reasons:* If the bystander feels that he and the victim are in an inequitable relationship, he should experience distress. *Empathy reasons:* When the bystander is forced to see another person suffer, he may empathize and become emotionally and physiologically upset.

Piliavin and Piliavin (1971) suggest that when the bystander observes another person suffering, he may become psychologically and emotionally aroused from empathetically experiencing the other's distress. The evidence in support of this contention is exhaustively presented in Piliavin and Piliavin (1973).

Functionally, of course, empathetic arousal and distress are virtually identical constructs; both terms describe a painful subjective state accompanied by physiological activation.

In any case, a variety of researchers have found that bystanders become markedly upset when they witness another being harmed.[2] Bystanders generally display such signs of arousal as sweaty and shaky hands, chain smoking, gasping, running around aimlessly, and other signs of strain. Bystanders also show strong galvanic skin responses (GSR) when they are forced to observe another suffer.[3]

Theorists believe that at least three equity variables intensify the arousal experienced by bystanders to an emergency.[4]

One's responsibility for the emergency: As we pointed out in the previous section, the more responsible a person feels for an inequity, the more distress he should feel. A not-so-innocent bystander may well experience both self-concept distress ("I am a bad person") *and* fear of retaliation distress ("I will be punished"). The truly innocent bystander should experience, at most, only mild fear of retaliation.

There is some evidence that the more responsible a bystander feels for the victim's plight, the more likely he is to help. Schwartz and Ben David (1976) recruited men from the Hebrew University of Jerusalem to participate in a "bio-feedback" study. Ostensibly, it was the students' job to (1) train rats to modify their heart rate (by administering carefully regulated shocks), and (2) to train themselves to control *their own* heart rates. While describing the dual training procedure, the experimenter casually warned the men that the rat they were training today was wild and uncontrollable. She admitted she was terrified of the rat. Then the experiment began. When it was well under way, an "emergency" occurred. There was a crash, followed by a single cry from the experimenter. The content of this cry was systematically varied: (1) Sometimes the experimenter blamed the bystander for her plight. (She cried, "What did *you* do?! The rat escaped! What did you do?") (2) Sometimes she attributed the plight to chance. ("What happened? The rat escaped! What happened?") (3) Sometimes she exonerated the bystander and blamed herself. ("What did *I* do?! The rat escaped! What did I do?")

Then the experimenter simply sat back and waited to see how long it took the bystander to come to her aid. As predicted, the hapless student was most eager to help when *he'd* been blamed for the emergency; he was moderately eager to help when the emergency was attributed to chance, and slowest to help when the victim blamed herself for the emergency.

Severity of the emergency: Piliavin, Rodin, and Piliavin (1969) propose that a bystander's arousal will increase as the perceived severity of the emergency increases (i.e., as the danger or potential danger to life or limb increases). The louder and more numerous the screams, the more the blood, the higher the flames, the more aroused the bystander will be. Piliavin et al. (1969) and Piliavin and Piliavin (1972) provide some support for this contention. These authors staged an emergency during a $7\frac{1}{2}$-minute express run on New York subway. On each run a male confederate (who pretended to be an invalid with a cane) collapsed. On half of the trials, he produced a thin trickle of very real-looking fake blood from the corner of his mouth as he fell. If the emergency was not too severe (i.e., the man merely collapsed) panicky behavior did not occur. On several of the severe "blood" trials, however, quite emotional and panicky behavior did occur. Other evidence[5] indicates that the heart rate of observers of a film depicting several industrial accidents accelerates less to the sight of losing a finger than to a man being impaled by a flying board and dying.

If we wished to translate "severity of the emergency" into Equity theory terms, we would equate severity with the size of the disparity between the relative gains of the participants. Evidence exists to support the contention that the greater the inequity that exists, the more distress participants will feel.[6]

Personality factors: Finally, the bystander's personality should combine with the situational factors discussed above to determine the degree to which he becomes distressed when he encounters a suffering human being.

The individual who has a strong self-concept would experience more distress when he causes or contributes to another's suffering than should a person who thinks little of himself. (See Glass, 1964.) The person who has been taught that exploitative behavior brings swift retaliation from man and God should experience more distress when he contributes to another's suffering than would the more leniently reared child. (See Aronfreed, 1961.)

Responding to the inequity: Once a participant faces the fact that his relationship with another is inequitable, Equity theory makes specific predictions as to how he will respond to the injustice. The bystander can restore *actual* equity to the unfair relationship (he can make reparation to the victim), or he can restore *psychological* equity (he can distort his perceptions of the emergency situation).

The Equity paradigm's conceptual alternatives are essentially identical to the bystander responses that Piliavin et al. (1969) and Piliavin and Piliavin (1971) describe. According to the Piliavins, bystanders typically make one of three responses: they get, or try to get, help for the victim; they refuse to help and instead spend their energy "reevaluating the situation" as one not requiring action, or they leave the scene. (Although avoidance responses cannot eliminate inequity, they can reduce its salience. Equity theorists have observed that such avoidance should occur when it is more costly to restore equity to a relationship than to abandon it.)[7]

THE DECISION PROCESS

Equity theorists and students of bystander behavior seem to agree on how individuals *can* respond to inequity. What determines which of these many potential responses an observer *will* make?

The reader will recall that Equity theory proposes two principles for predicting how an overbenefited person will respond to a needy victim. Whether a bystander helps the victim, justifies his suffering, or terminates their relationship, is said to depend on the *cost* for the alternative techniques available for restoring equity and the adequacy of those techniques.

The cost of helping: Equity theory states (Proposition I, Corollary 1): *Other things being equal, the more costly a person perceives an available equity-restoring technique to be, the less likely he will be to use this technique to restore equity.*

Piliavin and Piliavin (1971) make a similar proposal:

> An observer is motivated to reduce his arousal state as rapidly as possible, incurring in the course of his actions as few costs and as many rewards as possible. That is, his response will be determined by the outcome of a more

FIGURE 4.1. "Hold It! For All We Know, He May Be Making a Citizen's Arrest." (Drawing by Charles Addams. Copyright © 1974 The New Yorker Magazine, Inc. Reprinted by permission.)

The City Question

```
                          Wino?
              sidewalk.        Junkie?
                 on            Hurt?
                face           Sick?
                 on            Knife
                Man              in
                               pocket?
                               Danger?
                             Medicine
                        in
                     pocket?
                 May
                die
             without
             it?
             Forget
             him?

             Leave
             him
             to
             the
             cops?


         Or try to help?
```

Froman, R.
1971.

or less rational decision process in which he weighs the costs and rewards attendant upon each of his possible courses of action. (p. 6)

There is considerable evidence that rewards and costs are important in determining how a bystander will respond to an emergency.

What are the potential rewards for helping in an emergency situation? They include a feeling of competence, self-congratulation, thanks from the victim, praise and admiration from bystanders, money, and fame (see Figure 4.2).

The potential costs of helping include personal danger, effort expenditure, time lost, embarrassment, exposure to disgusting or sickening experiences (such as the sight of or contact with blood or other body fluids, wounds, deformities, seizures), and feelings of inadequacy or failure if help is ineffective.

---

*From the book *Street Poems* by Robert Froman. Copyright © 1971 by Robert Froman. Reprinted by persmission of the publishers, Saturday Review Press/E.P. Dutton & Co., Inc.

Be a Saturday hero.

A hero isn't just somebody who can dazzle a crowd. A hero is somebody who makes a difference. And it isn't really as hard as it sounds. All you have to do is give a little of your time each week and you can be a hero to a fatherless boy. He needs someone to look up to. Someone to show him he can grow up to be the man he'd like to be. You can be that someone any day of the week. Call your local Big Brothers today. And be a real hero.

Be a Big Brother.

FIGURE 4.2.   (Reprinted by permission of Big Brothers of America.)

Rewards for not helping consist of the rewards associated with maintaining personal freedom, freedom to continue doing what one likes without "getting involved," and lack of "involvement."

Potential costs for not helping include self-blame, public censure, and, in some instances, criminal prosecution.[8] In this regard, we should note that United States law provides fewer sanctions for the "Bad Samaritan" than does the law of any other civilized nation. For example, in Eastern Europe a bystander who neglects to help another, when he could do so without injury to himself, can often be prosecuted.

Piliavin et al. (1969) and Piliavin and Piliavin (1972) provide suggestive evidence that cost is an important determinant of whether or not bystanders will come to the aid of victims. These authors staged an emergency on a New York subway. An "invalid" with a cane collapsed on each run. In some cases he was bleeding from the mouth; in others he was not. The "invalid" lay there until someone came to his aid. The Piliavins assumed that it is less costly to approach an unbloody person than a bloody one. And, as they predicted, bystanders were more likely to help the "sanitary" victim than the bloody one.

A study by Darley and Batson (1973) provides further support for the proposition that potential Good Samaritans care very much about how much it costs to help. The authors found that seminary students were far more reluctant to assist a person slumped by the side of the road when they were in a hurry to deliver a sermon on the Good Samaritan than when they had "time to kill."

The adequacy of available equity-restoring techniques: A second derivation from Proposition IV of Equity theory states that a bystander's reaction to an emergency should depend on how adequate he perceives the alternative available techniques for restoring actual or psychological equity to be.

PROPOSITION IV: COROLLARY 1: Other things being equal, the more adequate an individual perceives an available equity-restoring technique to be, the more likely he is to use this technique to restore equity.

Weiss, Boyer, Lombardo, and Stitch (1973) provide suggestive evidence that the adequacy of a response is an important determinant of whether or not bystanders will come to the aid of victims. Weiss et al. found that observers were quicker to make a totally effective helping response than a partially effective one. In one study, the observers learned that intervention was totally ineffective, slightly effective, or completely effective in terminating the victim's suffering. In a second study, the observer learned that intervention was totally ineffective, effective about thirty-three percent of the time, or always effective in terminating his suffering. In both studies, Weiss et al. found that observers were less ready to make partially adequate responses than totally adequate ones. The victim, of course, probably prefers some help, inadequate or not, to none.

Compelling anecdotal evidence that bystanders take the costs and adequacy of help into account when deciding whether or not to help others comes from Lerner (1971a). In public demonstrations, Lerner uses a simple procedure to graphically illustrate why bystanders are often insensitive to even the most intense suffering of others.

First, Lerner reminds his audience that many Americans and Canadians are suffering and desperately need help. He then hands each member of the audience a folder containing a single case history from the active file of the university hospital. Each case history describes an American or Canadian family, in serious need of help, who for one reason or another cannot be helped by any official welfare agency. Each of the families lives under degrading conditions. The family needs money for food, clothes, soap, medicine to eliminate intestinal worms, heal sores, etc. The family is starving. Lerner points out that if the person will donate one hundred dollars a month, he can help this family avoid this primitive kind of human suffering. All that will be required of the affluent members of the audience is to give up a significant part of the money they spend each month on entertainment, liquor, movies, and dining out. Almost uniformly, audience members refuse to help.

With great sensitivity, Lerner explains why it is that individuals are so unwilling to help. First, the potential cost of such help is high. If the audience member contributes money this time, where can he stop? Can he and his own family enjoy their lives only when their lot is not better than that of all mankind? Second, the potential adequacy of such help is low. By paying one hundred dollars a month, the audience member can only help *one* family. Millions of victims remain. He cannot help them all. Perhaps if he were offered the chance to vote for an equitable tax system which, for one hundred dollars a month, would alleviate the suffering of *all* people, he might be far more willing to make an altruistic response.

The Recipient's Response to Exploitative and Excessively Profitable Relationships. We noted earlier that philanthropic acts may be less generous than they appear on the surface. Sometimes the wily philanthropist is, in fact, cheating the recipient, or returning only a portion of the benefits he owes him. Although the public may label such relationships "helping relationships," the participants know better. Such relationships are probably best labeled "exploitative or excessively profitable relationships." Since the victim's feelings and reactions to such exploiter/victim relationships were fully discussed in chapter 3, we will not consider them further in this section.

The Philanthropist/Recipient's Response to Reciprocal Relationships

$$\frac{(O_A - I_A)}{(|I_A|)^{k_A}} = \frac{(O_B - I_B)}{(|I_B|)^{k_B}}$$

Any relationship that endures for very long soon evolves into a reciprocal relationship. Neighbors take turns manning car pools, college students take notes for one another, colleagues exchange advice. In such stable relationships, participants alternate between helping others and being helped themselves.

In *The Gift*, Mauss (1954) brilliantly analyzes the impact of such reciprocal gift giving " in primitive or archaic types of society." His observations are equally applicable to our semiprimitive society.

Mauss uses the Melanesian institution of ritual gift exchange, the *kula ring*, as a framework for discussing reciprocal relationships. In the Massim area of the Pacific, tribal chiefs are linked in the *kula.*

By custom, a tribal chief is assigned to be donor on one occasion and a recipient on the next. In the *kula*, participants travel from island to island doling out and receiving gifts. The chiefs traveling in a clockwise direction circulate red spondylus shell necklaces (*soulava*). Those traveling in a counter-clockwise direction circulate finely cut and polished armshells (*mwali*). Malinowski (1922) observed:

> Each of these articles, as it travels in its own direction on the closed circuit, meets on its way articles of the other class, and is constantly being exchanged for them. Every movement of the Kula articles, every detail of the transactions is fixed and regulated by a set of traditional rules and conventions, and some acts of the Kula are accompanied by an elaborate magical ritual and public ceremonies . . . One transaction does not finish the Kula relationship, the rule being "once in the Kula, always in the Kula," and a partnership between two men is a permanent and lifelong affair.
>
> The Kula [Malinowski continued] is thus an extremely big and complex institution. . . . It welds together a considerable number of tribes, and it embraces a vast complex of activities, inter-connected, and playing into one another, so as to form one organic whole. (pp. 82–83)

FIGURE 4:3. "Any Relationship that Endures for Very Long Soon Evolves into a Reciprocal Relationship."

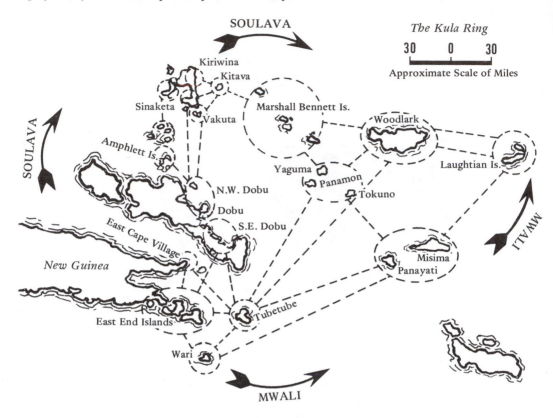

FIGURE 4.4. The Kula Ring. (From W. S. Dillon, *Gifts and Nations*, The Hague: Mouton, 1968, p. 89. Copyright © 1968 Mouton, The Hague. Reprinted by permission.)

Dillon (1968) observes that in the *kula,* as in our own society, "People who receive, want to give something in return. Both are involved in the quest for reciprocity." He points out that reciprocal exchanges are a source of social stability; they breed good feeling, liking, and co-operation. Experimental evidence supports Dillon's contention that *kula*-type reciprocal exchanges solidify social bonds.[9] Other experiments suggest that kindness generates not only liking, but a desire to reciprocate.[10]

"True" Exchange Relationships versus "Cunning" Exchange Relationships: In the area of altruistic behavior, scientists' personal longings often conflict with their scientific theories.

The scientist's personal reactions: When an acquaintance offers to help us "out of the goodness of his heart," our reaction is an immediate one: we feel intense gratitude and affection and resolve to return his kindness. If, on the other hand, when our acquaintance offers to help us he makes it brutally clear that he expects to collect—with interest—later, we will be far less touched by his generosity; we might even be less concerned about repaying his "kindness."

The data suggest that recipients are very influenced by the donor's apparent motives in offering help to them. They care very much whether the kindness is voluntary, accidental, or reluctant. They care very much whether the donor's act is an altruistic or a selfish one.

Why, in equity terms, should a recipient have such different reactions to the altruistic giver than to the giver who was forced to give or who had "ulterior motives"? There are several reasons.

First, the recipient may feel that goodness, unselfishness, and moral character are positive inputs to a relationship, in and of themselves. Thus, he may feel a good, unselfish benefactor *deserves* a bigger return than would a "bad" person who performed the same act.

Second, the recipient may be far more eager to maintain a relationship with a good person than with a bad one. A donor who helps out of the "goodness of his heart,"or out of friendship, is likely to behave generously in a wide variety of situations. Someone who acts kindly for selfish reasons, however, may adopt a more cunning strategy in slightly different circumstances. He may well act selfishly if no one is around to praise or to reward him. The genuine vs. the cunning donor, then, is proffering different benefits. The generous helper proffers specific benefits plus the promise of long-term generosity. The calculating helper proffers only specific benefits. It is not surprising then that the recipient is more eager to cement his relations with the former helper than with the latter.

There is evidence that recipients' reactions to donors are markedly influenced by their answers to two questions: Was the donor motivated to help? Was the donor motivated to help *the recipient*?

Was the donor motivated to help? In chapter 3 when we discussed exploiter/victim relationships, we concluded: *When an inequity is intentionally produced, participants in an inequitable relationship will experience more distress and will have stronger desires to restore equity to the relationship than if the inequity occurs inadvertently.* Let us now label this Conclusion II.

The same principle should apply in philanthropist/recipient relationships. When a philanthropist helps another, he should feel more entitled to reciprocation if he helped voluntarily than if he aided the recipient accidentally or reluctantly. Similarly, the recipient should have a stronger desire to restore equity to his relationship with the benefactor by reciprocating if he was helped voluntarily than if he was accidentally or reluctantly helped.

There is abundant support for Conclusion II.[11] A typical experiment is Frisch and Greenberg's (1972). The authors recruited students to participate in an experiment, ostensibly designed "to identify personality characteristics associated with success in the business world." Students were promised extra credit if they were successful on a task. During the course of the experiment, the students discovered that they had little chance of succeeding unless they received help from their partners. (Their partners possessed graph cards, which the students needed to successfully complete their tasks.) In all cases the partner helped the students. In some cases this help was intentional; in other cases it was not. In the High Intentionality condition, the partner sent the students the graph cards he needed along with a note: "I have some duplicates that probably belong to you. I'm sending them over since you can probably use them." In the Low Intentionality condition, the partner sent the needed graph cards, but they were accompanied by a note that made it clear that the partner did not realize that he was helping the student. The note said: "Some of my cards don't have the month on them. Can you help me and identify them for me?" Before the student could reply, however, the inadvertent benefactor sent him another note saying: "Forget it. I found the cards I was missing."

The student's eagerness to restore equity to his relationship with the partner (by repaying the help he had received) was then assessed. As predicted, students were more eager to pay back the intentional helper than the inadvertent helper.

Was the donor motivated to help him? Schopler and Thompson (1968) contend that the helper's motives are enormously important: if the recipient believes that the favordoer was genuinely motivated to help *him,* he is appreciative and is likely to reciprocate. If, however, he believes the favordoer was selfishly motivated to maximize his own gain, he will be less appreciative and less likely to reciprocate.[12]

The scientist's scientific reaction: Emotionally, then, scientists admire altruistic people, respond to them with appreciation, seek their company, and reward them. Intellectually, however, scientists suspect altruism does not exist.

Traditionally, humanists define *altruistic behavior* as "behavior that benefits another rather than the self"; something that is done out of the "goodness of one's heart." A few scientists believe that man does act unselfishly under very special circumstances. For example, Aronfreed (1970) contends that actions that are controlled by empathetic processes should be labeled "altruism." Aronfreed and Paskal (1966) point out that sometimes people place themselves in the shoes of a person needing assistance; they vicariously experience the other's satisfaction at getting what he wants (but is not able to achieve on his own), and vicariously experience his disappointment at not getting what he desires. In such circumstances a person may sacrifice himself for another.

The vast majority of scientists, however, are cynical. They interpret altruism in calculating terms. Equity theory, like every other social psychological theory, assumes that individuals learn to perform those acts that are rewarded.

James (1884) observed:

> Probably no one can make sacrifices for "right," without to some degree personifying the principle of right for which the sacrifice is made, and expecting thanks from it. . . . The old test of piety, "Are you willing to be damned for the glory of God?" was probably never answered in the affirmative except by those who felt sure in their heart of hearts that God would "credit" them with their willingness, and set more store by them thus than if in His unfathomable scheme He had not damned them at all. (pp. 204–205)

More recently, Blau (1968) has argued:

> To be sure, there are men who unselflessly work for others without thought of reward and even without expecting gratitude, but these are virtually saints, and saints are rare. Other men also act unselfishly sometimes, but they require a more direct incentive for doing so, if it is only . . . social approval. (p. 453)

Clearly, if altruistic behavior is in the same universe with all other behavior, it must be under the control of rewards and punishments.

In the next section, we will discuss altruistic relations in some detail.

The Philanthropist/Recipient's Response to Altruistic Relationships

A certain man . . . fell among thieves, which . . . wounded him . . . leaving him half dead. . . . there came down a certain priest . . . when he saw him, he passed by on the other side. And likewise a Levite . . . passed by on the other side. But a certain Samaritan . . . came where he was: and when he saw him, he had compassion on him, and went to him . . . and set him on his own beast, and brought him to an inn, and took care of him. And on the morrow when he departed, he took out two pence, and gave them to the host, and said unto him, "Take care of him; and whatsoever thou spendest more . . . I will repay thee." (Luke 10:30–35)

$$\frac{(O_A - I_A)}{(|I_A|)^{k_A}} > \frac{(O_B - I_B)}{(|I_B|)^{k_B}}$$

For most people, the true altruistic relationship—the relationship in which the philanthropist gives more to his fellow man than his fellow man "deserves" or can ever hope to return—is evidence of man at his best. The social workers who help their clients, the Schweitzers who give up luxurious lives to live among the lepers, the church members who donate turkeys to poor families at Thanksgiving are assumed to be good people. Their needy recipients are expected to be grateful. And, in part, the public's view is a correct one. Sometimes altruists do sacrifice in another's behalf; they voluntarily give more than they could ever hope to get in return.[13] And, sometimes, recipients are grateful for their aid. As Broll, Gross, and Piliavin (1973) point out:

> Simple reinforcement theories emphasize the positive aspects of receiving aid. Since help seeking and receiving help usually result in some tangible gain, obtaining help should be a positive experience for most needy people, at least when compared with such undesirable alternatives as failure or poverty. (p. 1)

Equity theory, however, suggests that altruistic relationships are extremely complex. Altruistic relationships are not always benign; sometimes altruists come to resent the needy's incessant demands for help; sometimes they come to despise the needy. Sometimes recipients, children, welfare clients, the disabled, or the elderly, come to resent their dependence; sometimes they come to despise their benefactor and themselves. (This contention is vigorously supported by a variety of researchers.)[14]

For Equity theorists, then, the observation that noble altruistic relationships produce mixed feelings in both the benefactor and the recipient is not so surprising. After all, the benefactor who gives and gives and gets little in return, "*is a participant of an inequitable and unprofitable relationship.*" His recipient is a participant in an inequitable, albeit profitable, relationship. Equity theory leads us to expect that both the benefactor and the recipient should feel at least slightly ill at ease in such relationships.

Let us now review what is known about how philanthropists and their recipients feel and respond in altruistic relationships.

The Philanthropist's Response to Altruistic Relationships: Why "Altruists" Must Be Ambivalent about Their Sacrifices. Society tells people they should behave altruistically—sometimes: One of society's most perplexing problems is to decide how the needy should be treated. On the one hand, people define need as a legitimate input, which entitles a citizen to the minimum outcomes for survival. They acknowledge that if one's fellow human being is so young, so disabled, so sick, or so old that he is unable to care for himself, society should care for him. [15]

Social observers may reproach individuals for not helping others as much as they "ought" to help, but the fact remains that people do help the needy to a remarkable extent. People give the "time of day" to passersby, dole out change at bus-stops, return lost wallets to their owners, and fix flat tires for stranded motorists. [16] Bystanders extend enormous help to those in dire straits. For example, Schwartz (1970) found that fifty-nine percent of the people he contacted were willing to consider donating bone marrow to a needy person. [17]

On the other hand, people do not consider need to be an entirely legitimate input and often resent the obligation to help. As Berkowitz (1972) notes: "Many of the subjects in our Wisconsin experiments seemed to resent having to work for the other person without reciprocity or compensation; they acted altruistically, but they didn't necessarily like it." (p. 33). The haves often complain that they should not be obligated to help the poor, the incompetent, the stupid, or the sick. At best they feel that any help they do cede should be considered not a gift but a loan. They feel that they are entitled to the recipient's gratitude and repayment in whatever ways he can manage. Thus, societal norms provide competing pressures; they say man should behave altruistically toward those in need, but that he is entitled to resent having to do so.

Society rewards people for behaving altruistically—sometimes: Generally, society supports altruistic behavior. The altruist and the hero, who internalized society's norms, may reward themselves for their unselfish behavior. Their fellows may reward them with love, praise, their name in the paper, medals, and a flowery epitaph. Yet, there is often a thin line between being an "altruist" and being a "sap." We know that at least sometimes people meet altruistic acts with ridicule and disdain. For example, Brown (1968, 1970) found that *if people believed that others would never know they had been slighted and exploited,* they were often quite willing to settle for less than they deserved. However, *if they know that others may discover their "largess,"* they feel they must "get theirs" lest they be thought a target for subsequent exploitation.

Since society's reactions to altruism are mixed, we might expect that altruists would have similarly mixed feelings about their altruism: they may end up feeling proud of and distressed about themselves at the same time. In view of these conflicting pressures, it is no wonder that altruists are often tempted to reduce that distress by restoring actual or psychological equity to their relationships.

The Recipient's Response to Altruistic Relationships. It is easy to see why the altruist has mixed feelings about being forced to contribute benefits to another with no hope of return. A little thought, however, makes it clear that help is a mixed blessing for the "lucky" recipient as well.

On one hand, the recipient knows that the altruist is showering him with far more love and material benefits than he is entitled to. He can't help but feel grateful.

On the other hand, the altruistic relationship is an unpleasant relationship for the recipient for three different reasons: it is inequitable, potentially exploitative, and potentially humiliating.

The altruistic relationship is an inequitable relationship: When the benefactor bestows undeserved benefits on a recipient, he places the recipient in an inequitable relationship. As we indicated in Proposition III, inequitable relationships are unpleasant relationships.

> In *The Godfather* (Puzo, 1969), Don Corleone created an eventually frightful debt merely by granting a favor to Amerigo Bonasera. On a similar different familial level, the legendary "Jewish mother" makes and acts out sacrifices for her children and for the rest of her life plays on their guilt. This type of long term control is not limited to the Western world. (Adams and Freedman, 1976, pp. 48–49)

Giving is, indeed, more blessed than receiving for having a social credit is preferable to being socially indebted. (Blau, 1968, p. 453)

The altruistic relationship is a potentially exploitative relationship: When a philanthropist grants benefits that his recipient cannot repay in kind, the recipient may well feel that he has become obligated to repay his benefactor in unspecified ways for an indefinite period. The recipient might reasonably fear that his benefactor may attempt to extract a greater repayment than the recipient would have been willing to give, had he been warned of the conditions of the exchange ahead of time.

Throughout time and geography, observers have noted that altruists often demand repayment—at usurious interest.

In the Fourth Century B.C., Democritus warned: "Accept favors in the foreknowledge that you will have to give a greater return for them."

Dillon (1968) provides a compelling example of the operation of how the generous gift/exploitation syndrome works. He describes Mr. B's (a French industrialist's) warm relationship with an Arab worker:

> In June 1956, an Arab worker at B's factory asked the *patron* for permission to leave work for two days to attend to problems of burying a brother, Ahmed. . . . B responded by offering to pay for the burial, by arranging to have an Arabic-speaking French *officier des affaires indigenes* (an ex-colonial officer) notify the kinsmen in Algeria, and by hiring an *imam* (Moslem prayer leader) to conduct the services. On July 16, 1956, the end of Bastille Day demonstrations by Algerians at the Place de la Republique, B. summoned Kazam and asked: "If your comrades tell you to go on strike during the vacation, when you are alone guarding the factory, what will you do, Kazam?" The *patron* told him that he was aware he would run the risk of being knifed (*coup de couteau*) by other Algerian members of an Islamic fraternal organization who were organizing sympathy strikes to protest French resistance against Algerian rebellion. . . . The *patron,* in describing this understanding with Kazam, his oldest Algerian worker, said:
>
> "We depend on each other. He has worked for me almost 12 years. Without him I could not count on the work of the other Algerians. He is top man and being the oldest, I depend on him to control the others. . . . Kazam knows that he can depend on me when he is in trouble." (p. 60–61)

When the industrialist offered his favors, he did not state that the price was to risk one's life. *Had* the Arab known, he may well have concluded that that exchange was not a profitable one.

In America, Gross, Piliavin, Walston, and Broll (1973) cite a similar example:

> Briar (1966), in summarizing extensive interviews with more than 100 welfare families, states that aid recipients do indeed give up freedom as part of the helping contract. When these families were asked about the legitimacy of refusing entry to a social worker at night, more than two-thirds of them acknowledged that a search warrant was legally necessary, but only half felt they had the right to refuse entry. Briar's data include other examples of experienced loss of freedom—the majority of respondents in his study felt obligated to follow social workers' suggestions on budgets, psychiatric visits, and marriage counseling. (p. 5)

The altruistic relationship is a potentially humiliating relationship: The recipient may be hesitant to accept charity for still another reason. He may fear that the benefactor's gift will establish the benefactor's moral and social superiority to the recipient. The recipient may be unwilling to accept such a menial status.

Observational evidence suggests that recipients fear that by accepting help they risk being assigned to a menial status; fears that are probably well founded. Social observers have noted that in a variety of cultures gift-giving and humiliation are linked. Small wonder then that people have learned to "look a gift horse in the mouth."

In her analysis of beneficence among East European Jews, Joffe (1953) notes:

> For a society within the Western cultural tradition, East European Jewish culture exhibits a minimum of reciprocal behavior. Wealth, learning and other tangible and intangible possessions are fluid and are channeled so that in the main they flow from the "strong," or "rich," or "learned," or "older," to those who are "weaker," "poorer," "ignorant," or "younger." Therefore, all *giving* is downward. . . . It is mandatory for the good things of life to be shared or passed downward during one's lifetime.
>
> The concept of the good deed, the *Mitzvah,* is not voluntary—it has been enjoined upon every Jew by God. . . . It is shameful . . . to receive succor of any sort from those who are inferior to you in status. To receive any (return gifts) implies that you are in a position to be controlled, for the reciprocal of the downward giving is deference. (pp. 386–387)

Listen to Oliver's (1967) description of an "honorary" feast given by the Siuai of Bougainville:

> After everything is assembled and with everyone waiting expectantly, the host indicates to the Guest-of-Honor his share of pigs, shell money, and delicacies.
>
> Long before he has eaten the small portion of pork . . . the Guest-of-Honor has begun to concern himself with plans to repay the feast, for unless he can honor his erstwhile host with a feast of equivalent or more than equivalent value he loses in reknown and, in the minds of fellow Siuai, becomes ranked lower on the social-political scale than his victorious rival. (pp. 392–393)

And, the American sociologist, Homans (1961) observes:

> Anyone who accepts from another a service he cannot repay in kind incurs inferiority as a cost of receiving the service. The esteem he gives the other he foregoes himself. (p. 320)

Reciprocal versus Altruistic Relationships

We have focused on two types of helping relationships; reciprocal relationships and altruistic ones. From our comparison of these two starkly contrasting types of relationships, it is clear that a single factor seems to have a critical impact on the benefactor/recipient relationship; i.e., *the beneficiary's ability to make restitution.*

Researchers who have investigated the interactions of Christmas gift givers, members of the *kula* ring, and the kindness of neighbors, have dealt with donors and recipients who know that eventually their helpful acts will be reciprocated in kind. Researchers who have investigated the interactions of welfare workers versus their clients, developed versus underdeveloped nations, and the medical staff versus the physically handicapped, have dealt with recipients who know they will never be able to repay their benefactors. The differing reactions of participants in reciprocal versus nonreciprocal relations underscores the importance of the recipient's "ability to repay" in determining how help affects a relationship. Ability to repay seems to determine whether favordoing generates pleasant social interactions or resentment and suffering.

The preceding observations, then, lead us to Conclusion III.

CONCLUSION III: Undeserved gifts produce inequity in a relationship. If the participants know the recipient can and will reciprocate, the inequity is viewed as temporary, and thus it produces little distress. If the participants know the recipient cannot or will not reciprocate, however, a real inequity is produced; the participants will experience distress and will therefore need to restore actual or psychological equity to the relationship.

Evidence in support of Conclusion III comes from four diverse sources:

1. *Ethnographic data:* On the basis of ethnographic data, Mauss (1954) concludes that three types of obligations are widely distributed in human societies in both times and space: (a) the obligation to give, (b) the obligation to receive, and (c) the obligation to repay. Mauss (1954) and Dillon (1968) agree that while reciprocal exchanges breed cooperation and good feelings, gifts that cannot be reciprocated breed discomfort, distress, and dislike.

In support of their contention, the authors survey a number of societies that have an exchange system in which everyone can be a donor *and* a receiver. (The *kula* ring is such an example.) Harmonious stable relations are said to be the result. They contrast these societies with those in which no mechanism for discharging obligations is provided. For example, Dillon notes:

Instead of the *kula* principle operating in the Marshall Plan, the aid effort unwittingly took on some of the characteristics of the potlatch ceremony of the 19th Century among North Pacific Coast Indians in which property was destroyed in rivalry, and the poor humiliated. (p. 15)

Volatile and unpleasant relations are said to be the result of such continuing inequities.

These authors, along with Blau (1955) and Smith (1892) agree that ability to reciprocate is an important determinant of how nations will respond to help from their neighbors.

2. *Experimental data: Liking for benefactors* (from "All in the Family"):

> **Mike:** No, no, no. Don't stop them. This is beautiful. It's the first time some truth is coming in their relationship. Let them kill each other.
> **Gloria:** Michael!
> **Lionel:** Now, wait a second!! What were you saying about saving another man's life?
> **Edith:** Well, this man saved another man's life. And the man who was saved, instead of bein' thankful, started gettin' madder and madder at the man who saved him. And the moral of the story was. . .
> **Mike:** All right, ma. What you're trying to say is that I resent Archie because I owe him so much. Well, I've told him a hundred times that I'll pay him back—every cent. —With interest. Excuse me.
> **Edith:** No, wait a minute, Mike, I ain't finished yet. There was more to the moral than that. The teacher said what the story really meant was that when you owe somebody an awful lot, you begin worryin' if you'll ever be able to pay him back, and that makes you resent that person even more. You see what I mean?
> (Mike stares at Edith for a beat)
> (Edith's point has registered)
> **Mike:** I'm going to the kitchen.*

Other evidence in support of Conclusion III illustrates that a beneficiary likes his benefactor more when he can reciprocate than when he cannot. Gergen and his associates investigated American, Swedish, and Japanese citizens' reactions to reciprocal and non-reciprocal exchanges.[18] Students were recruited to participate in an experiment on group competition. Things were arranged so that during the course of the game, the student discovered that he was losing badly. At a critical stage (when the student was just about to be eliminated from the game) one of the "luckier" players in the game sent him an envelope. The envelope contained a supply of chips and a note. For a third of the students (Low Obligation condition subjects) the note explained that the chips were theirs to keep, that the giver did not need them, and that they need not be returned. One-third of the students (Equal Obligation condition subjects) received a similar note, except that the giver of the chips asked the subject to return an equal number of chips later in the proceedings. The remaining students (High Obliga-

---

*From a teleplay by Michael Ross and Bernie West. Story by Susan Parkis Haven and Dan Klein and Michael Ross and Bernie West. Copyright © 1973 Tandem Productions Inc. All rights reserved. Reprinted by permission.

FIGURE 4.5. "There Is Evidence that a Beneficiary Likes His Benefactor More When He Can Reciprocate than when He Cannot."

tion condition subjects) received a note from the giver in which he asked for the chips to be returned with interest and for the subject to help him out later in the game.

At the end of the game, students were queried about their attraction toward various partners. The results support Conclusion III: those partners who provided benefits without ostensible obligation or who asked for excessive benefits, were both judged to be less attractive than were partners who proposed that the student make exact restitution later in the game.

Gergen, Seipel, and Diebold (in preparation) conducted a variation of the preceding study. Just as subjects were about to be eliminated from a game because of their consistent losses, another "player" in the game loaned the subject some resources with the expectation that they would be paid back. However, in subsequent play, only half of the subjects managed to retain their chips. Thus, half of the subjects were unable to return the gift; half were able to do so. In subsequent evaluations of the donor, recipients who were unable to repay the donor evaluated him less positively than did recipients who were able to repay. These results were replicated in both Sweden and the United States.[19]

The evidence, then, is consistent with Tacitus' observation (*Annals,* bk. 4, sec. 181) that, "Benefits are only acceptable so far as they seem capable of being requited: Beyond that point, they excite hatred instead of gratitude."

3. *Survey data: Liking for gifts:*   A third bit of evidence in support of Conclusion III is that individuals *prefer* gifts that can be reciprocated to gifts that cannot be repaid. Gergen and Gergen (1971) questioned citizens in countries that had received U.S. aid as to how they felt about the assistance their country received. The Gergens note that international gifts, when they are accompanied by clearly stated obligations, are preferred either to gifts that are not accompanied by obligations or gifts that are accompanied by excessive "strings." Presumably, gifts that can be exactly reciprocated (by fulfilling clearly stated obligations) are preferred to gifts that cannot be reciprocated or to gifts that require excessive reciprocation.

4. *Experimental data: Willingness to accept gifts:*   Finally, in support of Conclusion III there is evidence that individuals are more eager to accept gifts that can be reciprocated than gifts that cannot.[20]

For example, Greenberg (1968) told students that they would be participating in a study of the effects of physical disability on work performance. On an initial task, students were given a temporary handicap—their arms were placed in slings. This restriction made it almost impossible for them to perform the assigned task. The incapacitated student knew, however, that if he wished, he could solicit help from a fellow worker. Half of the students believed that the fellow subject would need their help on a second task and that they would be able to provide assistance. Half of the students believed that the fellow subject would not need their help and that, in any case, they would not be able to provide much help. The students' expectations about whether or not they could reciprocate any help provided to them strongly affected their willingness to request help. Students in the no-reciprocity condition waited significantly longer before requesting help than did those in the reciprocity condition. Greenberg and Shapiro (1971) replicated these findings.

Finally, Krebs and Baldwin (1972) provide a dramatic field demonstration of people's reluctance to accept charity. As Boston commuters left the subway station, two men, one white and one black, approached them. One of the men attempted to hand the commuter a dollar bill. The commuters obviously resented anyone's nerve in attempting to give *them* money. The commuters seemed to resent an offer of charity from a black "altruist" the most. Not one commuter would accept money from the black man. Only forty percent were willing to accept money from the white donor.

Summary

In this chapter we have explored three kinds of helping relationships. Although all three relationships are commonly labeled philanthropist/ beneficiary *relationships, the dynamics of the three are actually quite different.*

First of all we considered exploitative or excessively profitable relationships. For example, we considered exploitative relationships in which the ostensible philanthropist helped others merely because that was the most profitable way to help himself. We also considered a very special kind of excessively profitable relationship—the not-so-innocent bystander/victim relationship. We considered the case of the bystander who realizes that, by his actions or inactions, he has contributed to another's suffering. We reviewed factors which determine whether the "not-so-innocent bystander" would make actual restitution to the victim, justify his suffering, or leave the situation.

Next we considered reciprocal relationships. Such exchanges seem to breed good feelings and a desire to reciprocate.

Finally we considered the public's epitome of a "good" relationship, the altruistic relationship. We reviewed the factors that determine whether such relationships breed good feelings, or as they more frequently do, breed hostility, humilitation, and alienation.

ENDNOTES

1. For example, we were unsure how one type of philanthropist/recipient relationship, the bystander/victim relationship, should be classified. How did the bystander perceive things? When the bystander compared his relative outcomes to the victim's, he might have concluded that he, the bystander, was overbenefited and the victim was underbenefited. On the other hand, he might also have concluded that things were perfectly fair *as they stood;* he owes the victim nothing and the victim owes him nothing. Under these conditions, if the bystander were to volunteer to help, this would be a truly altruistic act. To deal with this problem, we have adopted the following strategy: we will first assume that, when the "not-so-innocent" bystander compares his relative outcomes to the victim's, he can only conclude that he is "overbenefited" and the victim is "underbenefited." (We will save our discussion of the reaction of the "truly-innocent-bystanders" for the section on "Altruistic relationships.")

2. For example, see Greenberg (1968), Latané and Darley (1970), Piliavin and Piliavin (1972), and Weiss et al. (1971, 1972, 1973).

3. See Bandura and Rosenthal (1966), Berger (1962), Lazarus et al. (1965), and Nomikos et al. (1968).

4. See Piliavin and Piliavin (1971), Piliavin, Rodin and Piliavin (1969), and Walster and Piliavin (1972).

5. See Lazarus, Opton, Nomikos, and Rankin (1965).

6. See Leventhal, Allen, and Kemelgor (1969), and Leventhal and Bergman (1969).

7. Of course, avoidance responses cannot eliminate the inequity; they can only reduce the inequity's salience.

8. See Ratcliffe (1966).

9. For example, Nemeth (1970), Berkowitz (1972), and Gross and Latané (1973) provide evidence that reciprocal helping relations stimulate friendly feelings.

10. See Greenberg (1968), Gross and Latané (1973), and Pruitt (1968).

11. See Frisch and Greenberg (1968), Garrett and Libby (1973), Gouldner (1960), Goranson and Berkowitz (1966), Greenberg (1968), Gross and Latané (1973), Leventhal, Weiss, and Long (1969), and Thibaut and Reicken (1955).

12. Data in support of this contention come from Brehm and Cole (1966), Heider (1958), Krebs (1970), Leeds (1963), Lerner and Lichtman (1968), Schopler and Thompson (1968).

13. Theorists commonly cite two reasons why altruists engage in such perplexing behavior: (1) strong social norms dictate that people must behave

altruistically in certain settings; (2) the altruists' feelings motivate them to behave altruistically. For some reason, they experience their own pleasure and pain less strongly than they empathize with their fellows'. (Psychologists do not really have a good understanding of this process.)

14. See for example, Alger and Rusk (1955), Bredmeir (1964), Briar (1966). Goldin, Perry, Margolin, and Stotsky (1967), Kalish (1967), Ladieu, Hanfmann, and Dembo (1947), and Lipman and Stern (1962).

15. See Berkowitz (1972a), Gouldner (1960), Lerner (1971), Leventhal, Weiss, and Buttrich (1973), and Pruitt (1972).

16. See Byron and Test (1968), Darley and Latané (1968), Feldman (1967), and Hornstein et al. (1968).

17. For a review of citizens' generous reactions to needy disaster victims, see Midlarsky (1968).

18. See Gergen (1969).

19. Other evidence in support of this contention comes from Gross and Latané (1973).

20. Berkowitz and Friedman (1967), Berkowitz (1968), Greenberg (1968), and Morris and Rosen (1973) support the contention that people are reluctant to ask for help they cannot repay.

CHAPTER
5

Equity Theory
and Business Relationships

Equity theory is a natural framework for analyzing business relationships.

First, in a business relationship it is usually fairly easy to specify who is in a relationship with whom. The employer knows he is in a relationship with his employees. The foreman knows he is in a relationship with his linemen. The linemen, who work side by side tightening identical bolts on identical auto bodies, surely feel they are in a relationship with each other.

Second, it is usually fairly easy to specify what the relevant inputs and outcomes are. Both employers and employees, if required to enumerate the inputs *they* consider to be important, can probably agree that intelligence, education, skill, training, experience, seniority, the possession of appropriate tools, effort, health, and so on, "count." (In special circumstances, they might also agree that such inputs as sex, ethnic background, social status, personal appearance, family responsibilities, the characteristics of one's spouse, and so on, are important.) Both employers and employees can probably agree that salary, and such fringe benefits as health insurance, a retirement program, and perquisites (such as the right to park your car in a privileged location) are valuable outcomes; they can also probably agree that dangerous working conditions, job insecurity, and monotony are negative outcomes.

Equity theorists have generated a fascinating array of equity predictions in the business area. Even more impressively, they have carefully tested their hypotheses in naturalistic business settings.[1]

At the time Equity theorists began their work, the prevailing assumption was that businessmen and employees were economic men— men who delighted in profit, the bigger the better. It is not surprising, then, that the two questions industrial psychologists found most intriguing were: (1) Do employers really care whether or not their workers are being fairly treated? (2) Do employees really care whether or not they are fairly treated? Or, are overpaid workers perfectly content with their lot? Is it only underpaid workers who long for justice?

Let us consider some of the voluminous data industrial psychologists collected in their attempt to answer these questions.

DO EMPLOYERS REALLY CARE ABOUT EQUITY?

Leventhal (1976a) has embarked on a research program designed to find out what motivates employers to behave in equitable/inequitable ways.

Leventhal's argument runs as follows:

A very few businessmen may follow equity rules because they are committed to abstract ideals of equity and justice. They pay their employees fairly because they believe people deserve to be paid fairly. Most employers, however, are not motivated by fairness and justice as ends in themselves. They follow equity rules because of the benefits they produce, both for the employer and for the company. The real question, Leventhal argues, is: Why do employers follow equity norms? What *specific* pattern of benefits are linked to equitable behavior?

Leventhal then reviews several "pay-offs" that employers may reap from equitable behavior:

1. *Conforming to business world norms:* Generally, the business world defines the equity rules as the appropriate allocation rules. Everyone takes it for granted that the better an employee's work, the higher salary he should get. Thus, one reason why employers treat their employees equitably is a practical one: they know that "to get along, you go along" with established practices.

2. *Attracting superior workers to the company; weeding out inferior ones:* Leventhal (1976a) points out that:

> Equitable distributions of reward make group membership more attractive for recipients who contribute more. Highly rewarded superior performers will

tend to remain in the group and poorly rewarded inferior performers will be inclined to terminate their membership. Consequently, over a period of time, an allocator who follows the rule of equity and rewards recipients in accordance with their performance will maximize group effectiveness by increasing the proportion of highly capable performers in the group. (p. 99)

There is evidence from Landau and Leventhal (in press) that employers are especially likely to follow the equity norm when they are eager to upgrade their work force. The authors asked students to play the role of a personnel manager. One of their workers, either a strikingly productive or a dismally unproductive worker, had received an impressive outside job offer. What would their counteroffer be? As expected, students offered highly productive workers more than the outside agency, and they offered nonproductive workers less than the outside agency. Clearly, this pattern of allocation would encourage good performers to remain in the group and poor performers to accept the offer and leave.

Landau and Leventhal obtained further support for the contention that employers are especially likely to follow the equity norm when they want to upgrade their work force. In a few groups, the authors told students to make counteroffers that would retain the best performers and weed out the rest. These students were even more inclined to distribute reward in accordance with performance than were other students. In particular they offered much less to poor performers. Clearly, they were attempting to induce poor performers to quit.

3. *Motivating workers to produce:* There is a third reason why even the most cynical of businessmen might choose to reward employees equitably: the belief that an equitable system is a profitable system.

Leventhal (1976a) notes:

In fact, it seems likely that an allocator who distributes rewards equitably frequently does so more because he desires to maximize long-term productivity than because he desires to comply with an abstract standard of justice. His decisions are based on an expectancy that equitable distributions of reward will elicit and sustain high levels of motivation and performance. (p. 96)

Leventhal cites a large body of theory and research that suggests the employer's expectation is a reasonable one: the employer who pays his employees equitably, who rewards those who work well and hard, and punishes those who do not, does motivate workers to produce.[2]

4. *Avoiding conflict:* Finally, employers may treat their workers equitably simply to avoid conflict.

Any time a manager sets himself up as a judge of other men's worth, he can expect to encounter trouble. The task is hard enough when his decisions are fair; woe to the manager whose decisions are unfair.

One reason, then, that employers treat employees fairly is their desire to maximize harmony and minimize dissension.[3] But how to do this?

At this point, Leventhal suggests a fascinating hypothesis. An employer could follow either of two strategies in his effort to be fair: he could apportion resources in the way that *he* thinks is fair, or he could apportion resources in the way that he knows *his employees* think is fair. But how to do that? Yuchtman (1973) observed that personnel managers and rank and file workers often disagree as to what is fair. Yuchtman found that managers in small factories preferred pay systems based on merit. Their workers preferred a more equal division of resources. One way, then, that an employer can accede to his employees is by giving them all a fairly equal share of the "pie."

Leventhal's contention is that the more employers value harmony, the more likely they will be to switch from an equitable allocation of resources to one that they think will satisfy the men.

> An allocator who hopes to minimize disruptive conflict will reduce the difference between recipients' rewards. . . . This suggestion is confirmed by the results of Leventhal, Michaels, and Sanford (1972). Their subjects recommended a distribution of earnings in work groups that would meet for a number of sessions. The subjects were told each group would be rewarded in accordance with its performance but that the experimenters were uncertain as to how group earnings should be divided among the members. To show their recommendation, subjects divided a monetary reward among the members of a hypothetical group two times. The first time, they divided the reward as they thought best and gave much higher reward to better performers. Subjects received different instructions concerning their second allocation decision. In two conditions, they were told to divide the reward so as to prevent conflict and hostility, either among the group members, or between the group members and the experimenters. In comparison to a control group, subjects in these conditions showed a marked tendency to inflate the rewards of poorer performers at better performers' expense. Thus, subjects whose goal was to minimize interpersonal conflict gave less weight to differences in recipients' work contributions and reduced the difference between the rewards of good and poor performers. However, it should be noted that subjects stopped short of giving equal reward to all recipients. They still gave substantially higher reward to better performers.* (pp. 109–110)

---

*From G. S. Leventhal, "The Distribution of Rewards and Resources in Groups and Organizations," in L. Berkowitz and E. Walster, eds., *Advances in Experimental Social Psychology*, vol. 9 (New York: Academic Press, 1976), pp. 99–110. Reprinted by permission.

Leventhal closes his essay by reminding readers that, because employers (like all people) are driven, not by abstract ideals, but by a desire for profit, they will treat employees equitably only so long as it is profitable to do so. Should social conditions make an equitable allocation system less profitable than some alternative system, employers will of course switch to the more profitable allocation system. (In the balance of his essay, Leventhal enumerates a potpourri of specific circumstances which currently temper businessmen's tendency to follow equity norms.)[4]

DO EMPLOYEES REALLY CARE ABOUT EQUITY?

The Leventhal research on employers' reactions to equity and inequity is provocative. Yet, by far the most provocative (and voluminous) research in the industrial area has dealt with the other half of the coin: the employee's reaction to equity and inequity.

Distress

In the previous sections, we reviewed evidence that people are most comfortable when they are equitably treated. Research conducted specifically in business settings indicates that the norms of the marketplace are not so very different from those of the rest of life.

One of the earliest industrial psychologists to observe that perceived injustice provokes dissatisfaction was Jaques (1961). In a study of British factory workers, Jaques found that underpaid workers showed "an active sense of grievance, complaints, or the desire to complain, and . . . an active desire to change jobs." But, more interestingly, he found that overpaid workers were distressed too; they showed "a strong sense of preferential treatment . . . with underlying feelings of unease."

Recent experiments support Jaques' observations. One especially impressive study was conducted by Pritchard, Dunnette, and Jorgenson (1972). Pritchard and his colleagues hired 253 Minnesota men to work for their "Manpower" firm. They made every attempt to make their work situation seem realistic. They told men that the company operated as an overload manpower firm, which took contracts for clerical work from small companies that felt they did not have the facilities to get a job done. The company name was displayed on all advertisements for the job, on the men's time cards, and on the checks they received.

The company hired the men to work as clerks for one week. At the time they were hired, all of the men were promised an equitable salary (approximately two dollars an hour). After they had gone through a day of orientation and had begun to work, however, their dismayed employer ruefully revealed that the recruitment flyers had been in error, that he could (or could not) remedy this, and that as a consequence they would be overpaid, equitably paid, or underpaid.

During the week the men worked, their satisfaction with their equitable/inequitable situation was measured in two ways. The men were asked to rate their feelings on the *Minnesota Satisfaction Questionnaire (MSQ)*. The *MSQ* measures men's satisfaction with their pay, their recognition, their general working conditions, and the extent to which their job uses their abilities. The men were also asked to express their feelings on the *Job Description Index (JDI)*. The *JDI* measures men's satisfaction with five dimensions: work, supervision, people, pay, and promotions.

The results were fairly clear: equitably treated men were more satisfied with their jobs than were either overpaid or underpaid men. Inequity, be it underpayment or overpayment, is an aversive state which causes significant job dissatisfaction.

Additional evidence that equitably paid workers are more satisfied than markedly underpaid or overpaid workers comes from a variety of sources.[5]

It seems, then, that in business, as in casual relationships, inequity provokes distress.

Once this fact was established, industrial psychologists proceeded to tackle their second question: How do inequitably paid workers handle their feelings? According to Equity theory, the two strategies available to them are the restoration of actual equity, or the restoration of psychological equity. An impressive body of literature indicates that workers seem to do both.

Restoration of Actual Equity

Altering Inputs. In the 1960s, Adams and his colleagues, in a series of elegantly simple papers and studies, excited a revolution in business research. Adams proposed the unthinkable: that capitalistic American workers would be uncomfortable earning too much, as well as too little,

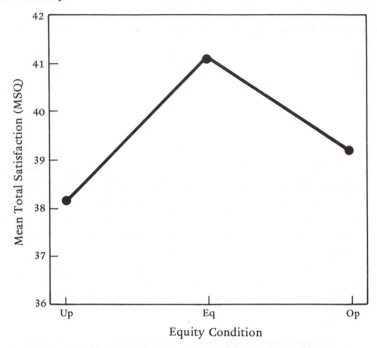

FIGURE 5.1. Mean Total Satisfaction (MSQ), Day 1, Experimentally Induced Equity/Inequity. (From R. D. Pritchard, M. D. Dunnette, and D. O. Jorgenson, "Effects of Perceptions of Equity and Inequity on Worker Performance and Satisfaction," *Journal of Applied Psychology*, 56, 1972, p. 89. Copyright © 1972 by the American Psychological Association. Reprinted by permission.)

and that their desire for equity would influence both the quantity and the quality of their craftmanship. From then on, business research was never again the same. Supportive studies and refutive studies followed one another pell-mell. Theoretical and methodological critiques succeeded each wave of research. To understand this body of research, then, let us begin at the beginning.

Adams and Rosenbaum (1962) pointed out that according to Equity theory: (1) employees who realize they are being overpaid *or* underpaid should feel distress; (2) overpaid and underpaid workers can reduce their distress in a variety of ways. For example, workers can restore actual equity by altering either the quantity or the quality of their work. Then, Adams and Rosenbaum make an ingenious observation; employees who are paid on a salary (or hourly basis) versus a piece-rate basis must restore actual equity in very different ways. The overpaid worker who is paid on an hourly basis can restore equity by increasing his inputs; he can produce more work and higher quality work. An underpaid worker can restore equity by doing the opposite; he can produce less and lower quality work. The worker who is paid on a piece-rate basis, however, must follow a somewhat different strategy if he is to set things right. An overpaid piece-rate worker can only restore equity if he produces less work of a higher quality. An underpaid piece-rate worker can restore equity by doing just the opposite; he can produce more work of a lower quality.

Adams and Rosenbaum (1962) tested the hypothesis that hourly and piece-rate workers would respond to inequity in quite different ways, in a now classic experiment. The authors hired New York men to be interviewers. Some interviewers were paid a flat salary ($3.50 per hour); others were paid on a per interview basis (thirty cents per interview).

The "employer" (an experimenter) then set out to make some interviewers feel overpaid and others feel equitably paid. In the Overpaid conditions, the employer studied the interviewer's employment folder, and then said:

> You don't have any (nearly enough) experience in interviewing or survey work of the kind we're engaged in here. I specifically asked the Placement Service to refer only people with that kind of experience. This was *the* major qualification we set. I can't understand how such a slip-up could have occurred. It's really very important for research of this kind to have people experienced in interviewing and survey techniques. [Agonizing pause.]
>
> We're dealing with a limited alternative, open-end kind of questionnaire. There's no "correct" answer to an item. Research in this area has shown that the nature of the response elicited by a skilled and experienced interviewer is more accurate and representative of the respondent's sentiments and differs substantially from the responses elicited by inexperienced people.
>
> Who interviewed you at Placement? [E scans the New York University phone directory, picks up telephone receiver and dials a number. Gets busy signal and slams receiver down. Pause, while E thumbs papers and meditates.]
>
> I guess I'll have to hire you anyway, but *please* pay close attention to the instructions I will give you. If anything I say seems complicated, don't hesitate to ask for clarification. If it seems simple, pay closer attention. Some of this stuff, on the surface, may appear to be deceptively easy.
>
> Since I'm going to hire you, I'll just have to pay you at the rate we advertised, that is ($3.50 per hour) (30¢ per interview). (p. 162)

In the Equitably paid conditions the employer simply said:

> Well, this is very good. We can use you for this work. You meet all the qualifications required for the job, which is good, because we often have to turn people down because they're poorly qualified. Poorly qualified people can really make a mess of a study of this kind. Why even the Census, where

they were dealing with simple demographic material, got fouled up. They hired inadequately qualified people, some of their housewives for example, and the result was the gross deficiencies in their data that were so widely criticized in the press, if you recall.

Well, anyway, I'm pleased you have the background we're looking for.

So far as pay is concerned, the people at the Placement Service have probably advised you that we pay $3.50 per hour (30¢ per interview). This rate of pay is standard for work of this kind performed by people with your qualifications. (p. 162)

Then the employer explained the interview to the men and sent them out to work.

Adams and Rosenbaum's results were striking. As predicted, when interviewers were paid by the hour, "overpaid" workers conducted far more interviews than did their "equitably" paid counterparts. When workers were paid by the interview, "overpaid" workers produced far less than their equitably paid counterparts. (In subsequent research, Adams (1963) and Adams and Jacobson (1964) demonstrated that these overpaid workers were also producing better interviews than their equitably paid colleagues.)

Lawler and O'Gara (1967) provide evidence that underpaid piece-rate workers will restore equity by increasing the quantity and decreasing the quality of their work. As in the Adams study, Lawler and O'Gara hired (Connecticut) men as interviewers. The "employer" then set out to make some interviewers feel equitably paid and others feel underpaid. In 1967, the "going rate" for interviews was $1.65 an hour. Thus, at the time men were hired, the authors offered them either an "equitable" salary (twenty-five cents per interview; the men soon learned that this averaged out to the traditional $1.65 per hour) or an "underpaid" salary (ten cents per interview; the men soon learned that this averaged out to only about sixty-five cents per hour). The men were then sent out to interview.

Once again, the results strongly supported Equity theory predictions: when men were paid by the interview, underpaid interviewers conducted far more interviews than did their equitably paid colleagues. Also, as predicted, the underpaid interviewer's work was of far lower quality than that of their equitably paid colleagues.

Adams and his colleagues, then, seem to have demonstrated that when workers *first* find out that they are being over or underpaid they feel concern and will set out to remedy things. This makes sense. When an employer first reveals to a worker that he is equitably or inequitably paid, the worker has every reason to accept the employer's word for it. But what would happen if the inequity were to continue—and to continue? With time, the overpaid worker would surely begin to wonder why, if he was so unqualified, his employer didn't fire him and hire a better worker. With time, the underpaid worker would be forced to ask himself why, if he was really so underpaid, didn't he quit his job and go elsewhere. It seems possible then, that a worker's initial reaction to inequity might be quite different than his long-term reaction.

The question of how overpaid/equitably paid/underpaid workers react over time is a fascinating one. And, luckily, it is a question that has been addressed by a few researchers.

Vroom (1964) and Lawler, Koplin, Young, and Fadem (1968) proposed an ingenious extension of the Adams et al. formulation. They agreed with Adams' contention that when individuals are overpaid (on a piece-rate basis) their immediate reaction may well be to try to right things by sacrificing income or effort. They predicted, however, that the overpaid workers' "sacrifice" would be a transitory one. In time, overpaid workers were bound to realize that restoring actual equity is far more costly than restoring psychological equity. Lawler et al. note:

> Because of the obvious negative consequences in economic terms of long-term low output, the prediction is that low output is not a viable long-term way to reduce feelings of overpayment. A preferable way might be for the subject to raise his evaluation of his own inputs (his qualifications) once he has begun the job or in some other way to alter cognitively his input-outcome balance. (p. 255)

Lawler et al. tested this hypothesis in a careful experiment. Men and women from New Haven were hired as interviewers. They were paid thirty cents an interview (which works out to about $3.50 an hour). À la Adams and Rosenbaum (1962), some of the interviewers were led to believe they were being equitably paid; others to believe they were being overpaid. Unlike Adams' and Rosenbaum's subjects, however, these interviewers were hired not for one session but for three sessions, spaced over a six-day period.

At the end of each day's work, the authors calculated the interviewers' productivity and the quality of their work. In addition, they asked the interviewers to complete a questionnaire. (The questionnaire was designed to tap the extent to which interviewers justified being equitably paid or overpaid. The data are reported in Figures 5.2 and 5.3.)

On the first day of work, overpaid interviewers responded as Adams said they would. Overpaid piece-rate workers interviewed fewer people but did a far better job on each interview than did their equitably paid colleagues. This was only true on the first day of work, however. By the second and third days, the overpaid interviewers had changed their strategy. By then, the overpaid and equitably paid interviewers had begun doing work of more comparable quantity and quality.

Equity had not become unimportant, however. The authors argue that the overpaid interviewers had simply switched to a more profitable mode of equity restoration: they had switched from the restoration of actual equity to restoration of psychological equity. Over time, overpaid interviewers became increasingly convinced that the employer was wrong and that they *were* qualified for their job. In fact, by their final day of work, overpaid interviewers (who had been told they were not qualified to earn thirty cents per interview) were actually more confident about their qualifications than were equitably paid interviewers (who had been told they were qualified).

Critiques of Adams. As happens whenever a study provokes great research excitement, the theorizing of Adams and his colleagues was followed by a flurry of critiques.[6] Let us review the most compelling of these criticisms.

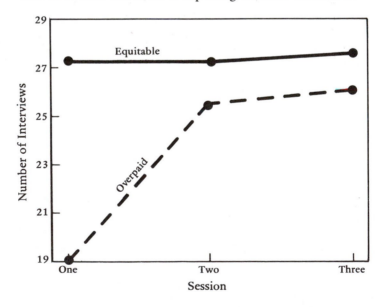

FIGURE 5.2. Mean Productivity Scores for the Equitable and Overpaid Subjects in Three Experimental Sessions. (From E. E. Lawler III et al., "Inequity Reduction over Time in an Induced Overpayment Situation," *Organizational Behavior and Human Performance*, 3, 1968, p. 260. Reprinted by permission.)

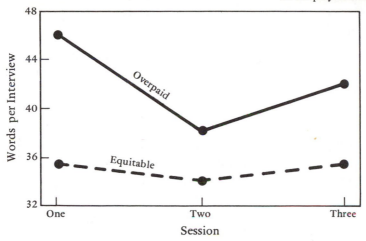

FIGURE 5.3. Mean Quality Scores for the Equitable and Overpaid Subjects in the Three Experimental Sessions. (From Lawler et al., "Inequity Reduction," p. 261.)

Essentially, critics charged that Adams and his colleagues, in their manipulation of overpayment/equity/underpayment, had inadvertently manipulated some far more powerful variables as well. They charged that Adams and Rosenbaum, in their equity/inequity manipulation, had also inadvertently (1) threatened the overpaid interviewers' self-esteem (2) threatened their job security, or (3) set more stringent production standards for overpaid than for equitably paid interviewers. And, their argument continues, it is *these* variables, rather than equity/inequity that produced the Adams results.

Self-esteem: The most viable criticism of the Adams data was broached by Friedman and Goodman (1967), Lawler (1968), and Pritchard (1969). Recall that in Adams and Rosenbaum, the experimenter manipulated "overpayment" by telling interviewers they were totally unqualified to earn $3.50 an hour; he manipulated "equitable payment" by telling interviewers that they were perfectly qualified.

As Pritchard (1969) notes, with devastating clarity:

> The essence of E's statement seems to be (1) what is an unqualified person like you doing here; (2) you will be a poor interviewer; (3) you will cause errors in my data; (4) I'm going to raise hell with the idiot who sent you over here; (5) I have to hire you, but I don't want to; (6) you will have to be extremely careful of these interviews; (7) you may think this stuff is simple, but it's not; and (8) I'm forced to pay you at the going rate, but you don't deserve it. E then proceeds to describe the extremely simple interviewing procedure. (p. 186)

Pritchard continues:

> It seems quite likely that the results of this initial contact with the "employer" was not only to induce cognitions of LH, HH inequity, but also to threaten the (overpaid) S's self-esteem. This threat could be relative to the subject himself—"I'll be a poor interviewer," and/or relative to E—"He thinks I'll be a poor interviewer." (p. 186)

Overpaid subjects may have performed so impressively, Pritchard argues, not because of their desire to restore equity, but because of their desire to convince the experimenter (and themselves) that they were capable employees.

Some support for the critics' contention comes from a study by Andrews and Valenzi (1970). These experimenters asked college students to witness a re-enactment of Adams and Rosenbaum. The students listened to a job applicant report to Mr. Scott, a potential employer. After some pleasantries about the weather, Mr. Scott began to examine the applicant's job folder. The more he read, the more upset he became. He muttered and shook his head in disbelief. Finally he reached for the phone and called Miss Evans (at the employment bureau) and complained bitterly that the applicant simply didn't measure up. After saying goodbye to Miss Evans, he turned to the applicant, and grudgingly announced that because of deadline pressures, he would have to hire him in spite of the fact that he was unqualified.

After witnessing this drama, the audience was asked to put themselves in the job applicant's shoes and say how they would have felt if they had been applying for that job. Thirty-five of the eighty students responded in terms of self-esteem (e.g., they checked such potential responses as, "I certainly don't like to be thought of as incompetent. He didn't seem to think much of me. Seems to me that other bosses I've worked for have liked my work well enough"). To out of the eighty responded in terms of job insecurity. (They checked such replies as: "There's a darn good chance I'll lose this job if I don't do well on my first try. I sure would hate to lose a job that pays $3.50/hour.") *Not one* student responded in terms of wage inequity. (No one checked such items as: "It seems unfair to the other interviewers that I get paid at the same rate they do. After all, I'm less qualified. Actually their pay should be higher than mine.")

There is also some experimental evidence that this alternative explanation of the Adams data may be a viable one.[7]

Threatened job security: A second possible interpretation of the Adams and Rosenbaum findings was discussed by Adams and Rosenbaum themselves, and by Arrowood (1961). When Adams and Rosenbaum hired interviewers, they told them they would be paid three dollars an hour for the duration of the job, which they implied *might* last for several months. Critics pointed out that overpaid workers (who felt they were unqualified for the job) might well have feared that their pay would be cut, or they would be fired. Equitably paid men (who knew they were qualified) would have no such worry. No wonder, then, the authors argued, that overpaid workers worked so conscientiously.

As reasonable as this alternative explanation sounds, subsequent research suggests that it is not a plausible alternative explanation for the Adams and Rosenbaum findings. The Adams and Rosenbaum effect appears to hold even when job security is assured or when workers know there is *no* chance of future employment.[8]

Differential production demands: A third, and final, interpretation of the Adams and Rosenbaum findings was proposed by Anderson and Shelly (1971), Opsahl and Dunnette (1966), and Pritchard et al. (1972).

In the course of the overpayment manipulation, Adams and Rosenbaum (1962) told men:

> *Please* pay close attention to the instructions I will give you. If anything I say seems complicated, don't hesitate to ask for clarification. If it seems simple, pay closer attention. Some of this stuff, on the surface, may seem deceptively easy. (p. 162)

They gave no such instructions to the equitably paid subjects.

The critics pointed out that these instructions gave overpaid workers the clear message that they were to produce, and to produce good quality work; equitably paid workers were given no such message. Thus, critics point out, overpaid workers might have produced so impressively, not out of a desire to restore equity, but out of a desire to conform to "experimenter demands." Although there is some evidence in support of this contention,[9] most reviewers have concluded on the basis of other evidence[10] that this interpretation of Adams' data is not a particularly viable one.

Conclusions. What is the current status of the Adams research? Things started out rather simply. Initially, Adams and his colleagues published a set of papers designed to support the Adams and Rosenbaum contention that overpaid/equitably paid/underpaid interviewers would try to restore actual equity by altering the quantity and quality of their work. Then came a flurry of critics' papers, designed to show that Adams got the results he did, not because workers desired to redress inequity, but rather because workers desired to maintain self-esteem, increase their job security, or conform with experimenter demands. Rebuttal followed rebuttal. Then things became more complicated. A variety of researchers began to speculate that if one ran the Adams and Rosenbaum study under slightly (or markedly) different conditions, one might get quite different results. And, sometimes they did. A flurry of research followed. Rebuttal after rebuttal followed *that* round of research. What, then, can we conclude from this remarkable collection of research? (1) Basically, Adams seems to be correct. Equitably treated workers do feel more comfortable than overpaid and underpaid workers. And, workers do often try to restore actual equity by altering their inputs. A substantial body of research supports these contentions. (See Table 5.1). (2) Additional evidence makes it clear that while, as Adams suggests, overpaid/equitably paid/underpaid workers can respond by

TABLE 5.1. **The Impact of Overpayment/Equitable Payment/Underpayment on Hourly and Piece-Rate Workers' Performance.**

	Hourly Workers	Piece-Rate Workers
Evidence Strongly Supports Adams' Predictions	Adams (1963b) Adams and Rosenbaum (1962) Arrowood (1961) Clark (1958) Cook (1969) Goodman and Freedman (1968) Kalt (1969) Pritchard et al. (1972)	Adams (1963b) Adams and Jacobsen (1964) Adams and Rosenbaum (1962) Andrews (1967) Evans and Molinari (1970) Garland (1972) Goodman and Freedman (1969) Lawler et al. (1968) Lawler and O'Gara (1967) Pritchard et al. (1972) Wood and Lawler (1970)
Evidence Provides Only Partial Support for Adams' Predictions	Evans and Simmons (1969) Freedman and Goodman (1967) Kessler and Wiener (1972) Lawler (1968a) *Weick and Prestholdt (1968) Wiener (1970) Wilke and Steve (1972)	Haccoun et al. (1973) Moore and Baron (1973)
Evidence Does Not Support Adams' Predictions	Anderson and Shelly (1970) *Freedman (1963) Gergen et al. (1974) Heslin and Blake (1969) Hinton (1972) Valenzi and Andrews (1971) *Weick (1964)	Hinton (1972) Moore (1968)

*Results actually in a direction opposite to that predicted by Adams.

trying to maintain *actual* equity, that is only one possible reaction. They might also use some quite different strategies to achieve equity. Let us consider two examples:

According to Table 5.1, both Valenzi and Andrews (1971) and Gergen, Morse, and Bode (1974) found "no support" for Adams' predictions. These authors found overpaid/equitably paid/underpaid workers produced work of approximately the same quantity and quality. A clear refutation of Equity theory, right? Well, not exactly. What the authors really found was this:

Valenzi and Andrews (1971) found no evidence that overpaid/underpaid workers would try to restore actual equity by painstakingly adjusting the quantity and quality of their work. What workers did do was far less subtle than this. The overpaid workers worked on; twenty-seven percent of the underpaid workers quit.

Gergen et al. (1974) conducted their equity study in the United States and Italy. They too found no evidence that overpaid/equitably paid/underpaid workers differed in work quantity and quality. What they did do was far simpler than that. Workers simply changed their perceptions of what constituted a fair wage.

While technically these studies must be classed as "failures" to support Adams' specific predictions, the results are, obviously, well in line with Equity theory predictions.

There is one final point that we should make. Adams and his colleagues contended that, *all things being equal,* overpaid/equitably paid/underpaid workers should be motivated to produce work of differential quantity and quality.

Numerous researchers have pointed out that in life "all things" are very rarely equal. Researcher after researcher has demonstrated that by slightly varying Adams' instructions, one could get individuals to focus, not just on their desire for an equitable salary, but on their desire for admiration, power, excitement, sex, security, revenge, etc. They correctly point out that under the right conditions, one's desire for equitable pay might be overshadowed by such conflicting desires.

Let us consider an example: Kessler and Wiener (1972) attempted to replicate Adams et al. They used a different equitable payment/underpayment manipulation: in the Equity conditions, the employer told the men that their qualifications "looked alright . . . average." In the Underpaid condition, the employer was far more flattering. He said:

> Well, you have really done a fine job. This is much better work than we usually see. Actually, it's too bad that you weren't around earlier when they were looking around for people with your high level of ability. We were

FIGURE 5.4. "Workers Simply Changed Their Perceptions of What Constituted a Fair Wage."

paying $3/hour then. In fact, there is a possibility we may do so again. Unfortunately, the rate for this job now is $2/hour. Although you are worth more, that's all I can pay. (p. 460)

Of course, the employer could have gone on and on from there. (To make our point clearer, let's go on.) The employer could have admitted to the student that he rarely encountered an applicant with his intelligence, skill, and maturity; acknowledged that it was the rare chance to contact potential leaders like that boy, who had the ability to do anything he wanted, that made his job worthwhile, etc., etc.

Now, a strict recital of Adams' formula might lead us to predict that these underpaid workers, who by now are convinced they are so talented that they should be running things, much less receiving three dollars an hour, would proceed to restore equity by producing shoddy work. But, our intuition surely would not. Would we really expect a student, basking in the employer's praise (and hopeful that maybe there's a good job waiting in the wings for a person with such ability) to "blow" it all by producing second-rate work? They didn't.

This study, then (which found that underpaid men produced less work but far higher quality work than their equitably paid colleagues) demonstrates the obvious but important point that human beings are interested in a variety of outcomes, including money, praise, and future job opportunities. If we arrange things so that one's desire for an equitable salary conflicts with his desire for these other potent outcomes, we may well find that equity behavior is diminished or even entirely eliminated.

Until now, we, like the industrial psychologists, have focused on just *one* of the four ways by which an individual can restore equity to a relationship: i.e., by altering his inputs. Let us now consider the evidence—admittedly sparse—that under different circumstances, workers will try to restore actual equity (by altering outcomes) or restore psychological equity (by distorting reality).

Altering Outcomes: A second way that employers/employees, caught up in a blatantly inequitable exchange, can restore equity to their relationship is to arrange a fairer allocation of resources. For example, a company troubled by "excess profits" can award their employees a bonus. Long exploited workers can organize and strike for higher wages.

There is considerable evidence that employers and workers do

FIGURE 5.5. "Workers Will Try to . . . Restore Psychological Equity (by Distorting Reality)."

try to arrange things so outcomes are distributed in a roughly equitable way.

One compelling bit of evidence comes from Schmitt and Marwell (1972). These authors hired Wisconsin students to work on a simple cooperative task. The students' jobs were identical; each student sat in a workroom equipped with a panel like the one in Figure 5.6. The panel contained a plunger, stimulus lights, switch, button, and two counters.

It was the workers' job to coordinate their responses. Either worker could start things off by pulling his plunger. This activated a white light on his partner's panel; the white light stayed on for three seconds. It was the second worker's job to wait until the light went off and then pull *his* plunger within .05 seconds. If everything went right, the pair received a small amount of money.

In an initial series of trials, the students were equitably paid. (They both earned .3¢ each time the team made a correct response.) Then, suddenly, the rules changed. All of a sudden, one of the workers began to earn .9¢ each time the pair made a correct response; his partner continued to earn only .3¢. Since the Schmitt and Marwell study went on for a long period (six–ten hours) and involved a sizable number of plunger-plunger responses (approximately 4,800), this seemingly small discrepancy (.9¢ vs. .3¢) could mount up.

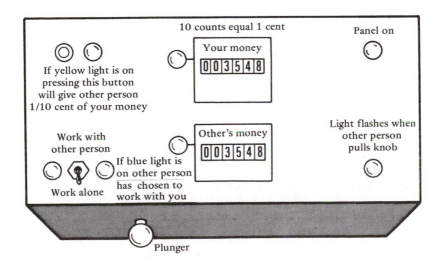

FIGURE 5.6. Diagram of Panel (9 X 18 in.). (From D. R. Schmitt and G. Marwell, "Withdrawal and Reward Allocation as Responses to Inequity," *Journal of Experimental Social Psychology,* 8, 1972, p. 210. Reprinted by permission.)

Schmitt and Marwell found that under these latter, inequitable, conditions, both the overpaid and the underpaid students would, whenever possible, voluntarily reallocate their money in a "fairer" way.

There is still other evidence that when individuals are suddenly granted the power to apportion (or reapportion) salaries, they do so on a roughly equitable basis.[11]

Restoration of Psychological Equity

Of course, individuals may respond to inequitable payment in a way quite different from those we have thus far discussed. Individuals can restore actual equity to their relationship but they can also restore psychological equity. Overpaid/underpaid workers can distort reality and convince themselves that they are being equitably paid.

Adams (1965) provides a concise depiction of how this process works:

> Person may cognitively distort his inputs and outcomes. . . . Since most individuals are heavily influenced by reality, substantial distortion is generally difficult. It is pretty difficult to distort to oneself, to change one's cognitions about the fact, for example, that one has a BA degree, that one has been an accountant for seven years, and that one's salary is $700 per month. However, it is possible, within limits, to alter the utility of these. For example, State College is a small, backwoods school with no reputation, or, alternatively, State College has one of the best business schools in the state and the dean is an adviser to the Bureau of the Budget. Or, one can consider the fact that $700 per month will buy all of the essential things of life and a few luxuries, or, conversely, that it will never permit one to purchase a Wyeth oil painting or an Aston Martin DB5. (p. 290)

Let us review some of the research which illustrates this process:

In an earlier section, we reviewed a study by Lawler and O'Gara (1967). These authors studied the behavior of underpaid (ten cents per interview) and equitably paid (twenty-five cents per interview) workers. Lawler and O'Gara made a very insightful prediction: they predicted, as Adams and his colleagues had, that some underpaid men would restore equity by actually adjusting their quantity or quality of work. But Lawler and O'Gara went further: they predicted that at least some underpaid men would reduce their distress by re-evaluating their inputs or their outcomes.

Some underpaid interviewers would choose to minimize their

own inputs. For example, they might convince themselves that the job was such a simple one, or they were so minimally qualified for interviewing, that they only deserved to be paid ten cents per interview (approximately sixty-five cents per hour).

Other underpaid workers might choose to restore psychological equity by exaggerating their own outcomes. They might convince themselves that in addition to sixty-five cents per hour, they were receiving numerous fringe benefits.

The data strongly supported Lawler and O'Gara's expectations. The author found that some underpaid men did come to perceive that they had relatively low inputs: underpaid men saw themselves as less qualified than did other men (this difference was not statistically significant, however); they also perceived their work to be relatively unimportant, simple, and unchallenging. Some underpaid men did exaggerate their outcomes: underpaid men rated the job as far more interesting than did other men.

Comparable evidence comes from a study conducted by Gergen, Morse, and Bode (1974). The authors conducted their research in Italy and in the United States. The fictitious Instituto per le Studie dei Processe Cognitive (in Rome), and The Institute for the Study of Cognitive Processes (in the U.S.), recruited students for an applied psychology study, ostensibly being conducted in the hope of improving air-ground communication. In the High Overpayment condition, workers were paid eighty percent more than they felt they deserved. In the Moderate Overpayment condition, they were paid forty percent more. In the Equity condition, they received just what they deserved. In the Moderate Underpayment condition, they were paid forty percent *less* than they deserved.

The students' task was a fairly difficult one. A "pilot" recited 120 words in a clear voice. These words, along with irritating "static," were broadcast to the students ("ground control") over a speaker. It was the students' job to identify as many of the words as they could. This job required intense concentration.

Contrary to the authors' predictions, they found *no* differences in the work of the overpaid/equitably paid/underpaid students. However, they did find sizable differences in their perceptions of the task's difficulty and in their definitions of a "fair wage" for such work. As we might expect, the more a man was overpaid, the more insistent he was that the air-ground communication task was a difficult one. Equitably paid and inequitably paid men did not differ in their perception of task difficulty.[12] However, as a glance at Figure 5.7 reveals, there is a tendency for equitably paid men to feel the job is slightly *easier* than do underpaid men. Neither we, nor the authors of this study, can offer a compelling explanation for this perplexing finding.

The authors' remaining results are more straightforward. As we might expect, the more a man is paid for performing a task, the more he feels he *deserves* to be paid.

There is other evidence that overpaid and underpaid workers may make themselves feel better by altering their perceptions of their own and their partner's inputs and outcomes.[13]

Leaving the Field

A job applicant who is offered a job at an unjust salary has only two choices: (1) he can accept the job; (2) he can reject it.

Until now we have considered only those special cases in which equitably/inequitably paid workers were committed to their jobs. We

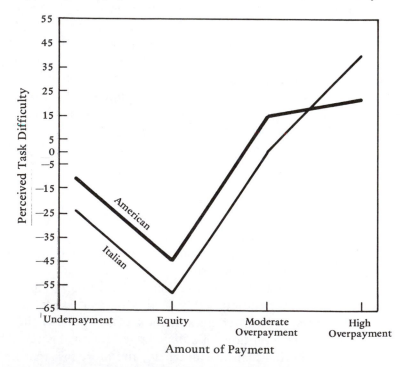

FIGURE 5.7. Estimate of Task Difficulty as a Function of Amount of Pay. (From K. J. Gergen, S. J. Morse, and K. Bode, "Overpaid or Overworked? Cognitive and Behavioral Reactions to Inequitable Payment," 1971. Reprinted by permission.)

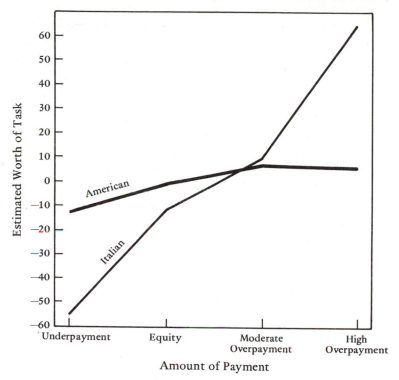

FIGURE 5.8. Estimated Worth of Task as a Function of Pay. (From Gergen, Morse, and Bode, 1971.)

considered cases in which applicants had already reported to their jobs or were busily engaged in working on their jobs when they discovered they would be equitably/inequitably paid. The researchers had carefully designed things to insure that employees, equitably paid or not, would stay on. (And it's lucky they did. Unless all the employees had agreed to stay on, the researchers would not have studied how equitable/inequitable wages affect workers' productivity and craftmanship.)

In real life, both employers and employees have more options than that. Employers and employees must continually decide whether they want to continue working together or to sever their relationship. The employer can keep an employee on, or he can transfer or fire him. The employee can accept his working conditions, or he can withdraw psychologically (coming in to work late, or not at all), request a transfer, or simply quit outright.

Equity theory would predict, of course, that the equity/inequity of the business relationship should have a big impact on a person's eagerness to stay in the situation or to leave the field. The

137

theory would predict that equitable relationships should be stable relationships while inequitable relationships should be fragile ones.

There are some experimental data to support these contentions:

One experiment, by Schmitt and Marwell (1972), was conducted to demonstrate that workers often engage in behavior that an economist might label as "seriously irrational" economically. (To an Equity theorist, however, such behavior seems perfectly reasonable.) The authors gave pairs of workers a choice: they could work individually (and make just a little money), or work cooperatively on a simple task (and earn quite a lot of money).[14] There was one catch, however. Sometimes (in the Equity conditions), the cooperating workers were paid the same amount of money (.3¢ or .4¢) each time the team made a correct response. Sometimes (in the Inequity conditions), the cooperating workers were paid markedly different amounts. In the small, medium, and large Inequity conditions, Worker$_A$ made two (.6¢ versus .3), three (.9¢ versus .3¢), or five times (2.0¢ versus .4¢) as much as his partner.

So workers had only two options: (1) they could work together and be equitably (or inequitably) paid at a high rate, or (2) they could withdraw, work alone, and be equitably paid at a low rate (.2¢ or .3¢).

As Schmitt and Marwell predicted, the inequitably paid workers behaved "irrationally"; the workers seemed to be more interested in equity than in money. When the pay schedule was equitable, and both cooperating workers received equal pay for equal work, they behaved rationally: they cooperated more than ninety percent of the time. As workers' payoffs became increasingly unbalanced, however, workers became more and more "irrational"; i.e., more and more likely to quit cooperating (and receiving inequitable, but high wages), and more and more likely to withdraw to the individual task (where they received equitable, but low wages). [In the Small Inequity conditions, fifteen percent of the workers withdrew. In the Medium Inequity conditions, twenty-five percent withdrew. In the Large Inequity conditions, forty percent withdrew.] Schmitt and Marwell point out that it was no mean sacrifice the students were making. For example, in the Large Inequity condition, one favored worker lost approximately $28.90 by his strategy; his disadvantaged partner lost $1.70.

A second bit of evidence that equitable relationships are more stable than inequitable ones comes from a study by Valenzi and Andrews (1971). Interestingly enough, the Valenzi and Andrews experiment was designed to test quite another hypothesis.

Valenzi and Andrews predicted that overpaid/equitably paid/ underpaid workers would differ in their productivity and craftsmanship. The authors found that they did not.[15] What Valenzi and Andrews did find, however, was fascinating.

The authors hired women to perform clerical tasks. They offered the women $1.40 per hour for the six weeks the job was to last. And, all women were equitably paid—on the first day of work. When the women reported back for their second day's work, however, the employer told some of them (those who had been assigned to be "overpaid" or "underpaid") that a problem had arisen. According to the project director, NIMH (the governmental agency that was presumably funding the clerical project) had notified them that NIMH insisted they follow their original budget, in spite of the fact that their needs had changed, the workers' classifications had changed, etc. The project director had finally decided that the only way they could comply with NIMH's complicated budget requirements was to randomly select a few of the clerks and pay them at a far higher (or lower) rate than the going rate. The overpaid clerks were told they would be paid $2.00 per hour. (The equitably paid clerks continued to be paid at the original $1.40 per hour rate.) The underpaid clerks were told they would be paid only $1.20 per hour. When faced with that information, all overpaid and equitably paid clerks stayed on the job; twenty-seven percent of the underpaid women quit.

Although the experimental evidence on the effect of equity/inequity on job stability is sparse, it does seem to provide some support for the contention that equitable relationships are more stable relationships than inequitable ones.

There is also a minute amount of naturalistic data in support of this contention. A very few researchers have interviewed management and workers in governmental agencies and in large corporations, in an effort to determine whether equitably paid employees are especially loyal employees. Most field investigators have concluded that they are.[16]

One early study was conducted by Finn and Lee (1972). Finn and Lee interviewed 170 professional and scientific employees of the Federal Health Service. These employees possessed B.A., M.S., and Ph.D. degrees in such specialties as biology, chemistry, microbiology, entomology, and zoology.

The authors asked the Health Service workers a very simple question: "Do you feel that you are being fairly paid at the present time in view of your training and experience, the work you do, and your capabilities?"[17]

The *equity* group consisted of the ninety-six men who answered "yes." The *inequity* group consisted of the seventy-six men who answered "no." (The authors argue that the inequitably paid men, i.e., the "underpaid" men, have a realistic basis for their perceptions.) The authors compared the educational levels, mean GS grades, personal variables, and supervisory ratings of the equity group versus the inequity group. They conclude that:

> Employees in the inequity subsample did indeed seem to have a legitimate basis for their perception of inequity; and in terms of the commonly accepted criteria for salary administration decision (including the official salary policy of the cooperating organization which emphasized "merit") there did not appear to be a justification for the substantially lower salary of the inequity subsample." (pp. 284–285.)

In a supplementary questionnaire, the experiments attempted to ascertain how willing equitably/inequitably paid men would be to abandon their job, should opportunity arise. The authors asked how tempted they would be to leave the Civil Service if offered six different inducements. These inducements included such things as: "an immediate salary increase of 20–30%," and "an opportunity for more interesting work." The authors found that, as expected, equitably paid individuals were far more hesitant to consider leaving their Civil Service jobs than were inequitably treated men.

Unfortunately, the Finn-Lee hypotheses have not yet been tested by other researchers.

Theoretically, equitable relationships should be far more stable than inequitable ones. Unfortunately, few investigators have explored whether or not, in practice, equity is a strong determinant of job stability.

In the absence of research, Equity theory can only offer a few hints as to how this process should work.

In an employer/employee relationship, in which the employee is overpaid, we might expect that it would be the employer who would most often terminate the relationship (or prod the employee into terminating it). In the absence of any employer pressure, an employee should find it easy enough to convince himself that he deserves his fine salary. Only one study, the Schmitt and Marwell (1972) study, found any evidence that when overpaid employees are uncomfortable enough about things they will voluntarily withdraw from an inequitable relationship.

In an employer/employee relationship in which the employee is underpaid, we might expect the employer to be fairly content with the existing state of affairs. In the absence of any employee pressure, he should find it easy enough to convince himself that his employees are getting all they deserve. It is the employee who should be motivated to leave. The equity job stability studies we have reviewed,[18] as well as a very complicated study by Dansereau, Cashman, and Green (1973), provide compelling evidence that underpaid employees are very likely to withdraw from an inequitable relationship.

Summary

In this chapter we explored the applicability of Equity theory to business relationships. Surprisingly, we found evidence that American workers feel more comfortable when they are equitably paid than when they are over or underpaid.

Next, we reviewed an impressive body of research conducted largely by industrial psychologists, which documents that hourly or piece-rate workers' belief that they are being equitably paid versus over or underpaid, will affect how much work they produce and how good that work is. Next, we reviewed a series of laboratory studies documenting that overpaid/underpaid workers do try to "set things right" by restoring actual or psychological equity. Finally, we pointed out that in nature, workers often have a simple remedy if they feel inequitably paid: they can quit their job and move on to one where they will be treated more fairly.

ENDNOTES

1. And from Baskett (1973) and Vershure (1974) as well.

2. See Collins and Guetzkow (1964), Homans (1961), Lawler (1971), Pondy and Birnberg (1969), Porter and Lawler (1968), Steiner (1972), and Weinstein and Halzback (1973).

3. Of course, employee morale, employee productivity, and company profits are all interrelated.

4. For example: the company president may know that it is more important to live up to the letter of the company-union contract than to treat his men as *he* thinks they should be treated. The timid shopkeeper may think it is more important to avoid trouble with the employee with Mafia connections than to treat him as he thinks is fair, etc. The foreman who is trying to teach a new lineman a difficult job may feel that it is more important to praise the new employee every time he shows even the most halting progress, than to treat him "fairly" *vis-à-vis* the other men.

141

5. See, for example, Giles and Barrett (1971), Homans (1953, 1961), Jaques (1956), Klein (1973), Patchen (1961), Stouffer et al. (1949), Vroom (1964), or Zaliznek et al. (1958).

6. See, for example, the excellent critiques of Goodman and Friedman (1971), Lawler (1968), Opsahl and Dunnette (1966), or Pritchard (1969).

7. See Lawler (1968a).

8. See Adams and Rosenbaum (1962), Arrowood (1961), and Lawler et al. (1968).

9. See Goodman and Friedman (1968).

10. See, for example, Andrews (1967).

11. See, for example, Adams' work (discussed in the previous section), Garrett (1973), Kahn (1972), Lane and Messe (1971), Lane, Messe, and Phillips (1971), Leventhal (1972a), Leventhal, Allen and Kemelgor (1969), Leventhal and Lane (1970), Leventhal and Michaels (1969, 1971), Leventhal, Michaels, and Sanford (1972), Leventhal, Weiss, and Long (1969), Messe (1969, 1971), Mikula (1972), Pepitone (1971), Shapiro (1972), and Smith (1970).

12. At least we assume they didn't; unfortunately, the authors do not report these data.

13. See Adams (1965), Lawler et al. (1968), Leventhal et al. (1964), and Weick (1964).

14. We described the Schmitt and Marwell task in an earlier section. The reader may recall that essentially it was the workers' job to coordinate the pulling of plungers. When the first worker pulled his plunger, a response light went on on his partner's panel. Then it was his turn to pull his plunger (anything within .05 seconds of the time his light went off). If participants did their jobs in the correct sequence, and at the correct times, they got a monetary reward.

15. The reader may recall that earlier we cited this study as one of the studies that "did not support Adams."

16. Unfortunately, in these studies, the authors were not careful to make the theoretically important distinction between individuals who feel inequitably overpaid and individuals who feel inequitably underpaid. They tend to equate "inequitable payment" with "underpayment."

17. Given the wording of the question and the author's subsequent discussion, it is likely that most of the men who said they were being "unfairly" paid, meant they were being unfairly *underpaid*.

18. Finn and Lee (1972), Schmitt and Marwell (1972), and Valenzi and Andrews (1971).

Equity Theory
and Intimate Relationships

INTRODUCTION

In the preceding sections, we have explored the ability of Equity theory to provide insights into casual relationships. We reviewed an extensive body of equity research, which documents that casual relationships will endure only so long as they are profitable to both participants. However, when Equity theorists turn to intimate relationships—those between close friends, lovers, mates, and parents and children—and suggest that these, too, must be dependent on the equitable exchange of rewards—objections are quickly raised. People indignantly insist that intimate relations are "special" relations and untainted by crass considerations of profit and social exchange.

In *Liking and Loving,* Rubin (1973) eloquently states this point of view:

> The notion that people are "commodities" and social relationships are "transactions" will surely make many readers squirm. Exchange theory postulates that human relationships are based first and foremost on self-interest . . . . Such characterizations contrast sharply with what many of us would like to think of friendship and love, that they are intimate relationships characterized at least as much by the joy of giving as by the desire to receive. But although we might prefer to believe otherwise, we must face up to the fact that our attitudes toward other people *are* determined to a large extent by our assessments of the rewards they hold for us.

Having said all this about the value of exchange theory, however, it is time to consider its limitations. For the fact is that, even when presented in its most enlightened form, a theory that presumes an overriding human desire to maximize one's own—and only one's own—profits inevitably falls short of providing a complete understanding of human relationships. Contrary to the guiding assumption of the exchange perspective, human beings are sometimes altruistic in the fullest sense of the word*. . . . There are many recorded instances—and countless other unrecorded ones—of people making great sacrifices for the sake of other people's welfare. . . . Examples here include the mother-infant relationship, kinship relationships between close neighbors, and the relationships of man to God.**

The principles of the interpersonal marketplace are most likely to prevail in encounters between strangers and casual acquaintances and in the early stages of the development of relationships. As an interpersonal bond becomes more firmly established, however, it begins to go beyond exchange. In close relationships one becomes decreasingly concerned with what he can get *from* the other person and increasingly concerned with what he can do *for* the other.[†] (pp. 82–87)

Anticipating inevitable opposition, then, we still contend that Equity theory will provide important insights into the daily workings of even the most intimate relationships. Who do people choose for friends? What kind of matches are happiest? What do parents "owe" their children? What do children "owe" their parents? Issues such as these will be illuminated by an awareness of the critical importance of exchange in intimate human relationships.

Before we present our "case" for Equity theory and intimate relationships, we must point out that while this is probably the most interesting of our chapters, it is, necessarily, the most theoretical and speculative. For thousands of years, philosophers, dramatists, and poets have speculated about intimacy. However, intimate relationships are so complex that, until recently, they have seemed to defy controlled analysis and experimentation. Few research data *are* available. Hopefully, as a general theory of human behavior develops, and as research methodology grows increasingly sophisticated, the possibilities for care-

---

*Alvin W. Gouldner, "The Norm of Reciprocity: A Preliminary Statement," *American Sociological Review*, 1960, *25*, 161–179.

**Elizabeth Douvan, "Changing Sex Roles: Some Implications and Constraints," paper presented at a symposium on "Women, Resources in a Changing World," The Radcliffe Institute, April, 1972.

†From *Liking and Loving: An Invitation to Social Psychology* by Zick Rubin. Copyright © 1973 by Holt, Rinehart and Winston, Inc. Reprinted by permission of Holt, Rinehart and Winston.

ful, controlled study of dynamic intimate interactions will grow too.[1] Accordingly, in this section we will suggest a number of equity hypotheses and avenues of research and we hope the reader will be stimulated to think of still others.

DEFINITION: WHAT IS INTIMACY?

Intimate /'int-ə-mət/ *adj.* [alter. of obs. *intime*, fr. L. *intimus*] **1** a:INTRINSIC, ESSENTIAL b:belonging to or characterizing one's deepest nature **2**:marked by a warm friendship developing through long association **3** a:marked by very close association, contact, or familiarity. b:suggesting informal warmth or privacy. **4**:of a very personal or private nature.

It seems best to begin our discussion with a definition of what we mean by intimacy. We began by asking ourselves: What are the characteristics of intimate relationships? Why are they so difficult to rationally examine and understand? Why are they so hotly defended as "special"? Supreme Court Justice Stewart once said of pornography that he couldn't define it, "But I know it when I see it." Most of us would echo his statement with regard to intimate relationships: we know them when we see them—but how to define them? Several possibilities occurred to us.

Certain relationships recognized by law, such as marital and family relationships, are generally considered intimate. (In fact, we will closely scrutinize such relationships later in the chapter.) Yet, most of us have witnessed *legally intimate* relationships that do not seem to merit the term. A husband and wife may share bed, board, and television set, but if they never share their hopes, fears, and affection, are they truly intimate? To us it seems not.

Pop culture, via advertisements, movies, television, and songs, provides us with myriad indicants of intimacy: bells ring, beautiful people gaze lovingly at one another, and constant harmony and happiness prevail. Clearly, these descriptors ignore the subtleties and intricacies of intimate relationships.

T-groups, Esalen community experiences, and sensitivity workshops claim to foster "instant intimacy—no strings attached" among participants. Yet, many would argue that it is the presence of just such "strings"—i.e., the presence of mutual *commitments* and responsibilities, which produce and sustain intimacy.

In the course of our dialogue, one fact emerged clearly; intimate relationships are varied and complex. Probably every person who has been intimate with another would offer a different definition of intimacy. Nor can *we* offer an air-tight definition. As a first approximation at a definition, however, we will conceptually define *intimates* as "loving persons whose lives are deeply intertwined."

When we reflect upon such relationships, relationships between best friends, lovers, spouses, and parents and children, it appears that they are generally marked by a number of characteristics. Let us enumerate some of these characteristics.

Characteristics of Intimate Relationships

Intimate Relationships: Relationships between loving persons whose lives are deeply intertwined.

Intensity of Liking (Loving). Intimate relationships are carried on by people who like or love one another. Of course, human relationships are complex. Sometimes intimates feel simple liking or love for one another, but more often their affection is interlaced with occasional feelings of dislike or even hatred. However, if an intimate relationship is to remain intimate, participants must basically like or love one another.

Depth and Breadth of Information Exchange. In casual relationships, individuals usually exchange only the sketchiest of information. Intimates generally share profound information about one another's personal histories, values, strengths and weaknesses, idiosyncrasies, hopes, and fears.

Altman and Taylor (1973) provide a painstaking analysis of the "Social Penetration" process. Their comparison of the extremes of intimacy provides a vivid example of the difference between the amount and kind of information exchanged in casual versus intimate relationships.

Stage 1: *Orientation:*

> Whether at a cocktail party, a small social gathering, or on a first date, individuals make only a small part of themselves accessible. . . . Their responses are not very rich or broad, are often stereotyped, reflect only the most superficial aspects of their modes of response, and demonstrate little personal uniqueness . . . they smile graciously and easily, are quick to nod agreement and understanding, offer greetings without hesitation, and exhibit a range of behaviors to present the image of a pleasant, understanding, likable person.

Stage 4: *Stable exchange:*

Achieved in only a few relationships, stable exchange continues to reflect openness, richness, spontaneity, and so on in public areas. . . . Dyad members know one another well and can readily interpret and predict the feelings and probable behavior of the other. . . . For the first time, perhaps, there is a considerable richness of communication in the central core areas and a high degree of mutual spontaneity, permeability, and dyadic uniqueness. In addition to verbal levels, there is a great deal of exchange of nonverbal and environmental behaviors, and less restrictiveness in facial expressions, gestures, body movements, touching and so on. They are more willing to allow each other to use, have access to, or know about very private apparel and belongings. (pp. 136–141)

On the basis of their review of the voluminous self-disclosure research, Altman and Taylor conclude that, with few exceptions, as intimacy progresses, "interpersonal exchange gradually progresses from superficial, nonintimate areas to more intimate, deeper layers of the selves of the social actors." (p. 6) The more intimate we are with someone, the more information we are willing to reveal to him and the more we expect him to reveal to us.[2]

Length of Relationship. Casual relationships are usually short-term. Intimate relationships are expected to endure, and generally do endure, over a long period of time. For example, Toffler (1970) cites husband-wife relationships and parent-child relationships as the most enduring of all relationships. " 'Til death do us part" is still our cultural ideal for marriage. As we cautioned in our introductory statement, exceptions to these conditions are easily found. A casual business relationship may last for generations, while an intimate relationship may run its course in a few months. As a general rule, however, intimate relationships tend to be long-term relationships.

This fact should have two important consequences for the way equity/inequity principles operate in intimate relationships.

Perception of inequity: It should be easier to calculate equity in casual relationships than in intimate ones. Over a short span it is easy to assess who owes whom what. Strangers in a bar need only remember who bought the last drink to determine who should pick up the tab for the next round. In intimate relationships it is far more difficult to calculate equity. Should the drinks I served my husband when we were dating "count" in determining who should pay for the case of Scotch we bought today? How far back in a relationship is it fair to go in making such calculations?

In the short-term relationships Equity theorists have studied heretofore, participants could usually distinguish with some ease what was equitable and what was not. We suspect, however, that participants in intimate relationships may have a far harder time even defining equity/inequity.

> Until their relationship reaches a certain point, they feel obligated to make a specific repayment for each favor received. Beyond this point, the closest of friends (as well as most lovers and spouses) do not feel obligated to give, or expect to receive, a specific repayment for each service rendered; rather, each feels the total amount of favors he gives and receives will average out over the course of their friendship. (Davis, 1973, p. 132)

Tolerance of perceived inequity: Participants in casual *vs.* intimate relationships may differ in their insistence that perceived inequities be redressed *immediately*. Casuals may be fully aware that unless existing imbalances are redressed soon, they will probably never be redressed at all. Intimates, committed to long-range interaction, should be more tolerant of momentary imbalances, since they know that they will have ample time in the future to set things right.[3]

The recent movie *Paper Moon* provides a comic illustration of this point.[4] Nine-year old Addie has convinced herself that Mose (a traveling con man) is her father. As long as they have a father/child relationship, she allows him to freely spend her money on himself. The moment she realizes that their "partnership" is about to end, however, her feelings change precipitously. She suddenly begins to insist loudly, "I want my $200!"

Value of Resources Exchanged. A variety of exchange theorists have observed that as a relationship grows in intimacy, the value of the rewards *and* punishments a pair can give one another increases.[5]

A friend's frown is better than a foe's smile.

James Howell, *Proverbs*

Value of rewards: Many theorists have observed that intimates' rewards are especially potent. For example, Huesmann and Levinger's (1976) elegant "incremental exchange model of dyadic interaction" has as its fundamental assumption: "that the expected value of a dyad's rewards increases as the depth of their relationship increases." (p. 6) Levinger, Senn, and Jorgensen (1970) point out that the same reward ("I'm glad I met you") is far more potent when it comes from an intimate than from a casual.

In addition, intimates possess a bigger storehouse of rewards than do casuals. Generally, people are more willing to invest their resources in an intimate relationship than a casual one. Thus, intimates usually provide their partners with more and more valuable rewards (time, effort, intimate information, money) than do casuals.

Value of punishments: Intimates' rewards may be unusually potent, but so are the punishments they can inflict on each other. For example, if a stranger at a party loudly announces that I am a selfish bore, I lose little; I can dismiss his words as those of a creep who doesn't really know what kind of a person I am. But if my best friend were to tell me the same thing, I would be crushed—she knows me, and still thinks that! As Aronson (1970) succinctly put it: "Familiarity may breed reward, but it also breeds the capacity to hurt."

Benefits of maintaining the relationship; costs of terminating it: Finally, we would like to note that intimates command one unique and potentially potent punishment: they can threaten to terminate the relationship. Earlier we indicated that people feel that intimate relationships *should* be long-term relationships. Best friends should remain friends through thick and thin. Husbands and wives should remain married "until death do us part." Parents should stand by their children. Thus, if an intimate is willing to suffer himself, he has the potential to deliver a devastating blow to his partner. He has the power to expose his partner to public humiliation; to make it clear to everyone that his friend, or spouse, or child is a "defective" person.

The intimate, who is willing to "cut off his nose to spite his face," can punish his partner in more practical ways. People take their relationships for granted; they come to depend on them. When a person precipitously terminates an intimate relationship, he abandons his partner to a lonely and painful unknown.

Variety of Resources Exchanged. As a relationship grows in intensity, the variety of rewards and punishments a pair can give one another increases.

Recent theoretical and empirical work by Uriel Foa and his associates, provides a useful framework for discussing this point. So, let us digress for a moment, and discuss their research in some detail.

Foa (and others)[6] have argued that the resources of interpersonal exchange fall into six classes: (1) love, (2) status, (3) information, (4) money, (5) goods, and (6) services.

According to the authors, all resources can be classified according to their "particularism" and "concreteness." The dimension *particularism* refers to the extent to which the resource's value is influenced by the person who delivers it. Since money is valuable regardless of its

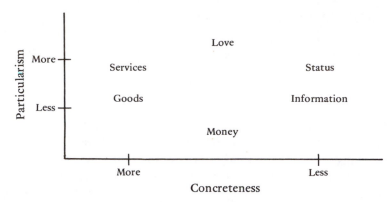

FIGURE 6.1. Foa's Typology of Resources of Interpersonal Exchange. (From U.G. Foa, "Interpersonal and Economic Resources," *Science*, 171, 1971.)

source, it is classed as *nonparticularistic*. Since love's value depends very much on who is doing the loving, it is classed as "particularistic."[7] The dimension *concreteness* refers to the resource's characteristic form of expression. Since services and goods involve the exchange of tangibles—things you can see, smell, and touch—they are classed as *concrete*. Since status and information are usually conveyed verbally, they are classed as *symbolic*.

We suspect that casual versus intimate relationships may differ markedly in both the variety and the types of resources participants commonly exchange.

We suspect that in casual exchanges, participants generally exchange only a few types of resources. In addition, since casual relationships are such short-term relationships, we suspect that casuals probably feel lucky if they can manage to negotiate an exchange of resources whose value is commonly understood. Casuals simply aren't "in business" long enough to work out any very complicated or troublesome exchanges. Thus we suspect that casuals' exchanges are generally focused primarily on nonparticularistic and concrete resources (i.e., money, goods, services, and information).

We suspect that in intimate exchanges, however, participants generally exchange resources from all six classes. Like casuals, intimates can exchange nonparticularistic and concrete resources. But, in addition, they can, and do, go to the trouble of negotiating more complicated exchanges. They can work out exchanges of symbolic and particularistic resources (love, status, services, and information). (It may even be that intimates are primarily concerned with such exchanges.)

If casuals usually exchange concrete and nonparticularistic re-sources, while intimates exchange not only these but a variety of other resources, whose value depends on each scrutineer's idiosyncratic eval-uation of both the giver and the reward, this fact provides a second reason why it is easier in casual than in intimate relationships to calculate equity. Casuals are exchanging resources of set value; thus, it is fairly easy to calculate equity. Intimates exchange these set value commodities, plus a potpourri of ambiguous value commodities. It is no wonder, then, that intimates may find the calculation of equity/in-equity a mind-boggling task.

Interchangeability of Resources. We venture into far shakier territory with our next characteristic of intimacy. We would speculate that, within a particular exchange, casuals tend to be limited to exchanging resources from the same class. Intimates, on the other hand, have far more freedom to exchange resources from entirely different classes. Let us describe the research that leads us to this prediction.

Research on the Foa typology suggests that equity is more easily established when an exchange involves similar resource classes (i.e., those that are close together on Foa's "circle"). A study by Turner, Foa, and Foa, (1971) showed that people prefer that two-way exchanges use resources of the same class: love given, love returned; services for services; money for money. We all know how disconcerting it is when, for example, we give of our time to help a neighbor (service) and are offered cash in return (money). We would feel far more comfortable if our neighbor offered to help us sometime (service) when we were in a similar situation.

In a theoretical extension of the Turner et al. results, Donnen-werth and Foa (1974) examined the effect of available resources on responses to inequity. They found that the intensity of a retaliatory response is inversely related to the similarity of resources in the ex-change. For example, they found that when an inequity is created in terms of love, and money is the only retaliatory resource available to the partner, far more money is needed to restore equity than if the original inequity was created in terms of money as well.

We thought about these findings, then reflected again on per-sonal experiences, and decided that these findings may not apply equally to casual and intimate exchanges. Casual relationships usually exist in a single context, where like is exchanged for like. If I lend my notes to the classmate I see three times a week, I expect to be repaid in kind the next time I miss a lecture. If I am invited to my neighbor's parties with great regularity, I know full well that unless I reciprocate and invite her to mine, I will be considered antisocial, unappreciative, and will very likely be dropped from her guest list. But inviting her to my parties is all I need do, unless I want the relationship to progress to deeper levels, perhaps to intimacy. (In that case, I would attempt to exchange with her some of the resources characterized above as typical of intimates: affection, status, disclosure of personal information.)

In contrast, intimate relationships exist in a variety of contexts. Participants have at their disposal the whole range of interpersonal resources, and freely exchange one type for another. Thus, the wife who owes her husband money can pay him back in a number of ways: she can defer to his conclusion that he is entitled to go golfing on Sunday (status), make him a special dinner (services), or tell him how much she loves him and appreciates his generosity (love). These responses may be less satisfactory to her husband than direct monetary repayment, but not necessarily so. Intimates spend much of their time negotiating the values and exchangeability of various behaviors; negotiating the "terms" of their relationship. This is what much of getting acquainted is all about.[8]

Foa's studies investigated the reaction of casuals to injustice. (The subjects' encounters were not to extend beyond the experimental setting.) Participants had no chance to work out between themselves the values of a given kind of injury and a given kind of retaliation. When the values are unclear, it is always safest to "do unto them exactly what they have done unto you."

Once again, our comparison of the variety of resources involved in casual versus intimate relationships leads us to the conclusion that it is easier for everyone to calculate equity in casual relationships than in intimate ones. We have just concluded that participants in casual relationships trade "in kind." Intimates may trade vastly different resources. It is easy enough to know that a round of beer on Monday night equals a round on Tuesday. It is far more difficult to decide if dinner at an expensive restaurant on Monday balances out three nights of neglect due to a heavy work load.

The Unit of Analysis: From "You" and "Me" to "We." We've seen how many of the unique characteristics of intimate relationships make assessments of equity, from outside as well as inside the relationship, a formidable task. Another characteristic of intimate relationships, which may add complexity, is that intimates, through identification with and empathy for their partners, come to define themselves as a *unit*; as *one* couple. They see themselves not merely as individuals interacting with others, but also as part of a partnership, interacting with other individuals, partnerships, and groups. This characteristic may have a dramatic impact on intimates' perceptions of what is and is not equitable.

Just what do we mean when we say that intimates see themselves as a "unit"? Perhaps the simplest way of describing this wholeness is by saying the unit is a "we." Examples of this "we-ness" are the joy and pride a parent feels at the success and happiness of his child ("That's my boy!"); the distress a wife experiences when her husband has been denied a hoped-for opportunity; the intense pleasure a lover feels while working to make his beloved happy.[9] Sir John Philip Sidney beautifully illustrated this sense of identification in his love poem, "My True-Love Hath My Heart":

> *His heart in me keeps him and me in one,*
> *My heart in him his thought and senses guides:*
> *He loves my heart, for once it was his own,*
> *I cherish his because in me it bides*
> *My true-love hath my heart, and I have his.*

Now, certainly in the examples above, the "identifiers" are directly affected by what happens to their partner: the parents may be supported in their old age by a successful son, the wife's household allowance as well as the husband's suffers when he is denied his hoped-for promotion, the lover may receive affection for his labors. But intimates' identification with their partners may cause them to experience genuine, "first hand" emotions aside from these returns. As we observed in chapter 4 ("Equity and Philanthropist/Recipient Relationships"), even casual, uninvolved observers can become distressed by the inequities they observe. How much easier for intimates, constituting socially defined units, to empathize with one another's circumstances.

A variety of theorists have noted that intimates' outcomes are linked. Rubin (1970) observes:

By helping one's partner, one is helping the *partnership* and thus helping oneself as well. Here again there is a reward involved, but it is not a reward to be gained at someone else's expense. It is, rather, a reward gained by and for the collective unit. (p. 85)

Society often thinks of and responds to intimate friends, lovers, and families and friends as units. Much empirical evidence exists for the folk wisdom that "A man is known by the company he keeps."[10] For example, Sigall and Landy (1974) found that subjects' impressions of a man were shaped by his girlfriend's characteristics. The boyfriend was rated most favorably when the woman was extremely attractive. He was rated least favorably when the woman at his side was ugly.

Blau (1964), too, argues that intimates' outcomes often become hopelessly intertwined. He speculates:

> The repeated experience of being rewarded by the increased attachment of a loved one after having done a variety of things to please him may have the effect that giving pleasure to loved ones becomes intrinsically gratifying. (p. 77)

What implications does the "we-ness" phenomenon have for the application of Equity theory to intimate relationships? There is one very important implication.

Throughout, we have stressed that if Equity theorists are to predict the behavior of individuals in a relationship, they must first be able to define the relationship: they must know who is interacting with whom. The student of intimate relationships must constantly ask what is happening in the intimate relationship at the moment of observation. Are the individuals relating to each other as individuals? Or, are they relating to others *as a couple*? If the intimates are relating as a couple to the rest of the world then the individual members are no longer the appropriate unit of analysis. It is the *couple's* inputs and outcomes which are important, and which form the basis for prediction of behavior of the individual members *as a twosome.*

Intimacy: A relationship between loving people whose lives are deeply entwined.

We have defined intimacy and discussed the unique character-istics of intimate relationships. Now, finally, we are ready to take a close look at three types of intimate relationships (close friendships, romantic relationships, and parent-child relationships), in order to try to determine whether or not equity considerations do apply in even the most intimate of relations.

Let us begin by examining close friendships. Then we will move on to somewhat more "exalted" relationships—romantic and marital relationships. Finally, we will end with an examination of the most "heroic" of relationships—parental relationships.

EQUITY IN CLOSE FRIENDSHIPS

When social commentators ask whether or not equity considerations operate in intimate relationships, they come up with conflicting an-swers.

On one hand, much of cultural folklore suggests that true friends do not care about equity. In ancient times, observers often commented on friendship's disinterestedness:

> *If men are friends, there is no need of justice between them.*
> Aristotle. *Nicomachean Ethics.* Bk. 8, ch. 1, sec. 5

Today, they still do. Douvan (1974) argues:

> Exchange is not the motive force in interpersonal relationships. Rather it is pleasure in the relationship itself, meeting and accepting each other as whole persons, affirming each other's selves. (p. 4)

On the other hand, throughout time people have, with unnerving inconsistency, casually taken it for granted that equity considerations do operate in friendly encounters. In Medieval times, Chaucer was commenting:

> *If thou be poor, thy brother hateth thee,*
> *And all thy friends do flee from thee, alas!*
> Chaucer. *Man of Law's Tale: Prologue,* 1.22

Today, routine deliberations such as: "We've simply *got* to have the Mattlocks over; we've been to their house for dinner six times and we've never had them here," or, "Oh, George, do give Mary a bottle of Scotch for Christmas; she chauffered the kids to skating classes *all* last year," attest to the pervasiveness of equity considerations in friendly relationships.

The Experimental Evidence

What people say they expect is confusing. Is there any evidence they behave with any more consistency? Is there any evidence that equity considerations really do operate in both casual and intimate friendships? Is there any evidence that they don't? The answer is: not really. Researchers are only now beginning to explore this controversial question.

Let us consider the existing evidence. We were able to locate only three studies that explored strangers' versus friends' reactions to equity/inequity. Morgan and Sawyer (1967), in a complex study, examined the bargaining styles of friends versus acquaintances.

If an Equity theorist is to make a prediction, his first questions must be: How did the scrutineer perceive the situation? What inputs did he perceive to be relevant? How valuable did he perceive these inputs to

"Eggplant casserole doesn't pay back for prime ribs."

FIGURE 6.2. **"Eggplant Casserole Doesn't Pay Back for Prime Ribs."** (From *Ladies' Home Journal*, August 1975, p. 128. Copyright © 1975 Downe Publishing, Inc. Reprinted by permission of *Ladies' Home Journal* and Chon Day.)

be? What outcomes did he perceive to be relevant? How valuable did he perceive them to be? Only when he has such information can a theorist predict how fair or unfair the scrutineer will perceive participants' relative gains to be. Unfortunately, as Morgan and Sawyer observe, it is impossible to tell how the boys in their study perceived the situation.

On one hand, we have every reason to believe that the boys assumed that they both possessed identical inputs. The boys were all from the same school, from the same grades (fifth and sixth), and were about the same age (ten–twelve). Presumably they were all from the same socioeconomic class (most received allowances of 50¢ a week). On these grounds, the authors conclude:

> Within the range of ages (10–12) in this research, preference for equality is uniformly strong ... boys generally regarded equality as the fair outcome. ... In Adams' (1963) terminology, equity calls for equal outcomes because the inputs are perceived to be equal. (pp. 145–146)

On the other hand, the boys may have perceived their inputs to be distinctly *unequal*. The authors paired friends and acquaintances whose grades were markedly discrepant. Then they gave the boys markedly discrepant potential for reward. Boys were seated at a game board like the one in Figure 6.3. One boy could win from 0 to 30¢. His partner could win from 0 to $1.50. Did boys see grades as a relevant input? Potential for reward? We do not know.

In any case, things were then made still more complicated. Operating on the assumption that friends have more similar inputs than acquaintances, the author decided to duplicate that condition experimentally. With the friend pairs, the smarter boys were seated at the side of the board with the lower potential payoff. (Thus, the dual inputs of I.Q. and payoff potential worked in opposite directions.) In the ac-

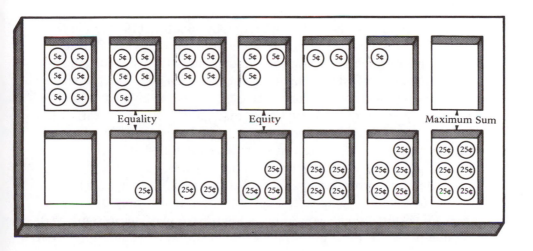

FIGURE 6.3. The Bargaining Board, with Quarters on the Near Side and Nickels on the Far Side. (In Practice, the Words in This Figure Do Not Appear on the Board—Only the Coins Themselves.) (From W. R. Morgan and J. Sawyer, "Bargaining, Expectations, and the Preference for Equality over Equity," *Journal of Personality and Social Psychology*, 6, 1967, p. 141. Copyright © 1967 by the American Psychological Association. Reprinted by permission.)

quaintance groups, the smarter boys were seated at the side of the board with the higher potential payoffs. (Thus, both inputs worked in the same direction.)

The authors then proceeded to study the bargaining behavior of the boys.

The results? When boys were allowed to reveal their expectations to their partners,[11] both friends and acquaintances tended to divide rewards equally. When participants had to guess at their partner's expectations, friends and acquaintances behaved quite differently. Acquaintances still insisted on strict equality. Friends did not; in most cases, the partner with the higher potential for reward was allowed to take it. As a team, then, the acquaintances made far less money than did the friends.

The authors' conclusion? They note:

> In fact, as Blau (1964) suggests, too quick or too strict concern with reaching equal balance in an interpersonal exchange appears to characterize nonfriends more than friends. Friends should be willing to tolerate temporary imbalances, while nonfriends want to keep their relation on more of a businesslike basis. (p. 148)

A second study was conducted by Benton (1971). Benton's experiment was designed to determine if boys and girls allocate resources any differently. He proposed that boys (whose "socialization history involves constant encouragement to engage in competitive games") would feel that performance ought to be taken into account in apportioning resources. He expected that girls ("whose education has emphasized nurturance and sympathy") probably wouldn't feel this way. Luckily for us, Benton systematically studied the reactions of boys and girls who were nonfriends vs. best friends.

Benton's procedure was straightforward. Children were invited, in pairs, to take a reading test. They were told that if they both passed the reading test, they would be allowed to play with some very desirable toys; if they both failed the test, they would not. What happened if one child passed and the other did not? The experimenter said that in those circumstances, they could both play.

As the reader who is familiar with the devious ways of psychologists might guess, the test was rigged. One child always passed the test while the other failed it. (Assignment to the role of "passer" and "failer" in each pair was random.) Thus, both children, regardless of their performance, won a chance to play with the desirable toys. Benton then observed how boys and girls went about deciding who could play with what. He asked children how acceptable various toy allocations would be. For example:

1:5 You get to play with the toy you like best;
     your partner gets to play with the toy he likes fifth best (out of
     fifteen toys).
2:4 You play with the toy you like second best;
     your partner gets his fourth choice toy.
3:3 Each of you gets to play with your third choice toy.
4:2 You get your fourth choice toy;
     your partner gets his second choice;
5:1 You get your fifth choice toy;
     your partner gets his first choice.

Benton's results are interesting: he found that boys, regardless
of whether their partner was a friend or nonfriend, tended to assume
that equity considerations should apply. (They assumed that the successful boy, who had made playing with the toys possible, ought to get
to play with the better toy.) Girls responded in exactly the same way,
but only when dealing with nonfriends. When girls' partners were
friends, they did not feel that equity considerations should apply.
(They preferred to divide things up "even steven" 3:3.)

The Morgan and Sawyer (1967) and Benton (1971) studies both
provide some evidence that both casuals and close friends, at least male
close friends, may be concerned about equity in their relationships.

A third study, by Traupmann (1975), went a little further. We
have already enumerated some of the ways in which casuals and
intimates differ:

1. intensity of liking (loving)
2. depth and breadth of information exchange
3. length of relationship
4. value of resources exchanged
5. variety of resources exchanged
6. interchangeability of resources
7. the unit of analysis: from "you" and "me" to "we"

Traupmann (1975) argued that such differences should affect
individuals' reactions to inequity. She proposed that strangers and
friends differ in their readiness to perceive inequity and their reactions
to it.

Traupmann invited college women who were either strangers
(women from different dorms) or friends (dormitory roommates) to
come to a verbal learning screening session. Presumably, researchers
were seeking women who were both intelligent and personable to
participate in a long-term, and very lucrative, verbal learning experiment.

Traupmann's "screening session" was carefully designed to convince women that they did possess the required inputs of "intelligence" and "personableness," and thus, deserved to be chosen for the long-term experiment. First, Traupmann gave two women a word list to study for ten minutes. Then she asked each woman to write down all the words she recalled. Both women were told they had done very well. It looked like they would both be chosen for the long-range experiment. Only one minor hurdle remained. Each woman would have to get a reasonable score on the "Personal Evaluation Form" if she was to participate. Her partner was to evaluate her "cooperativeness," "creativity," "ability to learn quickly," and "conscientiousness." In addition, her partner was to say whether she would or would not recommend her for the verbal learning experiment. Since each woman had done so well on the first test, and since her interaction with her partner had been so pleasant, she had no reason not to expect a reasonably good evaluation from her partner, and every reason to expect that she would be invited to participate in a lucrative three-week experiment. Then the blow fell. The experimenter reported that the woman had been given a very low rating by her partner; she had almost surely lost the opportunity to participate in the forthcoming experiment.

Traupmann predicted that friends and strangers would react in quite different ways to this inequity.

Perceptions of Fairness; Contentment/Distress. Traupmann observed that strangers versus friends should react very differently to two questions: (1) How equitable/inequitable was the relationship between you and your partner during the verbal-learning screening session? (2) How equitable/inequitable is your relationship overall? For strangers, the verbal-learning interaction *is* their relationship with their partner. For close friends, however, this incident is only a small part of their total relationship. Most intimates have a long history of pleasurable and equitable exchanges. If people could precisely partition out various segments of their interactions, we would expect strangers to feel that both this relationship (and their total relationship) was inequitable and distressing. We might expect intimates to feel this relationship was unfair and quite distressing, while at the same time feeling that their total relationship was fair and satisfying.

Traupmann, however, felt that the participants would not be capable of such fine distinctions. She predicted that if she asked women how fair their evaluation was, and how pleased or distressed they were with it, both their situation-specific experiences and their total experiences would be reflected in their report. There is some support for

Traupmann's prediction. Both strangers and friends were equally sure that their partner had treated them unfairly by giving them such a negative evaluation. However, strangers were far more distressed by their low evaluation than were friends.

Mode of Equity Restoration: Constructive Reactions versus Destructive Ones. Traupmann also predicted that strangers and friends would use very different strategies to restore equity.

Traupmann suggested that there are two radically different ways that people can respond to a perplexing inequity. (1) They can get together and discuss their differences. (For example, Person *A* can explain why she expected a good evaluation; Person *B* can explain why she didn't give her one.) In brief, they can negotiate about what should have been done and try to figure out some way to set things right, or (2) they can respond in a destructive way. The person who feels herself to be wronged can do everything in her power to hurt the other person.

As she predicted, Traupmann found that strangers and friends responded in totally different ways to inequity. Friends, more than strangers, were eager to try to talk to their partners about the inequitable situation. Friends, more than strangers, saw such a discussion as very likely.

Traupmann also found, as predicted, that strangers were far more likely to give their partner such a low "personal evaluation" that she, too, would be eliminated from the long-term experiment. Friends were not. They were more patient. They were more likely to give their partner a fair evaluation and allow her to stay in the lucrative experiment.[12] (Presumably, they expected to settle things later.)

What can we conclude from the Morgan and Sawyer (1967), Benton (1971), and Traupmann (1975) studies?

First, it appears that equity considerations apply in both casual and intimate friendships. Second, it appears that strangers find even momentary inequities distressing. Intimates do not. Third, strangers appear to be unwilling to tolerate temporary imbalances in the relationship. Intimates do not. Finally, it appears that when friends do set out to restore equity, they try to respond in ways that will not damage the relationship. Strangers seem to be far more likely to "let the Devil take the hindmost."

One can't be very confident about these conclusions, however. Far more research will have to be done before we feel comfortable about saying anything with certainty regarding equitable relationships among close friends.

EQUITY IN ROMANTIC AND MARITAL RELATIONSHIPS

Introduction

When Equity theorists contend that equity considerations apply not only in casual relationships, but perhaps even in close friendships as well, many readers can grudgingly agree. However, when Equity theorists proceed one step further, and suggest that equity considerations shape romantic and marital relationships, many readers rebel. They insist that these are "special" relationships.

For example, Erich Fromm is probably the most popular proponent of the notion that "true" love goes beyond exchange. In *The Art of Loving* (1956), Fromm admits that most flawed "human love relations follow the same pattern of exchange which governs the commodity and labor market." (p. 3) But, he contends, unconditional love, which is love given without expectation or desire for anything in return, is the truest, strongest, and best type of love.[13]

A variety of theorists agree with the contention that love transcends equity.[14]

An equally prominent group of theorists insists that equity considerations *do* apply in intimate relationships. For example, Scanzoni (1972) observes:

> These realities of courtship and marriage tend to be clouded . . . by the romantic love complex, which dictates that prospective partners are not supposed to weigh *reward* elements, at least consciously. Nonrational, romantic person-centered considerations are supposed to be paramount—lesser elements are too crass to be included. . . . Not that suppressing the reality of the process makes it disappear either before or after marriage. . . . Males and females socialized into their differing roles *prior* to marriage seek the different kinds of rewards from each other that they have learned are appropriate to their roles; they enter marriage because they perceive it will continue to supply these particular rewards and gratifications; they remain in the relationship so long as expected rewards are forthcoming; they withdraw from it if rewards diminish below and costs exceed desired expectations. (p. 54)

Patterson (1971) observes;

> There is an odd kind of equity which holds when people interact with each other. In effect, we get what we give, both in amount and in kind. Each of us seems to have his own bookkeeping system for love, and for pain. Over time, the books are balanced. (p. 26)

Other theorists agree that in love relationships, as in all other relationships, considerations of equity, and the marketplace, prevail.[15]

Faced with the compelling arguments that "intimate relation-ships *transcend* equity considerations" versus "intimate relationships *embody* equity considerations," we can only consider the evidence. There is some sparse evidence that equity considerations may operate both in mate selection and in the day-to-day interactions of an intimate rela-tionship.

Mate Selection

Psychological counselors often act as if marriage is a unique relation-ship. They ruefully acknowledge that in all of life *except* marriage, one must settle for what one can get. When they begin to talk about marriage, however, they act as if everyone is entitled to "the best."

For example, Herter (1974) warns young men to use "logic and common sense" in choosing a wife. He advises them to make sure that their wife possesses the following basic assets. She should:

1. Be beautiful.
2. Be younger than you.
3. Be shorter than you.
4. Be the same religion.
5. Be the same race.
6. Be willing to pretend to be equally intelligent or less intelligent than you.
7. Be a virgin at the time you meet.
8. Be willing to live with you for a year before marriage to see if things work out.
9. Be willing to let you participate in the sports you like.
10. Be tolerant of the work you do; be tolerant of your ambitions and abilities.
11. Be willing to have as many sons as you want.
12. Be sexually desirable.
13. Be free from diabetes.
14. Not be a regular drinker.
15. Have not used marihuana, LSD, or similar drugs.
16. Not have a family history of insanity.
17. Have large breasts.
18. Have consent of both parents.
19. Be a good cook.
20. Be a good sewer and knitter.
21. Not be a complainer or arguer.
22. Be clean and neat.
23. Not be overweight.
24. Not snore.

"Logic and common sense," says Herter.

Ann Landers (1975) gave similar advice when counseling women about how to go about selecting a mate.

By ANN LANDERS*

Dear Ann: Here's a message to all women in search of a man—object matrimony.

Most couples who are in love talk about how many babies they are going to have, what kind of house they want and where they'd like to vacation. They don't get to the vital issues until after marriage. Then they discover that one is at the North Pole and the other is at the South Pole.

If you want to find out if you and your beloved have a chance for a good life together, ask the following questions. If you don't like the answers, don't fool yourself into thinking he'll change later. He won't.

One. How does he handle problems and pressure? Does he go to pieces? Blame others when things go wrong? Or remain calm and search for the best solution?

Two. How does he feel about women? Does he believe they are inferior to men and can't possibly make important decisions?

Three. How does he feel about housework? Does he think it is below his dignity?

Four. How does he feel about children? Do they annoy him or does he enjoy them? What part does he feel a father should play in the rearing of children? Does he believe it's strictly the mother's job?

Five. Is he stingy when it comes to spending money on you but somewhat extravagant with himself?

Six. How does he feel about his job? Is he content to keep doing the same thing for the rest of his life? (If so, you can be sure he'll complain later that he never got a break.)

Seven. What is your social life like? Do you find yourself spending all your spare time with his family and friends and very little with yours?

Eight. Does he ask you which film you'd like to see and then somehow you end up seeing the one he prefers?

Nine. How does he handle the car when he's in a bad mood? Does he drive like a crazy man when he's ticked off? (This is a real symptom of immaturity.)

Ten. Does he become irritated if you are late but expect you to be understanding when he is late?

Eleven. How does he feel about birth control? Does he think the entire burden should be on the woman? If, for example, you are unable to take The Pill, would he be willing to accept the responsibility to protect you from an unwanted pregnancy?

Twelve. Has he ever slapped or punched you and later said he was sorry—and then done it again?

---

*From *The Wisconsin State Journal*, Madison (November 1975): 4. Reprinted by permission.

Thirteen. Does he treat his own mother and yours with respect?

Fourteen. How is his sense of humor? Can he laugh at himself or does he see something funny only at the expense of others.

Fifteen. How is his credit? Is he inclined to buy things on impulse, then have trouble paying his bills?

Sixteen. Is he truthful, or have you caught him in little lies which he has tried to wriggle out of?

Seventeen. Do you really enjoy his company—even when you are sitting silently?

Eighteen. Have you thought about what he'll be like in 24 years? Do you honestly want to live with him till death do you part? Sign me—*Sorry Now I Never Asked*

Dear Never: Thank you for allowing millions to learn from your experience. Those questions are superb guidelines to the true character of a man.

To Equity theorists, such "advice" is wildly impractical. Of course Everyman and Everywoman desires perfection. Unfortunately, they are not very likely to get it. Although a perfect man might be able to attract a perfect woman, and vice-versa, humans with human flaws had better resign themselves to the fact that they will have to settle for other people no better and no worse than themselves.

A variety of equity theorists have argued that equity considerations are important determinants of who dates whom and who marries whom. For example, Blau (1968) observes that people end up with the mates they "deserve." He points out that if one hopes to reap the benefits of associating with another, he must offer his partner enough to make it worthwhile for him or her to stay in the relationship. Thus, the more desirable a suitor is, the more desirable a partner he can attract. A less desirable fellow will have to settle for a less desirable "leftover." Thus, Blau argues, market principles insure that each person gets as desirable a mate as he "deserves."

Goffman (1952) puts the matter even more succinctly. He notes:

A proposal of marriage in our society tends to be a way in which a man sums up his social attributes and suggests to a woman that hers are not so much better as to preclude a merger or a partnership in these matters. (p. 456)

On the basis of such reasoning, exchange theorists[16] proposed a "matching hypothesis"—they proposed that the more equitable a romantic relationship is, the more likely it is to progress to marriage.

According to Equity theorists and matching theorists, equitable relationships should be far more stable than inequitable ones.

Is there any evidence that equity considerations are an important determinant of who dates whom and who marries whom? Is there

FIGURE 6.4. "... the More Equitable a Romantic Relationship Is, the More Likely It Is to Progress to Marriage."

any evidence that people do end up with partners who are no better and no worse than they "deserve"? No. Unfortunately, the Equity mate-selection hypothesis has never been tested directly. No theorist has calculated how equitable/inequitable dating couples' relationships are,[17] and watched to see if, in fact, the more equitable the relationship, the more likely it is to survive. There are some data that lend some credibility to the hypothesis that equity considerations do operate in mate selection, however.

Let us now examine the experimental evidence.

The Experimental Evidence

For years, Marriage and the Family researchers have explored the process of *homogamy:* the tendency for similar individuals to be drawn to each other. This literature provides evidence that if a person possesses *one* important input—say physical attractiveness, *or* a dependable character, *or* warmth, he will be more successful than his peers in attracting partners who possess that same asset.

Beauty. A number of researchers have demonstrated that couples tend to date and to marry those who are similar in physical attractiveness. Walster, Aronson, Abrahams, and Rottmann (1966) were the first to test the matching hypothesis. They proposed two hypotheses: (a) the more "socially desirable" an individual is (i.e., the more physically attractive, personable, famous, rich, considerate), the more socially desirable he or she will expect a "suitable" romantic partner to be; (b) couples who are similar in social desirability will more often continue to date one another and will better like one another than will couples who are markedly mismatched.

Figure 6.5 depicts graphically these predictions.

The authors' hypotheses were tested in a field study. College freshmen were invited to attend a "computer dance." They were told their partner would be assigned by a computer. The freshman's social desirability was roughly tapped by assessing one social input—physical attractiveness. (The authors hired four students to rate each person's looks as he or she waited to purchase a ticket to the dance.) The authors also tried to assess a few of the freshman's other social inputs; i.e., personality, intelligence, and social skills. (They gave each student a battery of personality and I.Q. tests during orientation week.)

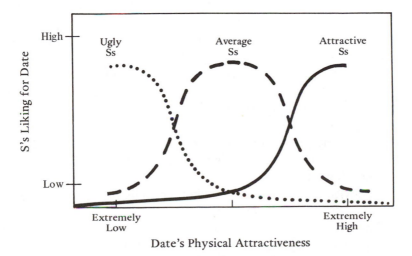

FIGURE 6.5. Amount of Liking Predicted for Dates of Various Attractiveness by Ugly, Average, and Attractive Students.

First, the authors predicted that students would expect the "all-knowing" computer to assign them partners of approximately their own social desirability. At the time the attractive, average, or unattractive freshmen signed up for the dance, they were asked how socially desirable they expected their date to be. (They were asked how physically attractive, how personally attractive, and how considerate they expected him or her to be.) The authors predicted that the more attractive the freshman, the more desirable he would expect an appropriate date to be. This prediction was confirmed.

Secondly, the authors also predicted that the more equitable a computer match was, the more viable the relationship would be. The freshmen who signed up for the dance were randomly assigned to a date. It was hypothesized that those students who obtained, by chance, dates of their own social desirability level (whether high, medium, or low) would like each other more than those who received dates whose social desirability level was far inferior or far superior to their own.

The validity of this hypothesis was tested in three ways. First, during intermission, students were asked how much they liked their date. Second, they were asked how eager they were to continue the dating relationship. Third, the authors interviewed all participants six months after the dance, in order to determine whether or not the couples had actually continued to date.

This time, the authors found no support for the matching hypothesis. Everyone, regardless of their own social desirability, liked the most desirable dates. The more physically attractive the date, the more he or she was liked. The Walster et al. results, or lack thereof, were substantiated by other investigators.[18]

This conclusion drew a storm of protest. Subsequent investigators pointed out that the computer dance situation was not an optimal setting in which to test the hypothesis. For example, Berscheid, Dion, Walster, and Walster (1971) pointed out that in the computer dance setting, individuals believed the computer had paired up couples. They may have assumed the computer knew something they didn't. In a normal dating situation, however, Berscheid speculated, individuals might be much more concerned with whether they were too good for their partner (and thus should be careful not to get too involved in a potentially awkward situation), or whether their partner was too good for them (and thus might reject them).

The authors conducted two experiments to determine if the matching principle would reveal itself under more favorable circumstances. In both experiments, "matchmakers" assessed the physical attractiveness of college students. Then the matchmakers gave students a chance to choose dates from a number of possibilities. Both experiments found support for the matching principle; as in the Walster et al. study, everyone preferred the physically attractive dates. Within this general trend, however, it was clear that highly attractive men and women did choose more attractive dates than did less attractive individuals.[19]

Kiesler and Baral (1970) were the first to confirm equity matching predictions in an experimental setting. The authors invited college men to see how well they could do on a new intelligence test. In the High self-esteem condition, men were led to believe that they were doing extremely well. (The experimenter smiled and nodded and mentioned how extraordinarily well they were doing.) In the Low self-esteem condition, men were led to believe that they were doing badly on the test. (The experimenter made it apparent that he was displeased with their performance. He frowned, looked away, and mentioned that other subjects had performed better.)

During a break in testing, the experimenter and the subject visited a nearby canteen to relax. When they entered the canteen, the experimenter recognized a girl (actually an experimental confederate). In one condition, the Attractive condition, the confederate was made-up to be very physically appealing; she wore becoming make-up and fashionable clothing. In the Unattractive condition, she was fairly unattractice; she wore no make-up, heavy glasses, and had her hair pulled back with a rubber band. Her skirt and blouse clashed and were sloppily arranged.

The girl sat down and began chatting with the experimenter and the subject. After a minute, the experimenter excused himself to make a phone call. While he was gone, the couple continued their conversation. Secretly, the girl attempted to assess how interested each man seemed to be in her. She kept track of whether he ignored her when she said she'd better be getting back to work, complimented her, offered her a cigarette, offered to buy her a snack or coffee, asked for her phone number, or asked her for a date.

Kiesler and Baral found strong support for the matching hypothesis. When the men's self-esteem had been raised, they behaved most romantically with the attractive confederate. When their self-esteem had been lowered, they behaved most romantically with the less attractive confederate. The study supports the matching contention that the more desirable a man feels, the more attractive a woman he will feel entitled to.

In one final study, Morse, Reis, and Gruzen (1973) found evidence that equity considerations become *increasingly* important as heterosexual interactions progress. The authors found that in an initial encounter, college men's interest in a female confederate was strictly a function of her attractiveness. The more beautiful she was, the more interested they were—period. But as time passed, things changed. The man's self-esteem (and probably his perception of how likely he was to win her approval) began to operate. Men with high self-esteem continued to express great interest in dating the most attractive girl. Men with low self-esteem began to express less interest in dating her.

Matching, **fait accompli.**   There is some correlational evidence that men and women of equal physical attractiveness do tend to pair up.

Silverman (1971), examined the degree of similarity in attractiveness exhibited by couples observed in naturalistic dating settings. Teams of observers (two males and two females each) went to such dating habitats as bars, social events, and theater lobbies where they could watch young dating couples. Each observer rated the dating partner of the opposite sex on a five-point scale. Silverman and his associates found an extraordinarily high degree of similarity in physical attractiveness between the dating partners. While the distribution of attractiveness scores of the men and women ranged from one to five (in intervals of .5), Silverman found that sixty percent of the couples were separated only by half a scale point; eighty-five percent of the couples were separated by one scale point, or less, and no couple was separated by more than 2.5 scale points.

In addition to rating the physical attractiveness level of the dating partners, the observers recorded whether the couples engaged in intimate touching (such as holding hands) during the period of observation. Silverman hypothesized that couples more similar in attractiveness would be happier with each other, and this would be reflected in their degree of physical intimacy. The data revealed that sixty percent of the couples who were highly similar in physical attractiveness level engaged in intimate physical contact of some kind, as compared to forty-six percent of the moderately similar couples, and twenty-two percent of those in the lowest similarity group.

Silverman's evidence of *fait accompli* matching along the physical attractiveness dimension is not as unequivocal as one would like. Despite the fact that observers did not know how the other observers rated the attractiveness of the other member of the dating pair, they did, of course, see the dating partners. Thus, it is possible that a "halo" emanating from one dating partner to the other may have produced artifactually similar ratings of dating pairs.[20] The *fait accompli* matching hypothesis might be best tested under conditions in which judges of participants' attractiveness are not aware of who is paired with whom.

Murstein (1972) did just that. Murstein secured photographs of ninety-nine steady or engaged couples. Then raters rated the physical attractiveness of each man and woman—separately. Murstein found evidence of matching along the physical attractiveness dimension. The steadily dating or engaged couples were far more similar in appearance than were artificially paired couples (which were formed by randomly pairing the physical attractiveness scores of the ninety-nine men and women with each other). Murstein concluded, "Individuals with equal market value for physical attractiveness are more likely to associate in an intimate relationship such as premarital engagement than individuals with disparate values." (p. 11)

Matching: More Complex Cases

In the preceding section, we reviewed evidence that individuals who possess one asset—physical attractiveness—have an advantage in attracting similarly attractive partners. Of course, individuals can contribute many other inputs to a relationship; i.e., a dependable character, warmth, etc.

Marriage and family researchers provide additional evidence that individuals who possess such assets as mental or physical health, high socioeconomic status, intelligence, and other social assets have an especially good chance of "capturing" partners with comparable assets.

Burgess and Wallin (1953) conducted the classic study of "homogamy in social characteristics" of engaged couples. The authors found evidence of homogamy (i.e., evidence that the engaged couples were very similar) on almost every characteristic they investigated. Of special interest to us is the fact that individuals were found to match up with partners who possessed similar assets and liabilities; i.e., such inputs as (1) physical assets (i.e., physical appearance and health); (2) mental health (i.e., "neuroticism" scores); (3) family's solidity (i.e., happiness of parents' marriage, etc.); (4) family background (including race, religion, parents' status, educational level, and income); (5) popularity (i.e., number of friends of the same sex as well as the opposite sex, tendency to "stay at home" vs. be "on the go," drinking habits, smoking habits, etc.).

Mental Health. Most clinicians agree that mentally healthy people and emotionally disturbed people tend to pair up. Perhaps Edmund Bergler

(1948), a psychoanalyst, presents the case most strongly:

> All stories about a normal woman who becomes the prey of a neurotic man, and vice versa [sic], or a normal man who falls in love with a highly neurotic woman, are literary fairy tales. Real life is less romantic; two neurotics look for each other with uncanny regularity. Nothing is left to chance as far as emotional attachments are concerned. (p. 11)

Equity theorists, of course, might interpret Bergler's data a little differently. It may well be that both normals and neurotics desire well-adjusted partners, but only normals are able to attract and hold them. Neurotics must settle for partners whose adjustment is as poor as their own.

In any case, there is some relatively hard evidence that people tend to date and marry those who are similar in level of adjustment. [21] For example, Murstein (1967a) asked engaged couples to complete the *Minnesota Multiphasic Personality Inventory (MMPI)*. Murstein recorded partners' overall *MMPI* profile scores and their score on such specific *MMPI* components as ego-strength, anxiety, and repression. Then, six months later, Murstein asked couples if they had made any courtship progress; if they were closer, the same, or further from becoming a permanent couple than before. Murstein found that the more similar in mental health couples were, the more viable their relationship was. Murstein (1967b) provides additional evidence that people end up being paired with partners who are as mentally healthy (or neurotic) as themselves.

Physical Health. Eugencists have observed that people are likely to marry partners with comparable physical disabilities. For example, in an article in the *Eugenics Quarterly,* Spuhler (1968) reviews forty-two studies of assortative mating. The studies investigated whether or not "like-married-like" based on 105 different physical characteristics, ranging from broad characteristics such as "general health" (which was assessed via nine different indicants), to specific ones such as "systolic blood pressure" and "ear lobe length." When we examine Spuhler's tabulation (see Table 6.1) we see that married couples are homogonously matched on five of the nine physical health indicants; i.e., general health, number of injuries, constitutional diseases, tuberculosis, and rheumatism. They are randomly matched on three traits, and they are heterogeneously matched ("selecting a mate unlike themselves") on only one trait—number of illnesses.

Intelligence and Education. A great deal of attention has been given to the fact that people tend to pair up with partners who are simlilar in

TABLE 6.1. Studies of Assortative Mating with Respect to Physical Characteristics. (From J.N. Spuhler, "Assortative Mating with Respect to Physical Characteristics," *Eugenics Quarterly*, 15, 1968, p. 134. Reprinted by permission.)

Character	Population or location	No.	r	Source
General health	English	630	0.27*	Elderton, 1908
	American	987	0.20*	Burgess and Wallin, 1944
Number of illnesses	American	100	−0.35*	Smith, 1946
Number of injuries	American	100	0.27*	Smith, 1946
Number of surgical operations	American	100	0.03	Smith, 1946
Number of chronic diseases	American	100	0.11	Smith, 1946
Total illnesses, injuries, and chronic diseases	American	100	−0.03	Smith, 1946
Constitutional disease	English	723	0.11*	Goring, 1909
Tuberculosis		41,786	0.32*	Pope, 1908
	English	723	0.01	Goring, 1909
	English	462	0.16*	Goring, 1909
Rheumatism	English	1,656	0.14*	Williams et al. 1914

*Significance level 1%.

education and intelligence. There is evidence that men and women marry partners of comparable intelligence[22] and evidence that they marry partners of comparable educational attainment.[23]

Matching: More Complex Cases. Thus far, we have reviewed only the evidence that documents the tendency of people to pair off with partners who possess similar traits. Of course, theorists have noted that couples can be "matched" in a variety of ways. For example, the handsome man (who is not especially dependable or warm) may use his assets to "buy" a beautiful partner, or he may decide to pursue a partner who is far plainer but far more dependable and warm than he is. Murstein, Goyette, and Cerreto (1974) provide a compelling description of the way such complex matching might operate:

A handsome man is seen with a woman of mediocre attractiveness. "I wonder what he sees in her?" may be the quizzical question of a bystander. Quite possibly, she possesses compensating qualities such as greater intelligence, interpersonal competence, and wealth than he, of which the bystander knows nothing. . . .

Another case of compensatory exchange might be indicated if an aged statesman proposed marriage to a young beautiful woman. He would probably be trading his prestige and power for her physical attractiveness and youth. (pp. 3–4)

The evidence is sparse, but that which does exist supports the contention that people do engage in such complicated balancing and counter-balancing in selecting mates. Let us review this research.

Beauty can "buy" high socioeconomic status: Elder (1969) proposed that beautiful women can have an advantage in attracting highly successful mates.

In the 1930s, the *Oakland Growth Study* rated fifth and sixth grade girls' physical attractiveness; they rated the girls' coloring, goodness of features, physique, and grooming, and sex appeal. Years later, Elder tracked down the girls and found out what had become of them. He found that the more attractive the preteen, the "better" she had done. The beautiful girls apparently used their beauty to "capture" mates whose "mobility potential" and "social status" far exceeded their own. Additional support for Elder's contention comes from Holmes and Hatch (1938).

Beauty can "buy" high socioeconomic status, a loving nature, and sacrifice: In a recent study, Berscheid, Walster, and Bohrnstedt (1973) encouraged *Psychology Today* magazine readers to fill out a questionnaire concerning their current dating, mating, or marital relations; 62,000 readers replied.

The authors selected a sample of 2,000 questionnaires for analysis. They stratified the sample on sex and age to approximate the national distributions. The final sample consisted of half men and half women. Within each sex, forth-five percent were 24 years old or younger, twenty-five percent were between 25 and 44, and the rest were 45 or older.

Berscheid et al. proposed that a beautiful woman or handsome man has an advantage in attracting a successful, loving, self-sacrificing, personable, and sexually tolerant mate. They argued that if a person had vastly "superior" inputs to his partner in one sphere, say physical attractiveness, he could use that to attract and keep a partner who contributed more than his share in other spheres. (For example, the aesthetically "inferior" partner might contribute more than his share of money, affection, or kindness and considerateness.)

Berscheid et al. tested their hypothesis in the following way. First of all, the authors asked respondents how attractive they and their partners were.

Describe your partner's physical appearance now:
Much more physically attractive than I.

Slight more physically attractive than I.
As attractive as I.
Slightly less attractive than I.
Much less attractive than I.

On the basis of the respondents' replies, they divided respondents into three groups: individuals who were far more attractive than their partners, those who were just about as attractive as their partners, and those who were far less attractive than their partners.

As predicted, the authors found that the more attractive a person is compared to his partner, the richer, the more loving, and the more self-sacrificing his partner was likely to be.

Income: The authors asked respondents to assess their own and their partners' socioeconomic status (i.e., occupational level, income, and educational level). As predicted, the more attractive an individual, male or female, is (compared to his partner), the richer his "inferior" partner is. (The Jacqueline Kennedy-Aristotle Onasis arrangement apparently was not an uncommon one.)

A loving nature: The authors asked respondents to assess the extent to which they provided each other with potent rewards of love and affection.

In almost every relationship one person loves more than the other. Who now loves most in your relationship?
I love more.
We love equally.
My partner loves more.

As predicted, the more an individual's beauty exceeds his partner's, the more loving a person the "inferior" partner is.

Self-sacrifice: Finally, the authors asked respondents how much effort they and their partners expended to please one another.

In many dating or marriage relationships, one partner makes more effort to please. Describe the effort you now make.
Great effort.
Considerable.
Minimal.
None.

Describe the effort your partner now makes to please you.
Great effort.
Considerable.
Minimal.
None.

As predicted, they found that the more an individual's beauty exceeds his partner's, the more kind and considerate the "inferior" partner is.

Apparently, then, the assett of beauty *can* be used to attract a beautiful partner; or it can be used to attract a partner who possesses quite different assets.[24]

Summary. We can conclude from the preceding studies that individuals *prefer* romantic partners who are more desirable than themselves. However, their romantic *choices* are influenced by realistic matching considerations. People tend to end up choosing partners of approximately their own social worth. Romantic choices appear to be a delicate compromise between one's desire to capture an ideal partner and one's realization that he must eventually settle for what he deserves.

The Operation of Equity in Day-to-Day Relations

The preceding evidence, then, leads us to believe that most couples *start off* in equitable relationships.

Relationships, however, do not always stay that way. In the course of a marriage, the marital balance may shift many times. Drastic marital shifts may be produced by a variety of factors:

Getting Acquainted. Regardless of how well engaged or newly married couples think they know one another, they are likely to make some marked discoveries about their own, and their partner's, characteristics once they begin living together. Participants may come to realize that the relationship they thought would be so equitable, is, in fact, grossly inequitable.

Day-to-Day Changes. Over the years, people change. The shy young bride may become less shy but far more witty and compassionate after raising four or five impish children. Her devil-may-care bridegroom may settle down and become far more dependable, but more irritable, than the man she married. Such mundane changes, too, may produce inequities.

Dramatic Changes. Sometimes dramatic changes occur in partners' "assets" and "liabilities." Eventually, the impoverished medical student is transformed into an affluent doctor. The once "good provider" may be laid off. The ugly-duckling wife may join Weight Watchers and emerge a desirable swan. The handsome soldier may become a scarred paraplegic. Such changes may, of course, drastically alter a relationship's balance.

The Dynamics of Equitable/Inequitable Relationships

One exciting question that Equity theorists have asked is: What effects do such inevitable changes in the equitableness/inequitableness of a relationship have on the dynamic equilibrium of a marriage? Equity theorists maintain that the smallest of changes in a marriage's balance should send reverberations throughout the entire system. This is a fascinating contention, but, unfortunately, not enough data yet exist to determine whether or not it is true.

Let us consider the research that does exist.

Berscheid et al. (1973) posed an intriguing question. They acknowledged that probably most married people, most of the time, do end up with the partners they "deserve." But, they asked, what happens when a person "beats the odds?" What happens when, through some fluke, day-to-day change, or momentous historical accident, a person ends up with a partner who is clearly "superior" or "inferior" to himself?

The authors made a series of predictions:

Hypothesis I: Mismatched Relationships are Unhappy Relationships. Interestingly enough, the authors predicted that both partners in inappropriate matches would be unhappy. It is obvious why the "superior" partner would be dissatisfied. Every time he looks around, he realizes that he is sacrificing rewards to which he is entitled. But, his "lucky" mate may not be so lucky either. The "inferior" mate is confronted with a wrenching dilemma. On one hand, he is eager to keep his prestigious prize; he is well aware that he has little chance of attracting so desirable a partner a second time. On the other hand, he is also painfully aware that his partner has little reason to stay with him.

For these reasons, the authors predicted that both the superior and the inferior partner in an inequitable relationship would feel uneasy about their relationship; they would both suspect that their alliance might be unstable.

Waller (1937) and Blau (1964) would make similar predictions. Citing the epigram that "in every love affair there is one who loves and one who permits himself to be loved," Waller points out that inequitable relationships are costly to both partners. The less dependent person feels guilty and uncomfortable about exploiting his or her mate. The more dependent person feels insecure and exploited. Waller predicted that such lopsided affairs come to sad ends.

Blau (1964) agrees. He notes:

> If a love relationship is to develop into a lasting mutual attachment, then the "lovers' affection for and commitment to one another (must) expand at roughly the same pace." That is, if one lover makes significantly greater inputs than the other into the relationship, this "invites exploitation or provokes feelings of entrapment, both of which obliterate love. . . . The weak interest of the less committed or the frustrations of the more committed probably will sooner or later prompt one or the other to terminate it." (pp. 84–85)

For these reasons, Berscheid et al. (1973) predicted that both the superior and the inferior partner in an inequitable relationship would feel uneasy about their relationship; they would both suspect that their alliance might be an unstable one. Support of this hypothesis comes from several experiments.

Walster, Walster, and Traupmann (1977) interviewed 500 University of Wisconsin men and women, who were dating "casually" or "steadily." First they asked students to consider all the things a man or woman could contribute to a relationship and all the things they *could* get out of a relationship and then to estimate how their relationship "stacked up" on the Walster (1977) *Global Measures of Participants' Perceptions of Inputs, Outcomes, and Equity/Inequity.*

Then they asked men and women: "When you think about your relationship—what you put into it and what you get out of it—how does that make you feel? How *content* do you feel? How *happy* do you feel? How *angry* do you feel? How *guilty* do you feel?

The authors found that the more equitable a couple's relationship, the more content and the happier they were. As Table 6.2 indicates, those men and women who feel they are getting far more than they really deserve from their partners are uncomfortable. They feel less content, less happy, and a lot more guilty than their peers. Of course, those men and women who feel they deserve a lot more than they're getting are understandably upset too. They feel a lot less content, less happy, and a lot angrier than their peers.

Berscheid et al. (1973) also provide some evidence in support of their hypothesis. The authors requested *Psychology Today* readers to fill out a questionnaire concerning their current dating, mating, or marital relations. They measured readers' perceptions of the equitable-

TABLE 6.2. The Effect of Equity/Inequity on Contentment/Distress.

	How Content*	How Happy*	How Angry*	How Guilty*
How Equitable/Inequitable Is the Relationship?				
Person is getting far *more* than he feels he deserves.	2.91	3.06	1.54	1.83
Person is getting somewhat *more* than he feels he deserves.	3.51	3.69	1.36	1.51
Person is getting just what he feels he deserves.	3.51	3.61	1.36	1.31
Person is getting somewhat *less* than he feels he deserves.	3.26	3.42	1.75	1.44
Person is getting far *less* than he feels he deserves.	2.70	2.98	1.98	1.39

*The higher the number, the more content, happy, angry or guilty the person feels.

ness/inequitableness of their dating, mating, or marital relationships *via* a single question.

> Describe your partner's desirability:
> Much more desirable than I.
> Slightly more desirable than I.
> As desirable as I.
> Slightly less desirable than I.
> Much less desirable than I.

Then they asked readers how satisfied they were with their marital relationships. As predicted, readers who were matched with "appropriate" partners were more satisfied with their relationship than were individuals whose partners were far more, or far less, desirable than themselves.

Hypothesis II: If You're #2, You Have to Try Harder. The authors' second prediction was equally provoking.

The authors proposed that all marriages are in a dynamic equilibrium. They argued that any time a disequilibrium occurs in a marriage, both the superior and inferior partners will automatically try to set things right. They will work to make their relationship actually more equitable, and/or they will try to convince themselves (and their partner) that their relationship is really more equitable than it seems.

Restoration of actual equity: One way participants in an inequitable relationship can restore equity is by inaugurating real changes in the relationship. The superior partner, who feels that he is contributing far more than his fair share to the relationship, will naturally be motivated to set things right by demanding better treatment from his partner. The inferior partner, who knows he is contributing less than his share, may reluctantly agree to cede such rewards.

For example, *Physical appearance:* The superior partner, who resents the fact that he's already contributing far more than his share to the relationship, can easily slip into becoming careless about the stylishness of his dress, his cleanliness, or his diet. *Day-to-day talk:* Or, the superior partner might begin to feel that he's entitled to conversation when he feels like it, and solitude when he doesn't; that he's entitled to be grumpy when he feels like it, but his partner isn't. *Financial security:* The superior partner might feel a little less pressure to work hard (or to save money) so that his partner can have the things she wants. *Expressions of love and affection:* The superior partner might become a little less careful to reassure his partner that he loves and admires her. *Self-sacrifice:* The superior partner might become especially reluctant to make sacrifices for his partner's benefit. When an argument arises as to whether they should go to a play or on a hunting trip, or who should take the car in for servicing, or whose mother they should visit at Christmas, he may be inclined to take a stronger stand than usual. *Sex:* The person who feels he's already putting too much into the marriage may feel reluctant to sacrifice himself to make his partner's sexual life fulfilling. He might feel that his partner should be as warm or as aloof as he prefers; that his partner should be willing to explore the sexual practices that he likes; that his partner should be tolerant of his extramarital affairs, but refrain from making him jealous and insecure.

Of course, the inferior partner's reactions would be quite different. The person who feels he's already getting very much more than he deserves might be especially eager to set things right by agreeing to treat his partner better.

There are a variety of ways, then, that a mismatched couple can restore actual equity to their relationship.

The data: Unfortunately most of the evidence in support of the contention that mismatched couples do try to "fine tune" their relationship, is anecdotal. There are some data suggesting that when a person's physical appearance changes drastically (through accident, plastic surgery, or dieting) his expectations may change too.

For example, Jones (1974), in "Marriage and the Formerly Fat: The Effect Weight Loss Has on Your Life Together," warned *Weight Watchers* magazine readers that:

> Marriage, like all relationships, is a balance. When one partner is overweight, the fact has been considered, perhaps unconsciously, in setting up the balance. Obviously, when you remove the obesity, you upset the balance. The relationship shifts and takes on a different complexion.

In the same article, Palmer adds:

> Gone are . . . the attempts to buy love through acquiescence and the overweight's traditional don't-make-waves-they-may-throw-you-out policy. In their place comes a new pride, an awareness of rights and a tendency to speak up for those rights. (pp. 23–50)

There is also a limited amount of survey data that supports the contention that any change in the equity of a relationship sends reverberations throughout the entire system.

For example, the depression afforded Komarovsky (1971) a tragic opportunity to study the impact of a dramatic change in the marital balance. Komarovsky reasoned that:

> In the traditional patriarchal view of the family, the husband is expected to support and protect his wife . . . she, in turn, is expected to take care of his household, to honor and obey him. (p. 2)

What happens, Komarovsky asked, when a man loses his job? Does he begin to lose authority?

During the winter of 1935–36, Komarovsky contacted fifty-eight families who were receiving public assistance. In all the families, before the depression, the husband had been the family's sole provider. When the depression hit, all this changed. The men lost their jobs and were forced to go on relief. Komarovsky interviewed family members to find out what impact, if any, this change had on the husband and wife's relationship. Komarovsky found that, in thirteen of the fifty-eight families, when the husband lost his ability to support his family, he began to lose his authority.

Two major types of changes occurred in families. (1) In some families, the couple's relationship began to evolve into a more egalitarian one. For example, in one family, the man began, for the first time, to take on part of the household duties. In another family, a Protestant father who had forbidden his children to go to a Catholic school, relented. (2) In a very few cases, the husbands' and wives' status was reversed. The dominant husband became totally subordinate. For example, in one family, so long as the husband was employed, his wife had treated him with careful respect. Once the depression hit, she no longer bothered to be so polite; she began to blame her husband for unemployment, ignore his wishes, complain about his behavior, argue with him, nag him constantly, and criticize him sharply, even in front of the children.

In another family, the husband admitted: "There certainly was a change in our family, and I can define it in just one word—I relinquished power in the family." (p. 31). His wife agreed and she observed: "He still wants to be boss. This is his nature, even though he knows it wouldn't be for the best. He says he is treated like a dog in the house, but that's not true." (p. 32)[25]

In a recent study, Walster, Traupmann, and Walster (in press) point out that Equity theorists make a clear prediction as to how equity/inequity should affect a couple's eagerness to engage in extramarital sex: i.e., the more "cheated" a person feels in his marriage the more concessions he should expect (and induce) his partner to make in the sexual area, and the more likely he should be to risk illicit extramarital sex.

To test this hypothesis, they retrieved the Berscheid et al. (1973) data and reanalyzed them.

As before, they considered Overbenefited respondents to be those whose partners were "much more" or "slightly more" socially desirable than themselves. Equitably treated respondents were those whose social desirability was equal to their own. Deprived respondents were those whose partners were "slightly less" or "much less" desirable than themselves.

Berscheid et al. assessed readers' willingness to engage in extramarital sex in two ways: They asked (1) how soon after they began living with or married their partner they first had sex with someone else, and (2) how many people they had extramarital affairs with.

The results (see Figure 6.6) provide some support for the Walster et al. hypotheses.

Overbenefited and Equitably treated men and women were very reluctant to experiment with extramarital sex. On the average, Overbenefited and Equitably treated men and women waited twelve to fifteen years before getting involved with someone else. Deprived men and women began exploring extramarital sex far earlier—approximately six to eight years after marriage. Similarly, the Overbenefited had the

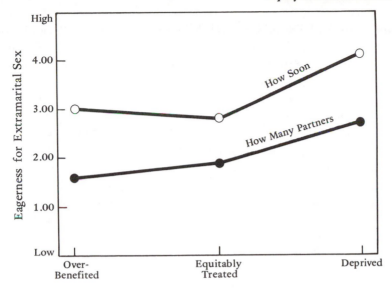

FIGURE 6.6. The Impact of Marital Overbenefit, Equity, or Deprivation on Men and Women's Eagerness to Engage in Extramarital Sex.

fewest extramarital encounters (zero to one). Equitably treated men and women had a few more, and the Deprived had the most extramarital liaisons of all (one to three).

Restoration of psychological equity: Of course, sometimes people find it harder to change their behavior than to change their minds. Sometimes couples, threatened by the discovery that their relationship is unbalanced and unstable, prefer to close their eyes and reassure themselves that "really, everything is in perfect order."

In intimate relationships, participants may find it fairly easy to restore psychological equity. We have discussed some characteristics of casual versus intimate relationships and concluded that casual/intimate relationships differed in such characteristics as:

a. Intensity of interpersonal attraction
b. Knowledge of other
c. Length of relationship
d. Value of resources exchanged
e. Costs of termination of relationship
f. Variety of resources exchanged
g. Interchangeability of resources
h. The unit of analysis: from "you" and "me" to "we"

We pointed out that the long-term, complex nature of intimate relationships means that even in the best of circumstances it is extremely difficult to calculate a relationship's equitableness/inequitableness. If participants expand their horizons, and try to calculate how equitable or inequitable a relationship will be over the course of a lifetime, such calculations become virtually impossible.

Probably, many couples then, when confronted with the fact that the balance of their marriage has changed, find it easiest to restore psychological equity to their relationship, and to convince themselves that these changes are not real changes, or that they are not really very important.

Leaving the field: Walster, Berscheid, and Walster (1973)[26] point out that if a couple's relationship becomes grossly inequitable, they should often be tempted to sever it. Of course, this is far easier for dating couples than for married couples. The dating couple who "breaks up" suffers, but as Bohannan (1971) documents, the married couple who divorces suffers even more: their parents and friends express shock, they may lose rights to their children, and their close friends may drop them; it is expensive to secure a divorce and to establish and maintain two households.

Divorce, then, is costly in both emotional and financial terms.[27] Yet, Equity theorists argue that if a marital relationship is unbalanced enough, and if couples can find no better way to set things right, participants may "leave the field." In 1973, 913,000 couples opted for annulment or divorce. Udry (1971) calculates that twenty to twenty-five percent of first marriages end in annulment, desertion, or divorce.

Equity theory, then, does provide a convenient paradigm for examining romantic and marital relationships. And, the sparse data that exist provide at least suggestive evidence that Equity principles do operate in determining who one selects as a mate and how they get along, day-to-day, and thereafter.

EQUITY IN PARENT-CHILD RELATIONSHIPS

If critics find the contention of Equity theorists that Equity principles operate in close friendships and romantic relations unsettling, they find the contention that Equity principles operate in parent-child relationships absolutely appalling. And, a number of eminent theorists share their objections.

For example, Douvan (1972) argues that the mother/infant relationship is an "integrative" or "heroic" relationship; one which goes beyond exchange. She comments:

> The mother does not say to the infant, "I give you fifteen units of maternal care so that you will return to me fifteen units of filial devotion, smiles, coos, contented gurgles." (p. 9)

Fromm (1956) agrees. He observes:

> Fatherly love is conditional love. Its principle is "I love you *because* you fulfill my expectations, because you do your duty, because you are like me. . . ." Motherly love by its very nature is unconditional. (pp. 35–36)

Yet, Equity theorists, and a few observers (often mothers), continue to assert that parent-child relations do embody equity considerations. For example, McBride (1973) notes:

> I sincerely believe that woman's obligation to make husband and child feel good in exchange for her physical and emotional security is as much an economic issue as whether all adult women can be absorbed into the work force. Acknowledging the monetary value of keeping a house clean or providing tax credits for child care will not put an end to domestic slavery if the one-sided, give-get nature of emotional exchanges is not also altered. Women deserve status and money, but they also *deserve* affection, personal affirmation, and understanding. (p. 140)

Regardless of whether the reader finds the suggestion that Equity principles operate in the most critical of human relationships, the parent/child relationship, "appalling" or "intriguing," he probably can agree that there may be some profit in trying to apply the same Equity principles that have been applied so successfully in other areas, to parent-child relationships. It would be exciting to see if Equity theory can give us a systematic paradigm for organizing the plethora of conflicting observations about parent/child interaction processes.

Let us begin by trying to cast parent/child relationships in equity terms.

Parental Inputs

Probably everyone can agree that parents invest an enormous amount in their children.

Society provides powerful and persuasive "norms" for child-rearing. Society tells parents (1) that they "ought" to have children [28] and (2) how they "ought" to raise them.[29]

For example, McBride (1973) complains that society tells parents, via women's magazines, newspaper articles, and government publications, what they "ought" to do with respect to every aspect of child-rearing: physical care, social development, instinctual satisfaction, moral education, need fulfillment, latent possibilities, cultural enhancement, and sexual gratification.

And, probably most parents do what they "ought"; probably most parents *do* invest tremendous amounts of money, time, effort, and emotional energy in their children. For example, the President's Commission on Population Growth and the American Future (1972) estimates that the typical American couple spends between $80 thousand and $150 thousand to rear two children and put them through college. Overshadowing parents' financial investments are the time, effort, and emotional energy they invest in their children.[30]

Do most parents, most of the time, feel that their momentous investments are repaid by the rewards of parenthood? Theorists are undecided.

Traditional observers generally assume that parent/child relationships are equitable relationships. They argue that parents' enormous investments are repaid by the rewards of parenthood.

Parental Outcomes: The Rewards of Parenthood

Traditional theorists contend that parents reap enormous intellectual and emotional rewards from their children. For example, Dr. Benjamin Spock (1957) maintains that, despite the sacrifices involved in raising children, most parents reap their greatest satisfactions in life from watching their children grow up and develop into fine people.

Waller (1938) (quoting "a pioneer nursery educator") argues that:

> All this talk about the sacrifices of parents for their children is totally unjustified. A father fosters his own personality development by working for his children and by missing his golf game to go on a picnic with his family. The mother is fulfilling the roles she laid down as a child when she spends most of her time "growing up" a challenge to her children. Everyone gains in the "process." (p. 33)

There is compelling evidence that parents do glean voluminous rewards from their children. In a variety of countries, demographers have conducted large-scale and careful studies to find out what rewards couples expect to get, and, in fact do get, from children. (The governments who sponsored these surveys hoped to use such information to prod couples into producing more—or fewer—children.)

The demographers compiled an overwhelming list of "parental

rewards." It appears that some parents, somewhere, sometime, find everything a child might do to be "rewarding." Hoffman and Hoffman (1973) took one look at the demographers' impressive, but unmanageable, compilations and decided that they must begin by presenting a meaningful conceptual scheme for classifying rewards. Only then could they present the demographers' potpourri of data in an orderly fashion. Thus, Hoffman and Hoffman undertook the herculean task of developing a classification scheme. They proposed the following one:

The Value of Children

Economic utility: In many countries of the world, people have children for economic reasons. Children can help around the house, in small home industries, in hunting, and in the fields.[31] In all cultures, children are expected to support their parents in illness or in old age.[32]

Adult status and social identity: Many people have children in an effort to demonstrate that they are truly adult, independent, and acceptable members of the community.[33]

Expansion of the self, tie to a larger entity, "immortality:" Many people have children in order to attain a kind of "immortality." For example, Swain and Kiser (1953) found that three-fourths of the parents they interviewed reported that one of their greatest parental satisfactions was in knowing that some part of them would live on in their children after they were gone. (Rainwater, 1960 confirms this observation.)

Morality: religion, altruism, good of the group; norms regarding sexuality, impulsivity, virtue:

> *. . . and God said unto them Be fruitful, and multiply, and replenish the earth.*
>
> Genesis 1:27,28

Parents sometimes have children in order to demonstrate to themselves (and others) that they are "moral" men and women. Others have children simply because "society expects them to." According to Udry (1971):

> As a child one learns that people grow up and have children, the children in turn, have children, and so on for generations. When one reaches adulthood, he also expects to have children, not especially for any particular gratification, but just because "people do." (p. 438)

Primary group ties, affection: People often have children in order to gain love and companionship.[34]

Stimulation, novelty, fun: People also have children because they find them intellectually and emotionally stimulating. For example, Waller (1938) points out that parents gain new insights into themselves, into others, and into life processes from watching children develop. Many parents also have children because of the "fun" they provide.[35]

Achievement, competence, creativity: Parents often feel a strong sense of accomplishment when they are able to produce a child, and eventually to meet the challenges and crises that inevitably arise during the child-rearing process.[36]

Power, influence, effectance: The power of parent over child is almost without parallel. Parenthood gives many people a unique opportunity to guide and control another human being. For example, Coles (1967) found that lower class black women felt that there was only one way they could have any effect in life—by becoming a mother.

Social comparison, competition: Some parents take pride in providing irrefutable evidence that they have sufficient sexual maturity, virility, and potency to reproduce.[37] Other parents take pride, not in the quantity of their children, but in the quality. For example, American parents often take pride in the fact that their child is a member of "Little League," "gets all A's," or is "my son, the doctor."

All in all, many parents clearly do feel that their staggering investments in their children are "paid back" by the rewards they receive from them. In 1957, the University of Michigan's Institute for Social Research interviewed a random sample of 2,460 Americans.[38] Among other things, the authors asked: "Thinking about a man's (woman's) life, how is a man's (woman's) life changed by having children?" Fifty percent of the fathers and forty-three percent of the mothers felt that parenthood had enriched their lives. Only ten percent of the fathers and twenty-two percent of the mothers felt that parenthood had changed their lives for the worse.

For these reasons then, many social commentators—especially traditional social commentators—conclude that parents are amply repaid for their emotional and monetary investments by the rewards they receive.

Some observers, however, are not so sanguine. They argue that parent/child relationships are inequitable relationships. They admit that parenthood does offer some of the rewards we have enumerated. But, they argue, these rewards are overshadowed by some serious costs that the traditionalists conveniently neglect to mention.

Parental Outcomes: The Costs of Having Children

Even in nonegalitarian marriages, the relationship between husband and wife is a matter of give and take toward each other. The relationship between a mother and her children is that she gives and they take. (Radl, 1973, p. 21)

LeMasters (1957) asked a sample of parents how they had felt following the birth of their first child. He found that in eighty-three percent of the families, the child's birth provoked an extensive or severe crisis:[39]

> The mothers reported the following feelings or experiences in adjusting to the first child: loss of sleep (especially during the early months); chronic "tiredness" or exhaustion; extensive confinement to the home and resulting curtailment of their social contacts; giving up the satisfactions and the income of outside employment; additional washing and ironing; guilt at not being a "better" mother; the long hours and seven days (and nights) a week necessary in caring for an infant; decline in their housekeeping standards; and worry over their appearance (increased weight after pregnancy, *et cetera*).
>
> The fathers echoed most of the above adjustments but also added a few of their own: decline in sexual response of wife; economic pressure resulting from the wife's retirement plus additional expenditures necessary for child; interference with social life; worry about a second pregnancy in the near future; and general disenchantment with the parental role. (p. 354)

A multitude of demographers and social commentators provide haphazard information about the "costs" of parenthood. Pohlman (1969), following Hoffman and Hoffman's lead, provides a classification scheme for describing these "costs."

Some Costs of Conception

Financial costs of children: Children are expensive. Optimists may claim that "two can live as cheaply as one," but no one has ever suggested that three, four, or more can.

Most couples find it extremely difficult to make ends meet. In some families, parents try to meet their financial obligations by "moonlighting" (taking on extra work). In others, they simply try to stretch their income more ways. According to economists, regardless of whether couples have none, one, or several children, they spend about the same proportion of their budget on housing, food, clothing, transportation, and medical care. What parents do sacrifice, is the *quality* of their housing, food, etc. For example, parents, especially those with many children, must settle for less elegant, less conveniently located, and more crowded housing. They must settle for smaller and cheaper cuts of meat, and more starch foods. They must wait until they are seriously ill before going to a doctor.[40] Demographers find that most parents who decide not to have any more children, do so for financial reasons.[41]

Psychological costs of children: Parents' psychological costs are often even more sobering: McBride (1973) contends that one of the heavy costs of parenthood is "loss of self."

Many parents come to resent the fact that no one seems to feel that *their* interests, needs, health, and beloved possessions are important. When a toddler repeatedly interrupts parents' intimate conversations, destroys their favorite books, scratches their cherished records, or disappears just as they are about to leave for important appointments, parents "childishly" feel that no one cares about *them.*

One of Radl's (1973) interviewees expressed this feeling as follows:

> After getting dinner, the dishes, and the kids' baths out of the way, feeling that I'd somehow miraculously survived this particularly chaotic day, I sunk tiredly into the sofa in the living room, and for a moment forgot my exhaustion and tension. I just sat enjoying the record my husband had put on. As I was finally starting to relax and feel human, the mood was shattered by a very loud and, as always, insistent "Mommy!" coming from the vicinity of the back hall. . . . Along with being annoyed at being disturbed and interrupted yet again, I felt ashamed of myself for having such selfish thoughts.
>
> If this kind of thing happened once a day, I wouldn't have thought anything about it; ten or twelve times—many more times even wouldn't have made me feel as if I were being attacked or punished even when I hadn't done anything to deserve disciplinary action. But the threshold had been reached somehow, and I'd gone past my normal tolerance level for routine interruptions. And those moments for myself while I was enjoying eight bars of music were well deserved and well earned. Stripping it away just then was like stripping me away *personally.* Pointing out to me that I don't really count, that time for me isn't even *secondary* to the needs, wishes, and whims of my family are these instances: instances where I have every reason to believe that I can relax only to have it demonstrated to me clearly that it isn't so. I resent this and I feel guilty over my resentment.*

---

*From S. L. Radl, *Mother's Day Is Over* (New York: David McKay Company, 1973), pp. 183–184. Reprinted by permission.

FIGURE 6.7. ". . . One of the Heavy Costs of Parenthood Is 'Loss of Self.' "

Costs of children to husband-wife relationships: For most people, the most important goal of marriage is "companionship."[42] In
many marriages, the arrival of children puts a severe strain on the
couple's emotional, sexual, and companionate relationship.[43]

There is no compelling evidence that children put such a strain
on *most* marriages, however. A number of investigators have found that
regardless of sex, race, age, or family income, childless couples are more
satisfied with their marriages than couples with children. They have also
found that couples with no children are happier than couples with three
or more children.[44]

However, a considerable number of other investigators have
found that there is no relationship between number of children and
marital adjustment.[45] In fact, a few investigators have even found that
childless couples are *less* happy than their counterparts with children.[46]

Thus, it appears that although many, and perhaps even most,
couples' relationships are marred by the arrival of children, some
parents do manage to avoid this "cost."

Some other costs of children: Pohlman (1969), along with a
variety of other authors, discuss the enormous day-to-day costs of
having children.

Concern about the child's development: Pohlman points out
that parents are responsible for the mental and physical health of their
children. Most parents find this an overwhelming assignment.

In relatively homogeneous and stable cultures, all that "good"
parents have to do is raise their children in traditional ways. In the
United States, physicians and child psychologists continually give parents conflicting advice. For example, the United States Children's
Bureau has published ten editions of *Infant Care.* Wolfenstein (1953)
reviewed changes in the advice given over the last forty years. Advice
has ranged from great strictness to permissiveness. Pohlman observes
that:

> As a result of all the change and diversity, the parent can be sure that any
> procedures he follows will be criticized by someone. And if the child does not
> turn out right, it is the parents' fault; mothers-in-law, preachers, and psychol-
> ogists are in general agreement on this. (p. 102)

Parents are also responsible for *constantly* checking on toddlers
to make sure that they aren't in trouble. Radl (1973) observes how
oppressive this responsibility can be:

> One day, Adam disappeared. The police combed the area for one agonizing
> hour before he was found by some neighborhood boys. He was only three
> years old; one minute he was in our fenced back yard, and the next
> minute—gone! I was terrified. . . . One father pointed out that he had never

thought much about hammers until he saw his two-year-old with one—the little boy was ready to hit his four-year-old brother on the head. A mother tells of her little boy running into the house with his head bleeding. It seems that he and a playmate were digging in the back yard. She had no idea where they got a pick ax, but they did, and a fight broke out. The result was a visit to the emergency ward. (p. 72)

Parents know that if they are negligent, just once, the consequences can be tragic. For example, in 1972, 5,000,000 children drank lethal amounts of medicine, cleaning solvents, and other poisons.

Time and hard work: In addition to watching their children to make sure they're safe, parents must prepare special meals for them, keep them clean, arrange special appointments for them, cart them from place to place, plus do their usual household chores. It is not surprising then to discover that parents (especially mothers) end up spending a startling amount of time on housework.

Wilson (1929) and Wiegand (1954), in two studies conducted a quarter of a century apart, interviewed women about their working patterns. From the authors' data (see Figure 6.8), we can draw several conclusions: (a) Women with no children have the lightest work load. (They spend thirty to fifty hours per week on housework.) (b) Women

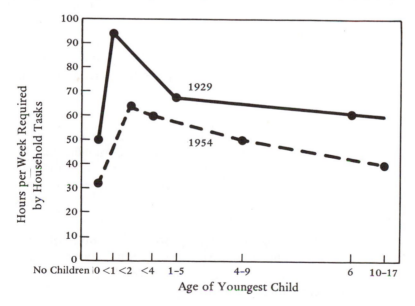

FIGURE 6.8. Hours Spent in Housework, Classified by Age of Young-est Child. (From Blood, 1962, 420. Adapted from Wilson, 1929, 29 and Wiegand, 1954, 18. Reprinted from E. Pohlman, *The Psychology of Birth Planning*, Cambridge, Massachusetts: Schenkman Publishing, 1969, p. 111.)

are forced to spend twice as much time (sixty-five to ninety-five hours per week) on housework after the arrival of their first child. (c) The younger the child, the more time a mother is forced to spend on housework. Mothers with preschool children spend fifty to sixty hours per week on housework. Things get slightly better as children get older. By the time children are between the ages of ten through seventeen, mothers spend only forty to fifty-five hours per week on housework.[47]

Confinement: Young parents complain that one oppressive cost of parenthood is being "tied down." For example, Dyer (1963) asked young mothers to name the most severe problem their first child's arrival had created. The wives most frequently mentioned how difficult it was to adjust to being tied down at home, and to have to give up outside activities and interests. Hoffman (1963) asked Detroit mothers how a woman's life is changed by having children. By far the most common reply was that children "tie you down."

Tiredness and physical exhaustion: In view of the preceding data, it should come as no surprise to discover that parents of young children often complain of fatigue. Pohlman (1969) points out that this tiredness "may be the result of sheer expenditure of energy. . . . However, fatigue may result from such other factors as feelings of confinement and isolation, jealousy, weariness from doing battle with children, and so on." (p. 124)

Other authors agree with Pohlman, that one of the costs of parenthood is fatigue. For example, Dyer (1963) reports that eighty-seven percent of wives complain that they are tired and exhausted most of the time.

Clausen and Clausen (1973) report:

> The early years of motherhood are frequently remembered as a period when one constantly yearned for a full night's sleep. In our longitudinal data at the Institute of Human Development, mothers with three or more children closely spaced, looking back at the early years of motherhood from the perspective of their late forties, are likely to recall those early years as years of extreme exhaustion and discouragement. (p. 189)

Mess, noise, confusion, and congestion: Finally, both Pohlman (1969) and Clausen and Clausen (1973) point out that, especially during the early years, parents must live surrounded by mess, noise, confusion, and congestion.

In summary, many parents clearly do feel that parenthood's costs outweigh its rewards. In 1963, Hoffman asked young Detroit mothers a straightforward question: "How is a woman's life changed by having children?" Four times as many mothers gave totally negative answers as totally positive ones.

On the basis of the preceding data, then, many irreverent social commentators have concluded that parent-child relationships are distinctly inequitable relationships.

Probably the question of whether most parents, most of the time, are in an equitable or inequitable relationship with their children is unanswerable. The preceding section makes it clear that parent-child relationships are complex, multi-faceted, and dynamic. If we asked parents if they were receiving less than, exactly what, or more than they "deserve" from their children, they would likely give us quite different answers at different stages in life, on different days, or even at different times of the day.

How Do Parents Restore Equity?

Instead of trying to decide whether most parent-child relationships are equitable or inequitable, it is probably more profitable to speculate about how parents and children should respond during those periods, on those days, at those hours, when the parent is feeling exploited, equitably treated, or overbenefited. If readers review the Equity theory and research described in "Exploiter/Victim Relationships" (chapter 3) and in "Philanthropist/Recipient Relationships" (chapter 4), they should be able to generate a number of predictions as to how parents should respond when they feel trapped in an inequitable situation. By way of demonstration, however, let us consider the common case where a parent feels that he or she "deserves" far more out of life than he or she is receiving.

In "Philanthropist/Recipient Relations" we pointed out that even the most altruistic of people should never be able to fully resign themselves to the fact that they must sacrifice themselves for another. We pointed out that, consciously or unconsciously, the altruist will always feel fleeting twinges of distress, and feel compelled to try to "set things right."

We can think of a variety of ways in which beleaguered parents try to set things right:

Restoration of Actual Equity

Demanding Practical Benefits

Relationships between the generations are also too often predicated on emotional rewards, with gratitude as payment. The mother exacts a price for her devotion; "You owe it to me, after everything I've done for you, all I've given up for you." (McBride, 1973, p. 140)

Sometimes parents feel their children owe them practical benefits. They expect their children to console them when they're blue, entertain their friends, run errands for them, call them every week, bring their children to visit on the holidays, and, of course, support them in their old age.

Demanding Respect and Status. The Bible exhorts us to "Honor thy father and thy mother." The truism that "parents are entitled to respect" is so ingrained in all of us, that often we do not realize that parental inputs are linked in any way to children's obligations to supply rewards. Sadly, when parents can no longer make a "parental contribution," we are poignantly reminded that a parental contribution is often a prerequisite for parental respect.[48]

Retaliation. According to Equity theory, exploited parents can restore actual equity in still another way—by retaliating against their children.

Theoretically, society forbids such equity-restoring reactions. During infancy (and well into the toddler stage), children are not considered responsible for their actions. When a child smiles, babbles and is charming, a parent is allowed to label him a "good child." When he soils his diapers, however, cries all night, or hits his best friend on the head with a truck, he is supposed to be forgiven since he "doesn't know any better." So, theoretically, parents are not allowed to restore equity by retaliating against their children.

In fact, however, parents often do. At some time or another, most parents get so angry that they ridicule, yell at, or hit their children. Then they feel guilty. Other parents do more than that. Collins (1968) notes:

> It is not uncommon to find battered children with broken bones, fractured skulls, brain damage, severe burns on the skin or in body cavities which have been caused by caustic substances, ruptured intestines, or other evidences of vicious attack. Doctors throughout the country who are active in the investigation and treatment of the battered child believe that the infliction of injuries by parents is a significant cause of death in infants and young children. Gill (1968) estimates that, in 1968, police, physicians, and child welfare agencies reported more than 7,000 child abuse cases. These parents, too, feel guilty. (p. 201)

In spite of taboos, then, some parents do restore equity via retaliation.

Restoration of Psychological Equity: Uneasy parents may restore equity to a parent-child relationship by trying to convince themselves that parenthood has more rewards than they had ever realized.

Simone de Beauvoir (1952) has noted that mothers are skilled at creating child-rearing rewards:

> What is in any case remarkable and distinguishes this relation of mother and baby from all other human relations is the fact that at first the baby itself takes no active part in it: its smiles, its babble, have no sense other than what the mother gives them; whether it seems charming and unique, or tiresome, commonplace, and hateful, depends on her, not upon the baby. (p. 180)

Parents, who find the current rewards of parenthood distressingly low, may try to convince themselves that things will get better by and by. The parents may soothe themselves by reminding themselves that once the child gets a little older, he will give them respect and companionship. ("He'll be so proud of us, when he introduces us to all his little friends." "We'll walk together on the beach and build sand castles.") They may imagine how much fun it will be, in their old age, when all their loving grandchildren congregate for Thanksgiving and Christmas dinners.

Leaving the Field.   In the very rare cases, a parent may psychologically or physically abandon his child. Parents *can* abandon their families. They can ship their children off to their parents, or to maiden aunts, or to boarding schools—or simply leave them on a doorstep somewhere. For most parents, however, this is not a realistic alternative. There are no socially acceptable ways of "divorcing" one's children. Once parents have children, they are committed to them until they become independent adults.

Summary

We began this chapter by pointing out that theorists are hotly divided as to whether or not equity considerations operate in such intimate relationships as close friendships, romantic and marital relationships, and parent-child relationships. We encountered a similar division when we asked colleagues, friends, or lovers about their ideas. People cling tenaciously to their own experiential facts. We were able to uncover almost no evidence, however, to allow us to arbitrate these conflicting claims. We found some evidence that equity considerations do seem to operate in close friendships and in romantic and marital relationships. We could only speculate, however, as to how equity principles might operate in parent-child relationships; no data exist. Obviously, if we are to get the glimmerings of an answer, we will have to undertake more research on this controversial question.

ENDNOTES

1. See Adams and Freedman (1976) for a lucid discussion of research possibilities for Equity theory and dynamic interactions.

2. Additional evidence in support of this contention comes from Altman and Taylor (1973), Huesmann and Levinger (1976), Jourard (1971), and Worthy, Gary, and Kahn (1969).

3. Sometimes, participants in a relationship unknowingly operate from quite different time perspectives. For example, a young husband may be operating on the assumption that things are fair right now. His bride may assume that, although things are grossly unfair now, "once he gets established in business," "once the baby grows up and leaves home," etc., her husband will make everything up to her. The advent of middle age, and her shattering discovery that things remain as is, or her discovery that the "indebted" spouse is about to leave, or die, may generate intense resentment and anger.

4. See Morgan and Sawyer (1967) for a further discussion of this point.

5. See Aronson (1970), Huesmann and Levinger (1976), and Levinger and Snoek (1972).

6. See Donnenwerth and Foa (1974), Foa (1971), Teichman (1971), and Turner, Foa, and Foa (1971).

7. See Foa and Foa (1974).

8. See Scanzoni (1972) for an elaboration of this point.

9. Boulding (1973) in *The Economy of Love and Fear,* presents a detailed and brilliant elucidation of this point.

10. See, for example Cartwright and Zander (1962), Deutsch (1962), and Sigall and Landy (1974).

11. For example, when they could reveal their answers to such questions as: What is the most you could win? What is the most he could win? What is the lowest amount you might win?

12. This difference was not statistically significant, however.

13. Even this champion of unconditional love, however, inadvertently finds himself in the equity camp. Although Fromm claims that equity considerations demean love relations, he is moved to promise his readers that if they love "truly" they will reap a handsome return. ". . . in truly giving, he cannot help receiving that which is given back to him. Giving implies to make the other a giver also. . ." (p. 21)

14. See, for example, Murstein et al. (1974), and Douvan (1974).

15. See, for example, Bernard (1964), Blau (1964), McCall (1966), Scanzoni (1972), and Storer (1966). At the beginning of this chapter, we pointed out that casual vs. intimate relationships differ in a number of ways. In that sense, we, too, agree that casual and intimate relationships are "different." However, we believe the same equity processes operate in both casual and intimate relations. The fact that casual and intimate relations differ in such characteristics as the time span of the relationship, the number of rewards involved in exchanges, the types of rewards involved in exchanges, and so on, should simply affect (1) how easy or

difficult it is to calculate equity in a casual vs. intimate relationship and (2) how casuals vs. intimates choose to restore equity.

16. See Backman and Secord (1959), Homans (1961), and Blau (1968).

17. In chapter 7, we will describe some of the techniques researchers might use to determine whether a dating couples' relationship was equitable or inequitable.

18. For example Brislin and Lewis (1968), Tesser and Brodie (1971), and Walster (1970).

19. Additional support for the Matching hypothesis comes from Huston (1973) and Stroebe et al. (1971).

20. See Sigall and Landy (1974).

21. See, for example, Gottesman (1965), and Murstein (1967a).

22. See Garrison, Anderson, and Reed (1968), Jones (1929), and Reed and Reed (1965).

23. See Garrison, Anderson, and Reed (1968), and Kiser (1968).

24. Since Berscheid et al.'s data are correlational, it is, of course, not possible to tell whether (1) individuals were able to attract an inappropriately beautiful person, because they possessed compensating traits, or (2) whether individuals, matched with inappropriately beautiful partners, quickly tried to *develop* compensatory traits in order to keep the partner. Both occurrences, of course, are predicted by Equity theory. (This latter process will be discussed in the next section.)

25. Similar results are reported by Bakke (1940a, b), who also studied the impact of the Great Depression on men and women's lives.

26. Along with Adams and Freedman (1976), Bernard (1964), McCall (1966), Scanzoni (1972), and Thibaut and Faucheux (1965).

27. See Bohannan (1971).

28. See, for example, Rainwater (1965), Stycos (1955), or Whelpton et al. (1966).

29. See, for example, Stendler (1950), Sunley (1955), and Wolfenstein (1953) for an elaboration of this point.

30. See, for example, Clausen and Clausen (1965), Hoffman and Hoffman (1973), or Pohlman (1969).

31. See Caldwell (1967, 1968), Dow (1967), Guthrie (1968), Fawcett and Arnold (1973), Heisel (1968), Martin (1970), and Pohlman (1969, see chapter 4).

32. See Mueller (1970), and Streib (1958).

33. See Sussman and Burchinal (1962a, b).

34. See Caldwell (1967), Heisel (1968), Martin (1970), Rainwater (1965), and Whelpton et al. (1966).

35. See Caldwell (1967, 1968), Heisel (1968), Komarovsky (1967), *Mysore Population Study* (1961), and Poffenberger (1969).

36. See Centers and Blumberg (1954), Gurin et al. (1960), Meade (1971), and Rainwater (1965).

37. See Kiser (1962), Rainwater (1960), and Stycos (1955).

38. See Gurin, Veroff, and Feld (1960).

39. Comparable findings have been reported by Dyer (1963), Jacoby (1969), and Silverman and Silverman (1971).

40. See Blood (1962), or Douglas and Blomfield (1958).

41. See Clare and Kiser (1951), Freedman et al. (1959), Rainwater (1960), and Whelpton et al. (1966).

42. See Blood and Wolfe (1960).

43. See Christensen (1968), Feldman (1962), and Radl (1973).

44. See Blood and Wolfe (1960), Burgess and Cottrell (1939), Lang (1932), Reed (1947), and Renne (1970).

45. See Bernard (1934), Davis (1929), Hamilton (1948), Karlsson (1951), Locke (1951), and Terman (1938).

46. See Blood and Wolfe (1960), and Farber and Blackman (1956).

47. Data from Myrdal and Klein (1956) provide additional support for these observations.

48. Komarovsky (1971) provides a poignant example of the fact that, although people are in accord that a father deserves respect "regardless," in fact, a father's ability to support his family is intimately tied to the respect his wife and children are willing to award to him. The families Komarovsky interviewed *said* such things as: "If a child is well brought up, he will certainly not lose respect for his father just because his father happens to be out of work." (pp. 75–76) Nonetheless, when the Great Depression hit, and these same fathers lost their ability to provide for their families, in fact, their prestige and status often deteriorated markedly.

CHAPTER

7

Confronting
Major Theoretical Issues

In chapters 1–6, we reviewed Equity theory and its applications. Let us now review the Equity sequence again, at a more leisurely pace.

THE EQUITY PARADIGM

1.

> PROPOSITION I: Individuals will try to maximize their outcomes.

2.

> PROPOSITION II: Groups can maximize collective reward by evolving accepted systems for "equitably" apportioning rewards and costs among members. Thus, members will evolve such systems of equity and will attempt to induce members to accept and adhere to these systems. Groups will generally reward members who treat others equitably and generally punish members who treat other inequitably.

3.

> The scrutineer perceives that Person A and Person B are in a "relationship."

4.

> The scrutineer assesses
>
> $$\frac{(O_A - I_A)}{(|I_A|)^{k_A}} = \frac{(O_B - I_B)}{(|I_B|)^{k_B}}$$

5.

> **PROPOSITION III:** When individuals find themselves participating in inequitable relationships, they become distressed. The more inequitable the relationship, the more distress individuals feel.

6.

> **PROPOSITION IV:** Individuals who discover they are in an inequitable relationship attempt to eliminate their distress by restoring equity. The greater the inequity that exists, the more distress they feel, and the harder they try to restore equity.

When one carefully examines the equity sequence, several major theoretical questions occur. In this chapter, we will confront these hard questions.

WHEN WILL A SCRUTINEER PERCEIVE THAT PARTICIPANTS ARE IN A RELATIONSHIP?

3.

> The scrutineer perceives that Person A and Person B are in a "relationship."

Equity theory deals with the reactions of observers or actual participants to equitable or inequitable *relationships*. The theory can make no prediction if the scrutineer does not perceive participants to be exchanging inputs and outcomes. Obviously then, one of the first questions Equity theorists must confront is: When will a scrutineer, either an outside observer or the participants themselves, assume that two individuals are in a relationship?

The Dyad

Partners in Actual Interaction. Thus far, Thibaut and Kelley (1959) provide the most compelling answer to this question. They state:

> Two individuals may be said to have formed a relationship when on repeated occasions they are observed to interact. By interaction it is meant that they emit behavior in each others' presence, they create products for each other, or they communicate with each other. In every case we would identify as an instance of interaction there is at least the possibility that the actions of each person affect the other. (p. 10)

According to Thibaut and Kelley's reasoning, then, one is probably most likely to perceive that he is in a relationship with those he encounters and interacts with on a day-to-day basis.

Luckily, a flood ·of theorizing and research on interpersonal association and attraction gives us a great deal of information as to the factors that determine with whom a person will interact.[1] A swift review of this literature indicates that two of the most potent factors in determining who we will form relationships with are:

Propinquity: The closer two individuals are located geographically, the more likely they are to interact with one another. For example, Festinger, Schachter, and Back (1950) arrived at the intriguing conclusion that an architect can control the social life of an apartment building's residents. In their study of two housing projects, the authors found that those residents who are forced, by architectural design, into contact with their neighbors, will be unusually popular. For example, residents whose apartments just happen to be situated near stairways, mailboxes, or community courts end up with more contacts, and more friends, than do isolated residents.

Reward versus Punishment: It should come as no surprise to discover that individuals gravitate to people who provide important rewards and drift away from people who are unable or unwilling to do so. People seek out those who reduce their anxiety and fears, offer admiration and affection, bolster their self-confidence, assure them that their opinions and life styles are appropriate, and help them attain a multitude of other goals; they forgo the company of those who do not.

Evidently, then, individuals are most likely to interact and to establish firm relationships with people who are close at hand and with those whose company is so rewarding that it is worthwhile to seek them out.

Partners in a Fantasied Interaction. Although for the scientist it is very important to distinguish what is real from what is fantasied, in our everyday life the distinction between reality and fantasy may be neither important nor easy to make. An individual may react in comparable ways regardless of whether he is actually interacting, or merely imagining what it would be like to interact, with another. An example will illuminate this point. A colleague once complained that Equity theory was too limited. He pointed out that we are in actual relationships with very few of the four billion people in the world. Thus, Equity theory had nothing to say about our reactions to most people. "For example," he argued, "I am *not* in a relationship with Nelson Rockefeller. It would never occur to me to compare my relative outcomes to his. Thus, although I probably receive less than I deserve in life, and Rockefeller certainly receives far more than he deserves, that knowledge is in no way distressing. Even worse, since Rockefeller and I aren't in a relationship, Equity theory has nothing to say about how I will react to

FIGURE 7.1. ". . . those Residents Who Are Forced, by Architectural Design, into Contact with Their Neighbors, Will Be Unusually Popular."

Rockefeller." We were all about to acquiesce, when he continued, hammering home his point: "Now, perhaps if I worked alongside Rockefeller, I'd be angry. For example, he's not as smart as I am, he has less education, and he doesn't work as hard. But his outcomes certainly are a lot better than mine." The critic expanded, commenting on the former Vice President's palatial home, his luxurious hideaway retreats, etc. But what was fascinating, was that as he continued to focus on this fantasy relationship, he became angrier and angrier, finally summing up by vehemently saying, "So, if I *did* compare my relative outcomes to Nelson Rockefeller's, I'd be damn mad!" This scenario suggests an intriguing hypothesis. If one spends time speculating or fantasizing about what it would be like to be in an actual relationship with another, one may very well experience the same reactions a person enmeshed in a real relationship experiences. Equity theorists have not investigated this possibility. They have sensibly chosen to begin at the beginning and attempted to explain the reactions of real people in real relationships. The next generation of Equity researchers may be more daring, and may begin to investigate individuals' reactions in fantasy relationships.

Equity with the World

Austin (1973)[2] acknowledges that Equity theory is designed to predict individuals' behavior in dyadic relationships. However, he argues that the theory can, and should, predict an individual's behavior in many coexisting relationships.

Conventional Equity researchers would argue that the injustices one inflicts on a partner (or suffers at his hands) should motivate one to right things with his partner—and only his partner. By definition, the equitableness of a relationship depends solely upon how much Participants A and B contribute to the AB relationship, and how much reward they can draw out of it. If Person A exploits Person B, A cannot restore equity to the AB relationship by making restitution to Person C who has in no way suffered from A's exploitation. Such a "philanthropic" act would only create a second inequitable relationship; this time with Partner C.

On the surface, this argument is a compelling one. However, Austin argues that such a traditional Equity analysis is deceptively simple. If one is to predict Person A's reaction to an inequity, he must specify (a) who Person A perceives himself to be in a relationship with, and (b) how A calculates his own and his "partner's(s')" inputs and outcomes. Outside observers may agree that A is in a separate relationship with Person B and Person C. Unfortunately, Participant A may disagree. He may compare himself with the "appropriate" partner (*B* or *C*), but then again, he may recalcitrantly insist on comparing himself with both partners at once (*B* plus *C*), or with "others in general." If Person *A* does neglect the partner with whom Equity theorists think he should compare himself, and chooses instead to compare himself with a different person—or collection of persons—Equity theory *would* make transrelational predictions.

Specifically, Austin proposed two hypotheses:

1. If a person is over or underrewarded, he will naturally be eager to restore equity to the *AB* relationship, and thereby maintain both situation-specific equity and equity with the world. Sometimes, however, Person *A* will be unwilling or unable to restore equity to the *AB* relationship. Under these conditions, *A* may settle for paying back (or victimizing) a totally different partner in a totally different situation, and at least maintaining equity with the world.
2. If Person *A* knows he will have to interact frequently with his second partner (*C*), and thus will be held strictly accountable for his actions, he should be careful to maintain a strictly equitable relationship *with that person.* Were he to try to maintain equity with the world, he should anticipate that his second partner would call this situation-specific injustice to his attention. However, when *A* is secure that he will never see his second partner again, he may be quite willing to abandon the equitableness of his relationship with a specific partner in order to maintain equity with the world.

Austin tested his hypotheses in the following experiment. He asked pairs of women to participate in a study of decision making. Both women worked on the same task and, by design, they performed the task equally well. Then, the experimenter asked one of the women to serve as a "decision maker" and to divide the $3.00 fee between herself and her partner ("the worker"), on the basis of their task performance. Since most of us are imbued with a belief in "equal pay for equal work," the workers naturally assumed they would receive $1.50. By experimental predesign, however, one-third of the workers were underrewarded (they received only $1.00), one-third were equitably rewarded (they received $1.50), and the remainder were overrewarded (they received $2.00). With that, the experiment ended.

Sometime later, each woman was asked to participate in a second experiment. This second experiment was run in a similar fashion to the first. As before, she and her partner—a second woman, of course—worked on identical tasks; once again, both performed equally well. This time, however, the supposedly random draw assigned the woman herself to be the decision maker.

Accountability manipulation: Half of the time (in the No-accountability conditions) women were led to believe that they would never see their second partner again. Half of the time (in the High-accountability conditions) women expected that at the end of their session, they would have a chance to discuss their decision with their second partner.

Austin's results were exactly as predicted. When women expected to confront their second partner, they invariably split the $3 equally. When they expected that they would never have to see her again, they were willing to sacrifice situation-specific equity, to some extent, in order to maintain equity with the world. Women who had been cheated in the first experiment took more money than they deserved on the second. (On the average, they took $1.72 of the $3.00.) Those who were equitably treated in the first experiment took almost exactly what they deserved ($1.51). Those who were over-rewarded in the first experiment gave their partner more than she deserved in the second situation. (They took approximately $1.44.)[3]

A number of theorists share Austin's view that Equity theory should broaden its perspective. For example, Anderson, Berger, Zelditch, and Cohen (1969), Zelditch et al. (1970), and Berger et al. (1972) point out that individuals can make two distinctly different types of comparisons. These are *local comparisons,* by which a person can compare himself with one other particular individual; and *referential comparisons,* by which an individual can compare himself, not with any particular Other, but with a generalized Other. (For example, they note, if *A* is an airline mechanic, he might compare himself with "people who are highly skilled mechanics.") They argue that Exchange theorists must begin to concentrate less on social comparisons and focus more intensely on referential ones.

Social Comparison Processes. Heretofore, Equity theorists have had to face only the simple question: When will Person *A* perceive himself to be in a relationship with Person *B*? If future Equity theorists decide they wish to predict not only Person *A's* reactions to Person *B,* but also to try to predict Person *A's* reactions to groups of people or even with people in general, they will have to confront a more difficult question: When will Person *A* perceive himself to be in a relationship with Group *B*?

A number of eminent theorists have tried to answer that sticky question.[4] (For a comprehensive review of this literature, consult Austin, in press.) In essence, these theorists conclude that people tend to compare themselves to three types of others: (1) people with whom they are in actual association, (2) people they admire and look up to, and (3) people they perceive to be very similar, or very different, from themselves along some dimension. When theorists try to be more specific than this, about all they can say is that many individuals compare themselves with a surprising variety of groups. We do not yet know what causes a person to choose one social comparison group at one time, and then choose another group at another time.

During the earlier stages of their research, Equity researchers wisely chose to test their paradigm in the most clear-cut of relationships; the actually existing dyadic relationship. However, future researchers may wish to be more daring and to begin to explore the borderline areas of fantasy relationships vs. actual relationships and single person versus group interactions.

HOW DOES A SCRUTINEER DECIDE WHICH *INPUTS* ARE RELEVANT IN A GIVEN SITUATION?

4.

$$\frac{(O_A - I_A)}{(|I_A|)^{k_A}} = \frac{(O_B - I_B)}{(|I_B|)^{k_B}}$$

Potentially, a scrutineer could perceive *anything*—bravery, cowardice, humility, arrogance, strength, or weakness—to be a valuable input. How, then, can a scrutineer possibly decide exactly which inputs should count in a given situation?

The Equality–Proportionality Controversy

Aristotle[5] argued that there are two major types of social justice: equal justice and proportional (i.e., distributive) justice.

Equal Justice. (Rewards are distributed equally among men.) Sometimes only one input counts—a man's "humanity." In certain situations, people assume that "all men are created equal" and that whether a man has behaved badly or well, he is entitled to the same treatment. For example, Aristotle notes:

> For it makes no difference whether a good man has defrauded a bad man or a bad man a good one, or whether it is a good or a bad man that has committed adultery; the law . . . treats the parties as equal. (p. 1131[b])

In our own time, a similar view is expressed by the statement:

> We hold these truths to be self-evident, that all men are created equal, that they are endowed by their Creator with certain unalienable Rights, that among these are Life, Liberty, and the pursuit of Happiness.

In *Ethica Nicomachea*, Aristotle discusses such situations and provides judges with a mathematical procedure for equating participants' outcomes when things go awry. Basically, this explanation is straightforward:

> The problem of "rectificatory justice" . . . is only that of rectifying a wrong that has been done, by awarding damages; . . . The parties are treated by the court as equal . . . and the wrongful act is reckoned as having brought equal gain to the wrong-doer and loss to his victim; it brings A to the position A + C, and B to the position B − C. The judge's task is to find the arithmetical mean between these, and this he does by transferring C from A to B. Thus (A being treated as =B) we get the arithmetical "proportion"

$$(A + C) - (A + C - C) = (A + C - C) - (B - C)$$
$$(A + C) - (B - C + C) = (B - C + C) - (B - C).$$

Aristotle then spends agonizing time over these simple instructions. Students well versed in mathematics will be perplexed at his difficulty in explaining this simple process. For example:

> In some states they call judges mediators, on the assumption that if they get what is intermediate they will get what is just. The just, then, is an intermediate, since the judge is so. Now the judge restores equality; it is as though there were a line divided into unequal parts, and he took away that by which the greater segment exceeds the half, and added it to the smaller segment. And when the whole has been equally divided, then they say they have "their own"—i.e., when they have got what is equal. The equal is intermediate between the greater and the lesser line according to arithmetical proposition. It is for this reason also that it is called just (δίκαιον), because it is a division into two equal parts (δίχα), just as if one were to call it δίχαιον; and the judge (δικαστής) is one who bisects (διχαστής). For when something is subtracted from one of two equals and added to the other, the other is in excess by these two; since if what was taken from the one had not been added to the other, the latter would have been in excess by one only. It therefore exceeds the intermediate by one, and the intermediate exceeds by one that from which something was taken. By this, then, we shall recognize both what we must subtract from that which has more, and that we must add to that which has less; we must add to the latter that by which the intermediate exceeds it, and subtract from the greatest that by which it exceeds the intermediate. . . . Let the lines AA′, BB′, CC′ be equal to one another; from the line AA′ let the segment AE have been subtracted, and to the line CC′ let the segment CD have been added, so that the whole line DCC′ exceeds the line EA′ by the

segment CD and the segment CF; therefore it exceeds the line BB′ by the segment CD. (pp. 1132 a & b)

	A	E		A′
	B			B′
D	C	F		C′

Proportional Justice. (Rewards are distributed in proportion to men's merit.) Sometimes simple "humanity" is not enough. Men vary in their inputs and people assume that the greater one's inputs, the better the treatment he deserves. In describing this form of justice, Aristotle observes:

> . . . awards should be "according to merit"; for all men agree that what is just in distribution must be according to merit in some sense, though they do not all specify the same sort of merit. . . . The problem of distributive justice is to divide the distributable honor or reward into parts which are to one another as are the merits of the persons who are to participate. If A (first person):B (second person)::C (first portion):D (second portion). . . . This, then is what the just is—the proportional; the unjust is what violates the proportion." (pp. 1131 a & b)

If our student mathematician thinks Aristotle floundered when explaining how to divide things up evenly, he will be aghast at Aristotle's tortured explanation of how to apportion outcomes proportionately.

Unfortunately, Aristotle does not provide any precise guide as to when equality, and when proportionality, is the appropriate standard of social justice.

Equality versus Proportionality: Aristotle and several current theorists[6] assume that equality and proportionality are entirely different varieties of justice. Social critics have both praised and damned these alternative forms of social justice.

Social inequality has had its passionate defenders; Aristotle, Hobbes, and Rockefeller among them. For example, Isocrates praised the primitive Athenians for recognizing that there are two forms of equality; i.e., "the division of advantages indiscriminately among all citizens vs. the division of the same advantages according to each man's deserts." He commended the Athenians for inviolably adhering to the latter principle of justice.[7]

Social equality has had its equally passionate advocates. For example, in the eighteenth century Rousseau[8] argued that natural man's state was equality, and the evolution of society ravaged his idyllic state.

> ... the strongest did most work ... the most ingenious devised methods of diminishing labour: while both laboured equally, the one gained a great deal by his work, while the other could hardly support himself. Thus natural inequality unfolds itself [Later] .... the rank and condition of every man assigned him; not merely his share of property and his power to serve or injure others, but also his wit, beauty, strength or skill, merit or talent [become important] .... To be and to seem became two totally different things; and from this distinction sprang insolent pomp and cheating trickery, with all the numerous vices that go in their train. (pp. 217–218)

Social psychologists, however, contend that people are less consistent than Isocrates or Rousseau might think. Sometimes they adhere to one, and sometimes to another, of these two "entirely different" types of social justice. More confusingly, sometimes they even try to combine the two.

There is ample evidence in support of their contentions. Sometimes individuals do allocate rewards in accordance with others' task inputs.[9] Sometimes they do ignore differences in others' task inputs and divide rewards equally.[10] Sometimes they do try to combine the two. For example, Chertkoff (1970), Schelling (1960), Gamson (1961), Komorita and Chertkoff (1973), and Leventhal (1976) observe that participants frequently decide to "split-the-difference" when debating whether to divide goods equally or proportionally.

Since it seems obvious that in different situations individuals define fairness differently, researchers soon began to concentrate on isolating the demographic, personality, or situational variables that determine whether individuals perceive equality or proportionality to be most fair.

Age: Some theorists argue that age is a crucial determinant of how people define fairness. However, evidence in support of this contention is mixed. Lane and Coon (1972) argued that preschoolers are incapable of comparing their own input/outcome ratio with another child. Children simply cannot perform such a complex task. Masters (1968) agreed. Lerner (1974) found that kindergarteners do simply divide things equally. Morgan and Sawyer (1967) found that even at ten through twelve years of age, boys prefer to share and share alike.

Accumulating evidence, however, makes it clear that even preschoolers are capable of behaving equitably. Leventhal and Anderson (1970), Lerner (1974), and Leventhal, Popp, and Sawyer (1973) document that preschool children are capable of assessing merit and giving more reward to the better of two performers.

Sex: Other theorists propose that sex is a crucial determinant of how a person will allocate rewards. Vinacke (1969) proposed that males and females differ in two important ways in their allocations: (1) men tend to be exploitative while women tend to be accommodative, and (2) coalitions of males tend to apportion group benefits unequally. (The man whose initial inputs were greater tends to receive the larger share of the resources.) Coalitions of females tend to ignore initial differences and to split group resources equally.

Support for Vinacke's contention that males are more exploitative than females comes from a number of studies.[11] Support for Vinacke's contention that females focus on harmonious relations and share prizes, while men focus on quality of performance and divide them unequally, comes from still others.[12]

In a recent essay, Leventhal (1973) proposes a compelling alternative interpretation of the Vinacke data. Leventhal proposes that men and women do not differ in their motivation to behave equitably; both want to maintain equitable relations. Leventhal observes, however, that individuals must sometimes sacrifice equity in order to pursue more important goals. This is where men and women differ. For a man, succeeding at a challenging task is an important alternative goal. For a woman, succeeding at affiliative goals is important. According to Leventhal, recognizing these motivational differences enables us to account for the way men and women apportion rewards.

If Leventhal's reasoning is correct, we should be able to predict how men and women will apportion resources when they win or lose. When males perform better than their partners, they should insist that others recognize their success by allocating a large share of the community resources to them. When they fail, they should be less eager to have success and failure marked by the reward allocation. When women perform better than their partners, they should divide rewards equally; when they perform worse, they should take less than half of the reward.[13]

Vinacke (1969) provides a comprehensive review of other personality and situational factors that influence how individuals allocate reward.

When Equality? When Proportionality? Apparently, then, a wide range of specific personality and situational factors determine whether people adopt equality or proportionality as their standard. Can we specify any general factors that determine when people will be motivated to define equal or proportional inputs as relevant? A cost-benefit analysis of the process provides some insights.

It is much simpler to apportion resources equally than proportionately. In order to divide things equally, all the allocators have to do is look around and decide who is entitled to share in the spoils. Then, each group member gets an equal share. In order to divide things proportionately, the allocators must decide who should share in the spoils, enumerate all the inputs that may be relevant in the situation, negotiate as to which inputs "count" and how much, and calculate appropriate shares.

Given this analysis, we should be able to specify several general variables that probably affect the willingness of people to apportion resources equally versus proportionately in ambiguous situations.

Time constraints: When a decision must be made quickly, an equal division becomes more attractive. When participants have unlimited time to bargain, they will be more likely to consider a proportional division.

Communication costs: When negotiation is extremely costly, an equal division becomes more attractive.

Potential benefits: When the amount involved is small, an equal division becomes more attractive. It isn't worth it to haggle over a small amount.

Significance for future decisions: When the allocation is a one-time-only affair, an equal division is more popular. If, however, the decision will set a precedent for future allocations, individuals will be more likely to consider a proportional division. For example, Brickman and Campbell (1971) note:

> It is interesting to note that contrast between the division of reward on athletic teams in salaries . . . versus prize money or bonuses for winning . . . salaries are of course traditionally highly uneven, with players receiving what it is believed that their skills deserve. Prize money, on the other hand, is traditionally divided into equal shares and given to all members of the team regardless of their contributions to winning. (p. 297)

Other considerations: Leventhal (1976a) argues that if an individual's primary goal is to maximize production, he should favor the proportionality norm, since, in the long run, equitable allocations maximize group productivity. If, however, an individual's primary goal is to maintain solidarity and minimize antagonism, he should favor the equality norm, because equal allocations foster interpersonal harmony.

Leventhal cites voluminous evidence in support of these contentions. The reader interested in a sophisticated discussion of this point should see Leventhal (1976).

Are Equality and Proportionality Really Entirely Different Forms of Justice? Several authors argue that it is profitable to treat equality and proportionality as two entirely different forms of justice.

> What is being argued for, therefore, is a consideration of the concept of justice in at least its two major senses. In the one, justice in a relationship exists when resources are allocated on the basis of investments. This the author and others have referred to as *equity* (*sic.* proportionality). In the other, justice exists when resources are allocated independently of investments and according to a norm or principle of *equality*. It is suggested, furthermore, that both senses of justice in human relationships can be and have been demonstrated. To speak of equality as a special case of equity overlooks more than it reveals and is a move toward unwise parsimony.* (p. 264)

In spite of the fact that most theorists seem to feel that equality and proportionality are markedly different types of justice, we would argue that Aristotle's, and the more contemporary theorists', examples fit nicely within Equity theory. In the view of Equity theorists, Aristotle is simply describing two different types of situations. In the first collection of situations, participants assume that the only relevant input is a man's "humanity." Since all men possess equal humanity, all men are entitled to equal outcomes. In the second collection of situations, participants assume that the relevant inputs are ones on which men vary; they assume that inputs such as Marxian need, legal advantage, task performance, bravery, investments, and political acumen are relevant. Thus, they conclude, different men deserve different amounts of reward.

In his review of the many theories of social justice that have been proposed, Brandt (1962) reminds us that not just such inputs as humanity, task effort, or need can be viewed as inputs.

Lerner (1974) enumerates four systems of justice: "the Marxian justice of need, the justice of equity, the justice of parity, and the justice of laws." Leventhal (1976*b*) reviews still other bases of justice.

Deutsch (1974) cogently observes that societies have defined almost everything to be a valuable input at one time or another.

> Justice has been viewed as consisting in the treatment of all people:
> 1. As equals.
> 2. So that they have an equal opportunity to compete without external favoritism or discrimination.

---

*From *The Psychology of Power,* by Ronald V. Sampson. Copyright © 1965 by Ronald V. Sampson. Reprinted by permission of Pantheon Books, a Division of Random House, Inc.

3. According to their ability.
4. According to their efforts.
5. According to their accomplishments.
6. According to their needs.
7. According to the supply and demand of the market place.
8. According to the requirements of the common good.
9. According to the principle of reciprocity. (p. 4)

These reviews make it evident that somewhere, sometime, people have assumed that almost *any* input legitimately entitled its possessor to reward. Regardless of which inputs a society believes are relevant in a given situation, the same theoretical framework, Equity theory, predicts that men will feel equitably or inequitably treated and how they will respond to their treatment.

Equity and Social Justice

Since most of us have been socialized in American values, we naturally assume the investments that Americans deem relevant are somehow the only legitimate, or even possible inputs. It is difficult for us to believe that "capital" and "hard work" aren't *really* inputs in every society, or to believe that someday "good guitar playing" could be a crucial input in the business world. Potentially, society can define *anything*—bravery, cowardice, humility, arrogance, beauty, or ugliness—as a valuable input. In fact, great diversity already exists. In traditional societies, a distinguished lineage entitled one to esteem. In revolutionary societies, the same lineage entitles one to disdain—or assassination.

If that is the case, a practical question naturally occurs to us. Who gets to decide whether equality or proportionality prevails? If

DOONESBURY   **by Garry Trudeau**

FIGURE 7.2. (Copyright 1975, G. B. Trudeau/Distributed by Universal Press Syndicate. Reprinted by permission.)

proportionality prevails, who gets to decide whether such inputs as good breeding, skin color, sex, or tap dancing ability prevail? Equity theory's Proposition II states: *Groups can maximize collective reward by evolving accepted systems for "equitably" apportioning rewards and costs among members. Thus, members will evolve such systems of equity and will attempt to induce members to accept and adhere to these systems.* Equity does not explain how society's members make that decision. But we can speculate. In general, the following scenario seems to make the most intuitive sense.

> In a society, members have a vested interest in evolving some system for allocating the community's social and material goods.
>
> Every member also has a vested interest in persuading others that the inputs he happens to possess are relevant and important ones, and that he thus is entitled to maximum reward.
>
> The more powerful an individual or coalition of individuals is, the more successful it will be in (1) capturing the lion's share of community goods, and (2) persuading others to acknowledge the equitableness of the unbalanced allocation.
>
> Over time, the powerful who control community resources will evolve a social philosophy to buttress their right to monopolize community goods. And, over time, the entire community will come to accept this justification of the status quo.
>
> So long as society's distribution of power remains the same, members will accept the existing standard of equity. If marked shifts in the distribution of power occur, however, the emerging groups will be motivated to push for a new, more profitable, definition of equity.

Is there any compelling evidence in support of this scenario? No. Almost no researchers have experimentally investigated the impact of power on social justice. What we can do, however, is to review the sparse evidence of relevance to each of the five contentions.

In a society, members have a vested interest in evolving some system for allocating the community's social and material goods. In chapter 2, "The Heart of Equity Theory," we pointed out that Equity theory's first and most basic proposition is "man is selfish." The belief that man is selfish does not imply, however, that man is totally unrestrained in his pursuit of material benefits. Hobbes (1588–1679) pointed out that if men were unregulated in their pursuit of pleasure, the result would be an unprofitable "war of all against all." Locke (1632–1704) observed that social associations not only check the "Warre of all" but allow men to secure positive benefits as well. In any case, all existing societies have found it profitable to evolve some rough guidelines for allocating community resources.

Every member also has a vested interest in persuading others that the inputs he happens to possess are relevant and important ones, and that he thus is entitled to maximum reward. A wide range of theorists have observed that men's assessments of "justice" are heavily colored by their own self-interest. For example, Aristotle (translated in Ross, 1966) cynically notes:

> Awards should be "according to merit"; for all men agree that what is just in distribution must be according to merit in some sense, though they do not all specify the same sort of merit, but democrats identify it with that status of freemen, supporters of oligarchy with wealth (or with noble birth), and supporters of aristocracy with excellence. (p. 1131[a])

There is recent evidence in support of Aristotle's contention. McGinn (1973) argues that in almost any situation there is some ambiguity as to what is "equitable." For example, in a work situation, should effort count? Or only quality of performance? Should one's previous experiences with an individual be taken into account? Or should each new encounter be treated separately? McGinn proposes that in ambiguous situations, participants will scan the possible alternatives and select those "rules" that give them the biggest "equitable" outcomes.

Support for McGinn's contention comes from a variety of research.[14] For example, Komorita and Chertkoff propose that when coalition members can legitimately divide resources equally or proportionately, self-interest will shape their perception and advocacy of equity. They state:

Assumption 3: A person strong in resources is more likely to expect and advocate the parity norm as the basis for reward division, while a person weak

THE WIZARD OF ID   by Brant parker and Johnny hart

FIGURE 7.3. (*The Wizard of Id* by permission of Johnny Hart and Field Enterprises, Inc.)

in resources is more likely to expect and advocate the equality norm.[15] (p. 152)

In the same vein, Karsh and Cole (1968) report that older Japanese workers prefer traditional pay systems (which pay workers on the basis of seniority)—a system that benefits *them*. In contrast, younger workers favor a system that rewards individual productivity rather than seniority and age. Obviously, such a modern system benefits *them*.

The more powerful an individual or coalition of individuals is, the more successful it will be in (1) capturing the lion's share of community goods, and (2) persuading others to acknowledge the equitableness of the unbalanced allocation.

The definition of power: Tawney (1939) defines *power* as:

> The capacity of an individual, or group of individuals, to modify the conduct of other individuals or groups in the manner which he desires, and to prevent his own conduct [*sic*] being modified in the manner in which he does not. (p. 229)

Basically, Tawney suggests (and we agree) that there are only two ways a person can induce others to do the things he wants: he can promise to reward them if they comply and threaten to punish them if they do not.

People are very inventive. Over time, humans have found a myriad of ways to exercise power; to reward, withhold reward, or punish others in order to get what they want. Politicians offer political patronage, mothers proffer love, courtesans offer sex, teachers offer good grades, and bosses offer bonuses for compliance. Truckers park their rigs, Lysistrata withholds affection, children refuse to budge until they're placated, shrews make sarcastic comments, bullies beat their wives, generals wield atomic warheads to induce others to go along. Sages use knowledge, con men use cunning, orators use persuasive power, lawyers remind others of their commitments.

Deutsch (1974) points out that the power to embarrass is another potent source of power. Alinsky (1971), a master at inventing such tactics, illustrates with the following hypothetical example:

> Imagine the scene in the U.S. Courtroom in Chicago's recent conspiracy trial of the seven if the defendants and counsel had anally trumpeted their contempt for Judge Hoffman and the system. What could Judge Hoffman, the bailiffs, or anyone else do? Would the judge have found them in contempt for farting? Here was a tactic for which there was no legal precedent. The press reaction would have stunk up the judge for the rest of time.

Other tactics of embarrassment and ridicule include picketing slum landlords, key stockholders and management personnel of recalcitrant firms, and other such wielders of power in situations which are embarrassing to them— e.g., at their homes, at their churches or synagogues, at their social clubs. (p. 141)

Some people are adept at turning weakness into power. The "helpless" maiden aunt threatened to commit suicide if her relatives didn't toe the mark. The wild-eyed, drunken teenager's irrationality scares his partner in a game of "Chicken."

And, if an individual is not strong enough to get the things he wants, he may form a coalition with like-minded individuals in order to do better.[16]

Evidence that the powerful can "capture the lion's share" of community goods: If we accept Tawney's general definition of power, our contention that, "The more powerful an individual or coalition of individuals is, the more successful it will be in (1) capturing the lion's share of community goods" necessarily follows. However, it is of interest to document that individuals who possess the specific bases of power we have enumerated *do* get a larger share of community goods than their fellows.

Collins and Guetzkow (1964) conclude, on the basis of a review of correlational evidence: (1) "High power persons will be successful in a larger percentage of the influence attempts which they do make than low power persons."[17] (2) "High power persons will be less affected by the efforts of others to influence them."[18]

There is also abundant laboratory evidence that powerful people and powerful coalitions can command a relatively large share of community goods, and existing power models can make reasonable predictions as to the impact that various degrees, and various distributions, of power will have on a person's or group's bargaining success.[19]

Can the powerful persuade their rivals that they deserve the lion's share of goods? The preceding theory and data document that the powerful can force others to cede a large share of the community's social and material goods to them. But can they persuade their rivals that they deserve the lion's share of goods? Unfortunately, there is no evidence in direct support of the contention that:

POWER

ability to capture the lion's share of community goods, and

ability to persuade others to acknowledge the equitableness of the unbalanced allocation.

219

However, there is substantial evidence that:

POWER ⟶ *ability to capture the lion's share of community goods*

↓

ability to persuade others to acknowledge the equitableness of the unbalanced allocation.

Theorists have observed that people possess an intense need to perceive this as a fair and equitable world; a world where both the enormously benefited and the underbenefited deserve their fates. For example, Lerner (1971a) has observed that even the most impartial of observers possess an intense desire to believe that people get what they deserve and deserve what they get. In an impressive body of research, he documents the eagerness of observers to convince themselves that exploiters deserve their excessive benefits and victims deserve their unwarranted suffering.[20]

The Assembly in New England in the 1640s passed a series of resolutions on the Indian question:

1. The Earth is the Lord's and the fullness thereof.   Voted.
2. The Lord may give the Earth or any part of it to his chosen people. Voted.
3. We are his chosen people.   Voted.

(Reported in Mason, 1971, p. 242)

Equity researchers have documented that, under the right conditions, *both* "exploiters" and their victims tend to be capable of convincing themselves that the most unbalanced of the most inequitable of exchanges is, in fact, perfectly fair.[21]

Over time, the powerful persons who control community resources will evolve a social philosophy to buttress their right to monopolize community goods. And, over time, the entire community will come to accept this justification of the status quo. Perhaps, among theorists, Karl Marx (1818–1883) (reprinted in 1947) has most eloquently argued that there is an inevitable connection between power, monopoly of community resources, and the evolution of a justifying philosophy. He notes:

> The ideas of the *ruling* class are in every epoch the ruling ideas: i.e., the class, which is the ruling material force of society, is at the same time its ruling intellectual force. The class which has the means of material production at its disposal, has control at the same time over the means of mental production, so that thereby, generally speaking, the ideas of those who lack the means of mental production are subject to it.

The individuals composing the ruling class . . . rule also as thinkers, as producers of ideas, and regulate the production and distribution of the ideas of the epoch. For instance, in an age and in a country where royal power, aristocracy and bourgeoisie are contending for mastery and where, therefore, mastery is shared, the doctrine of the separation of powers proves to be the dominant idea and is expressed as an "eternal law."

. . . during the time that the aristocracy was dominant, the concepts honour, loyalty, etc., were dominant, during the dominance of the bourgeoisie the concepts freedom, equality, etc. . . .

For each new class which puts itself in the place of one ruling before it, is compelled, merely in order to carry through its aim, to represent its interest as common interest of all the members of society, put in an ideal form; it will give its ideas the form of universality, and represent them as the only rational, universally valid ones. (pp. 39–41)

More recently, Kipnis (1972 *a,b*) has been fascinated by the impact of power on men's social relations and social philosophy. Kipnis argues that as soon as men acquire power, they become tempted to use that power to enrich themselves; inevitably they succumb to temptation. Power thus leads to corruption of several sorts. According to Kipnis, the powerful (1) monopolize community goods, (2) are tempted to develop an exploitative morality (they soon conclude that they are exempt from ordinary morality), (3) develop an exalted and vain view of their own worth, (4) become alienated from their fellow man, and (5) come to despise him. In a series of laboratory experiments, Kipnis (1972) amasses weak evidence in support of the sequence he proposes.

So long as society's distribution of power remains the same, members will accept the existing standard of equity. If marked shifts in the distribution of power occur, however, the emerging groups will be motivated to push for a new, more profitable, definition of equity. Researchers have investigated the effects of various distributions of power on the development of contractual norms (i.e., on the definitions of "social justice" groups develop).[22]

Some theorists have argued that social upheaval, in and of itself, motivates citizens to take a close look at their power position and to wonder whether they can improve their lot. For example, they argue that during both unusually good times or major depressions, citizens come to realize that "traditionally valued inputs" are not inevitably linked to "appropriate outcomes." During such chaotic times, the naked power basis underlying society's laboriously articulated philosophy of social justice often becomes evident. It becomes painfully evident that people are receiving far more or far less than they deserve. Such an observation may well stimulate people to wonder why things shouldn't be reformed still further. Why shouldn't Equity be defined in a way that is more beneficial to them?

Theorists in a wide variety of periods have observed the connection between social change and social reform.[23] For example, Rousseau (1712–1778) (reprinted in 1913) argues:

> Most peoples, like most men, are docile only in youth; as they grow old they become incorrigible. When once customs have become established and prejudices inveterate, it is dangerous and useless to attempt their reformation. . .
>
> There are indeed times in the history of States when, just as some kinds of illness turn men's heads and make them forget the past, periods of violence and revolutions do to peoples what these crises do to individuals: horror of the past takes the place of forgetfulness, and the State, set on fire by civil wars, is born again, so to speak, from its ashes, and takes on anew, fresh from the jaws of death, the vigour of youth. Such were Sparta at the time of Lycergus, Rome after the Tarquins, and, in modern times, Holland and Switzerland after the explusion of the tyrants. . . . But such events are rare. (p. 39)

Mason (1971) cites more contemporary examples in which political revolutions have undermined traditional definitions of social justice.[24]

Concluding Comments: The Impact of Power on Social Justice

> It is a truism that political philosophy has traditionally concerned itself with the search for some kind of moral justification for the power and coercion of governments. (Sampson, 1968, p. 140)

If the scenario we have sketched is accurate, it has two unsettling implications for the social reformer.

1. Social reformers naturally assume that they stand somewhat outside of their own society. They feel they possess a special sensitivity for, and special willingness to work toward, universal justice. The preceding dismal scenario, however, suggests that reformers, like their fellows, are likely to be trapped by the status quo. Rather than having a special sensitivity for universal social justice, they may simply possess a special sensitivity to the pressures of emerging groups for "fairer" treatment.

One generation of reformers' biases often become startlingly evident in the next generation, when the next generation of reformers encounters yet another power balance. The masses of serfs, merchants, second sons, migrant workers, blacks, women, middle Americans, youths, or elderly now assert *their* claims. The new generation of reformers realizes that the principles of justice that their fathers found so compelling were, in fact, unduly influenced by the prevailing power balances. They, too, try to articulate an objective system of universal justice. They, too, end up rationalizing the status quo.

We would simply suggest that we inveterate social reformers must acquire some humility, and admit that we are all inexorably shaped by our society. Today, we can easily feel appalled at the way nobles exploited their serfs, slaveowners exploited their slaves, or men exploited their women. But these landowners, slaveowners, and male chauvinists were not fundamentally different people than we are; they were simply responding to different pressures, and a different status quo. The prevailing power balances, then, surely affect even the most aloof reformer's conception of social justice.

2. Our scenario also suggests that even if a social reformer did transcend his society, and propose an objective theory of social justice, it would have very little chance of being accepted.

Let us consider an example: John Stewart Mill (reprinted in 1971) observed that at one time, sex and physical power determined men's outcomes:

> People are not aware of how entirely, in former ages, the law of superior strength was the rule of life; how publicly and openly it was avowed, I did not say cynically or shamelessly—for these words imply a feeling that there was something in it to be ashamed of, and no such notion could find a place in the faculties of any person in those ages, except a philosopher or a saint. (p. 22)

In 1869, Mill, who was a generation ahead of many other social philosophers, argued that such inputs as sex, race, and physical strength should not be determinants of one's social opportunities. Instead, such inputs as intelligence, industry, and interest should determine one's outcomes. Mill's advanced vision was not accepted by his contemporaries. For example, Freud was an enthusiastic admirer of Mill's. Yet, Sampson (1968) wryly notes:

> The irony could hardly be greater. Mill is singled out as the man above all others of his epoch who succeeded in surmounting contemporary prejudices; and then rebuked for his supreme achievement in unmasking the most

disastrous of prejudices to which Freud succeeded in clinging his life long.* (p. 50)

What Sampson (1968) is referring to is Freud's criticism of Mill:

On the other hand, . . . he lacked in many matters the sense of the absurd; for example, in that of female emancipation and in the woman's question altogether. I recollect that in the essay I translated a prominent argument was that a married woman could earn as much as her husband. We surely agree that the management of a house, the care and bringing up of children, demands the whole of a human being and almost excludes any earning, even if a simplified household relieve her of dusting, cleaning, cooking etc. He had simply forgotten all that, like everything else concerning the relationship between the sexes. That is altogether a point with Mill where one simply cannot find him human. His autobiography is so prudish or so ethereal that one could never gather from it that human beings consist of men and women and that this distinction is the most significant one that exists. In his whole presentation it never emerges that women are different beings—we will not say lesser, rather the opposite—from men. He finds the suppression of women an analogy to that of negroes. Any girl, even without a suffrage or legal competence, whose hand a man kisses and for whose love he is prepared to dare all, could have set him right. It is really a still-born thought to send women into the struggle for existence exactly as men. If, for instance, I imagined my gentle sweet girl as a competitor it would only end in my telling her, as I did seventeen months ago, that I am fond of her and that I implore her to withdraw from the strife into the calm uncompetitive activity of my home. It is possible that changes in upbringing may suppress all a woman's tender attributes, needful of protection and yet so victorious, and that she can then earn a livelihood like men. It is also possible that in such an event one would not be justified in mourning the passing away of the most delightful thing the world can offer us—our ideal of womanhood. I believe that all reforming action in law and education would break down in front of the fact that, long before the age at which a man can earn a position in society, Nature has determined woman's destiny through beauty, charm and sweetness. Law and custom have much to give women that has been withheld from them, but the position of women will surely be what it is: in youth an adored darling and in mature years a loved wife.** (pp. 49–50)

Other commentators assailed Mill's equalitarian views with equal bitterness.[25]

In the time honored tradition, both the beneficiaries and the victims of the status quo joined in defending the status quo. Even those

---

*From *The Psychology of Power,* by Ronald V. Sampson. Copyright © 1965 by Ronald V. Sampson. Reprinted by permission of Pantheon Books, a Division of Random House, Inc.

**From E. Jones, *Sigmund Freud: Life and Work,* Vol. 1 (New York: Basic Books, 1960), pp. 192–193.

FIGURE 7.4. "... I Implore Her to Withdraw from the Strife into the Calm Uncompetitive Activity of My Home."

women who were chaffing most at society's restrictions, insisted that although a "slight adjustment" in the way resources were allocated was clearly in order, major revisions were, of course, unthinkable. Thus, Caroline Norton[26] a tireless campaigner for the Infant Custody Bill of 1839, could not bring herself to support general rights for women. She wrote:

> The wild and stupid theories advanced by a few women, of "equal rights" and "equal intelligence," are not the opinions of their sex. I, for one (I, with

225

millions more), believe in the natural superiority of man, as I do in the existence of a God. The natural position of woman is inferiority to man. Amen! That is a thing of God's appointing, not of man's devising. I believe it sincerely, as a part of my religion. I never pretended to the wild and ridiculous doctrine of equality. (pp. 149–150)

Mill (1806–1873) would not have been surprised at this. In *On the Subjection of Women*[27] he observed:

But was there any domination which did not appear natural to those who possessed it? There was a time when the division of mankind into two classes, a small one of masters and a numerous one of slaves, appeared, even to the most cultivated minds, to be natural, and the only natural, condition of the human race. (p. 27)

It hardly seemed less so to the class held in subjection. The emancipated serfs and burgesses, even in their most vigorous struggles, never made any pretension to a share of authority; they only demanded more or less as limitation to the power of tyrannising over them. So true is it that unnatural generally means only uncustomary, and everything which is usual appears natural. The subjection of women to men being a universal custom, any departure from it quite naturally appears unnatural. (p. 28)

In our time, James Baldwin (1955) has seconded Mill's observation:

It is the peculiar triumph of society—and its loss—that it is able to convince those people to whom it has given inferior status of the reality of this decree. (p. 20)

Recent experimental evidence, of course, has supported Mill's and Baldwin's contention. Experimental evidence that both the over-benefited and the underbenefited tend to accept their fortuitous position comes from a fascinating study by Stephenson and White (1970).

They invited ten-year-old boys to participate in a miniature car racing game and divided them into privileged and deprived groups. The privileged group was allowed to race the cars all of the time. The deprived group was only allowed to pick up the cars when they skidded off the track. The authors were interested in the effect that providing a fairly coherent justification versus providing no justification for the boys' status discrepancy would have on the boy's reactions to injustice. In the Justification conditions, the boys were told that the boy who had made up the best new words from the phrase "the racing cars" had been chosen to do the racing. In the control groups, boys were told a coin flip had determined which boy raced and which boy picked up. In the No-justification condition, boys were told that the experimenter had intended to allow the boy who made up the best words to race the cars, but by mistake had chosen the boy who had done the worst. As the author expected, both the overprivileged and the exploited boys accepted the justification.

More importantly, the authors were interested in the extent to which justified versus unjustified privilege and deprivation would perpetuate itself. After the boys had played with the cars (or picked them up), the experimenter asked them to take a motor racing quiz. This quiz, by design, was impossibly difficult. The boys knew that a score of six out of eight would earn them a prize (a model car). Since the boys were asked to score their own questions from an answer sheet, cheating was very easy. Overprivileged boys had been given a phony rationale for their privileged position. They were more likely to cheat to maintain it than were boys who did not possess this convenient rationale. Similarly, the deprived boys, when they had some rationale for their deprivation, were less likely to cheat to gain a toy than when they did not.

If the preceding scenario is correct, the message seems clear. Logic is a good ally for the social reformer; power is a better one. There seems to be little chance that the majority will recognize the claims of exploited minorities, unless these minorities can amass sufficient power to enforce their demands for equal treatment. Minority members can (and have) used a variety of techniques to make majority members realize that sharing with them is a more profitable strategy than hoarding. They can use praise, passive resistance, sabotage, or moral opprobrium or approbation. But unless the minority has some real power to affect the outcomes of the majority, their case seems hopeless. The powerful can probably always generate a philosophy to satisfactorally justify the most unequal of outcomes.

HOW DOES A SCRUTINEER ASSESS
PARTICIPANTS' OUTCOMES FROM A RELATIONSHIP

4.

$$\frac{(O_A - I_A)}{(|I_A|)^{k_A}} = \frac{(O_B - I_B)}{(|I_B|)^{k_B}}$$

Our wants and pleasures have their origin in society; we therefore measure them in relation to society; we do not measure them in relation to the objects which serve for their gratification. Since they are of a social nature, they are of a relative nature. (Marx, 1933 p. 33)

Equity theory deals with individuals' *perceptions* of reality. According to Equity theory, Person *A* or *B's* outcomes are "the positive and negative consequences that a scrutineer *perceives* a participant has received in the course of his relationship with another."

Equity theory does not attempt to specify all the things that a scrutineer might consider to be rewarding or punishing. Nor does the theory attempt to predict how highly a given scrutineer will rate a given set of rewards and punishments. One scrutineer may rate Outcomes ($X + Y - Z$) at +5,000. Another may rate the very same Outcomes at −5,000. The theory simply states that *once we know how the scrutineer perceives A and B's outcomes*, we can proceed to make predictions.

Although Equity researchers have not been motivated to tackle the knotty questions (What determines *what* individuals value? What determines *how much* they value these things?), other social psychologists have been.

What Do Men Value?

Theorists such as McDougall (1908), Murray (1938), and Maslow (1970), have tried to compile definitive lists of universal human needs. Presumably, anything that satisfied these primitive needs could be classified as reward; anything that thwarted them as punishment (or cost).

Of course, few theorists were optimistic enough to think they could conceive of a list of things that all people, under all circumstances, at all times would find rewarding or punishing. They did hope, however, that they could enumerate the things that appear to be "transituational reinforcers or punishers"; things that most men, in most circumstances, at most times find rewarding or punishing.

McDougall (1908) was the first to try to compile a list of the "principle instincts of man." Later, Murray (1938) offered a more comprehensive taxonomy of human *viscerogenic* and *psychogenic* needs:

Viscerogenic Needs

1. n Air
2. n Water
3. n Food
4. n Sex
5. n Lactation
6. n Urination
7. n Defecation
8. n Harmavoidance
9. n Noxavoidance[28]

10. n   Heatavoidance
11. n   Coldavoidance[29]
12. n   Sentience[30]

Psychogenic Needs

1. n   Acquisition
2. n   Conservance
3. n   Order
4. n   Retention
5. n   Construction
6. n   Superiority
7. n   Inviolacy
8. n   Dominance
9. n   Deference
10. n   Similance
11. n   Autonomy
12. n   Contrarience
13. n   Aggression
14. n   Abasement
15. n   Blamavoidance
16. n   Affiliation
17. n   Rejection
18. n   Nurturance
19. n   Succorance
20. n   Play
21. n   Cognizance
22. n   Exposition

Maslow (1970) argued that man's needs are arranged in a hierarchy. An individual's first concern must be to satisfy the needs lower in the hierarchy. Only when these prepotent needs are satisfied, can he begin to focus on those needs higher in the hierarchy:

1. *Physiological needs:* These are the most prepotent of all needs; they must be satisfied if the person is to function. This category includes the need for food, water, air, sleep, rest, activity, and stimulation.
2. *The safety needs:* Once the physiological needs are satisfied, the safety needs emerge. These include the need for safety from physical harm, for security, for freedom from fear, for structure and order, and for stability.
3. *The belongingness and love needs* are the next to emerge. These include the need to have satisfying relationships with parents, peers, and neighbors.
4. *The esteem needs:* Individuals possess two types of esteem needs. First, they need self-esteem and self-respect; they need to have a high and stable evaluation of themselves. Second, people need to

have esteem and recognition, appreciation, or respect from other people.

5. *The need for self-actualization:* The person needs to do "what he is uniquely fitted for. . . . A musician must make music, an artist must paint, a poet must write, if he is to be ultimately at peace with himself." (p. 46)

McDougall's, Murray's, or Maslow's taxonomies give us some inkling of what things people generally classify as rewarding or punishing. They give us some idea of the myriad of rewards or punishments that scrutineers might perceive Persons *A* and *B* are receiving in their relationship.

What determines how highly a scrutineer values these patterned rewards and punishments?

How Much Do Men Value Various Specific Rewards and Punishments?

Why do some men rate a specific outcome (say $X + Y - Z$) as "extremely good" (+5,000), while other men rate the same outcome as "only slightly good" (+10)?

Classical theory and research gives us some glimmerings as to the factors that determine how highly a scrutineer will evaluate various objective outcomes.

Thibaut and Kelley (1959) point out that individuals vary startlingly in how positively or negatively they rate the same material outcome. According to these authors, individuals possess two different standards.

Comparison Level (CL): First, everyone possesses a *Comparison Level* (or *CL*). Everyone possesses some sort of standard (the *CL*) as to what he expects from a relationship. What determines how much an individual expects from a relationship? According to the authors:

> The location of *CL* on the person's scale of outcomes will be influenced by all the outcomes known to the member, either by direct experience or symbolically. It may be taken to be some modal or average value of all known outcomes, each outcome weighted by its "salience," or strength of instigation, which depends, for example, on the recency of experiencing the outcome and the occurrence of stimuli which serve as reminders of these outcomes. Because these factors are likely to be absent or weak in the case of relationships and interactions that are unattainable, the latter will ordinarily have little weight in determining the location of *CL*. (p. 21)
>
> The comparison level depends in general upon the outcomes which are

salient (actively stimulating or vividly recalled) at any given time. If we assume that all the recently experienced outcomes are salient, then the better they have been, the higher the *CL* and the less the satisfaction with any given level. Thus *CL* tends to move to the level of outcomes currently being attained. In other words, the person adapts to the presently experienced levels: after a shift upward to a new level, the once longed for outcomes gradually lose their attractiveness; after a downward shift to a new lower level, the disappointment gradually wears off and the once dreaded outcomes become accepted.* (pp. 97–98)

Thibaut and Kelley's contention that a scrutineer's evaluation of a given outcome will be shaped by his *CL* is a compelling one.[31]

CL_{alt} : According to Thibaut and Kelley, individuals possess a second important standard—the *Comparison Level for Alternatives* (or CL_{alt}). This is the standard that the person uses in deciding whether or not to remain in a relationship.

The authors define CL_{alt} as follows:

CL_{alt} can be defined informally as the lowest level of outcomes a member will accept in the light of available alternative opportunities. It follows from this definition that as soon as the outcomes drop below CL_{alt} the member will leave the relationship. The height of the CL_{alt} will depend mainly on the quality of the best of the members' available alternatives, that is, the reward-cost positions experienced or believed to exist in the most satisfactory of the other available relationships.

As in the case of *CL*, the outcomes that determine the location of CL_{alt} will be weighted by their *salience* (how strongly they are instigated). Unlikely outcomes in the alternative relationship will usually have little weight in fixing the location of CL_{alt} because, again, the salience of such outcomes will ordinarily be rather low. (pp. 21–22)

Like Thibaut and Kelley, Equity theorists have predicted, and found, that individuals *do* doggedly pursue the most rewarding relationships available and do abandon those below their CL_{alt}.[32] Thibaut and Kelley go one step further; they provide a precise rule for predicting *exactly* when an individual will abandon a relationship.

The theorizing of McDougall (1908), Murray (1938), Maslow (1970), and Thibaut and Kelley (1959), provide some useful guidelines as to the things scrutineers may find rewarding or punishing, and the factors that determine how highly scrutineers will value various specific rewards and punishments. However, at this point in time our knowledge is limited; it is still the case that if one wishes to ascertain (1) the scrutineer's perception of A and B's outcomes, and (2) how highly the scrutineer evaluates these outcomes, the best strategy is still to ask him.

HOW CAN AN INVESTIGATOR ASSESS
PARTICIPANTS' PERCEPTIONS OF
EQUITY/INEQUITY?

We have pointed out that "Equity is in the eye of the beholder" and that every scrutineer will have his own ideas as to whether or not a relationship is equitable. Given such chaos, how can we ever hope to use the Equity formula? How can we ever hope to anticipate how a scrutineer will evaluate A and B's contributions to a relationship, their outcomes from a relationship, and the equitableness of a relationship? These measurement problems turn out to be far simpler than one would anticipate.

Measurement in Experimental Research

The Equity experimenter can only test his hypothesis if he knows how subjects perceive the experimental situation. Equity experimenters have used two techniques to insure that they know how their subjects perceive inputs, outcomes, and equity/inequity.

Interviewing Subjects.   Sometimes experimenters interview the subjects or the subjects' peers to find out how they perceive things. The investigator painstakingly describes the experimental setting. Then he asks subjects (1) to enumerate all of the inputs they think are relevant in such settings and their value, (2) how they think they, and their partners, "stack up" on these traits, and finally (3) to rate the value of various possible outcomes. Once the experimenter possesses these data, he can use the Equity formula to calculate the equitableness/in-equitableness of the experimental relationship for that subject. Of course, if all subjects agree in their ratings of inputs, outcomes, and equity/inequity, the average subject's perceptions can be used to cal-culate the equitableness of the experimental relationship.

Relying on Cultural Uniformities.   The experimenter may follow a simpler procedure. He can carefully devise a situation that is so clear-cut that everyone perceives things the same way.

In every society, there are some cultural norms and standards that are so basic everyone simply takes them for granted. Thus, Equity experimenters usually can easily devise a situation that virtually all subjects perceive in the same way. (For example, probably all students would agree that if two equally talented students work equally hard, and do an equally good job, they are entitled to equal salaries. They would also probably agree that if one of the students works twice as hard as the other, and thus does twice as good a job, he is entitled to twice the salary.) Most experimenters have chosen to test their hypotheses in such straightforward settings.

If an experimenter relies on the "obviousness" of the setting, opponents may, of course, charge that his assumptions were wrong. For example, they could charge that, for some reason, students did not perceive talent, hard work, and productivity to be positive inputs, or that they did not perceive money to be a reward. When a critic feels that a rival experimenter's assumptions are incorrect, a simple strategy is available. He has only to check subjects' perceptions of the relevance and value of the presumably valuable inputs and outcomes to determine whether the experimenters' assumptions were correct, or whether his criticisms are.[33]

Measurement in Natural Settings

Some people have assumed that although Equity theory can easily be tested in experimental settings, it is impossible to apply it in natural ones. They have pointed out that a staggering number of inputs and outcomes might be involved in any real, ongoing relationship. Thus, they conclude, Equity calculations are impossible in natural settings.

For example, some critics have assumed that a researcher could assess a scrutineer's perception of A's and B's inputs and outcomes in only one way: first, the interviewer would have to compile an exhaustive list of A's and B's potential inputs to their relationship. Then the interviewer would have to find out (1) which inputs the scrutineer thought were relevant, (2) how valuable an asset (or liability) he thought each potential was, (3) how much Persons A and B contributed of each relevant input. Then the interviewer could proceed to compute I_A and I_B. He would then have to repeat the entire process to secure an index of A and B's outcomes. Since such a laborious procedure is obviously impractical, such critics have assumed that the Equity formula can not really be used in natural settings.

Of course, it is totally unnecessary to calculate the equitableness of a natural relationship via such a complicated procedure. Equity researchers have used far simpler procedures for finding out how much scrutineers think Persons *A* and *B* are contributing to their relationship, what they are getting out of it, and whether their relationship is equitable or inequitable.[34]

For example, Equity researchers have used the following procedures to ascertain how Participants *A* and *B* perceive their own intimate relationships.

The Walster (1977) Global Measures: Participants' Perceptions of Inputs, Outcomes, and Equity/Inequity. Recently, Smith[35] interviewed newlyweds. He attempted to measure couples' perceptions of their own and their partners' inputs, outcomes, and equity/inequity in a straightforward way.

Smith began his interview by briefly explaining to the newlyweds what he meant by inputs and outcomes:

[Inputs] : People often differ markedly in how much they *contribute to* a marriage. For example, in one marriage the wife may contribute an enormous amount to her marriage. She may be beautiful, intelligent, personable, do all the housework, take care of the children, *and* work outside the home. In other marriages, the wife may contribute very little to the relationship.

[Outcomes] : People may also differ in how much they get *out* of their marriages. For example, one wife may feel she gets a great deal out of her marriage. She may get to sleep late in the morning, enjoy her children when she wants to . . . and delegate the child care to hired help when she does not, spend her afternoon touring art galleries, shopping or just doing what she pleases, etc. Another wife may feel she gets very little out of her marriage. She may be alone a good deal of the time, have little money to spend, and have no household help . . . We are interested in *your* marriage.*

Assessing Perceived Equity/Inequity: After explaining to newlyweds what inputs and outcomes are, Smith then asked the newlyweds to make a global estimate of *their own* and *their partner's* inputs and outcomes.

Assessing Inputs. All things considered, how would you describe your contributions to your relationship? (Circle the correct response.)

+4. My contributions are extremely positive.
+3. My contributions are very positive.
+2. My contributions are moderately positive.

---

*Reprinted by permission of David J. Smith.

+1. My contributions are slightly positive.
−1. My contributions are slightly negative.
−2. My contributions are moderately negative.
−3. My contributions are very negative.
−4. My contributions are extremely negative.

All things considered, how would you describe your partner's contributions to your relationship?

+4. My partner's contributions are extremely positive.
+3. My partner's contributions are very positive.
+2. My partner's contributions are moderately positive.
+1. My partner's contributions are slightly positive.
−1. My partner's contributions are slightly negative.
−2. My partner's contributions are moderately negative.
−3. My partner's contributions are very negative.
−4. My partner's contributions are extremely negative.

Assessing Outcomes. All things considered, how would you describe your *outcomes* from your relationship?

+4. My outcomes are extremely positive.
+3. My outcomes are very positive.
+2. My outcomes are moderately positive.
+1. My outcomes are slightly positive.
−1. My outcomes are slightly negative.
−2. My outcomes are moderately negative.
−3. My outcomes are very negative.
−4. My outcomes are extremely negative.

All things considered, how would you describe your partner's outcomes from your relationship?

+4. My partner's outcomes are extremely positive.
+3. My partner's outcomes are very positive.
+2. My partner's outcomes are moderately positive.
+1. My partner's outcomes are slightly positive.
−1. My partner's outcomes are slightly negative.
−2. My partner's outcomes are moderately negative.
−3. My partner's outcomes are very negative.
−4. My partner's outcomes are extremely negative.

Assessing Participants' Perceptions of Equity/Inequity. Once Smith had assessed the newlyweds' perceptions of their own and their partner's inputs and outcomes, he could calculate how husbands and wives rated the equity/inequity of the marriage. Smith simply had to substitute the newlyweds' ratings of their own and their partners' inputs and outcomes in the Equity formula:

Husband's perception of Equity:

$$\frac{(O_H - I_H)}{(|I_H|)^{k_H}} - \frac{(O_W - I_W)}{(|I_W|)^{k_W}} \qquad {}_{36}$$

Wife's perception of Equity:

$$\frac{(O_W - I_W)}{(|I_W|)^{k_W}} - \frac{(O_H - I_H)}{(|I_H|)^{k_H}} \qquad {}_{37}$$

The respondent was classified as Underbenefited if his Relative Gains fell short of his partner's. He was classified as Equitably Treated if his Relative Gains were equal to his partner's. He was classified as Overbenefited if his Relative Gains exceeded his partner's.

The Traupmann-Utne-Walster (1977) Scales: Participants' Perceptions of Inputs, Outcomes, and Equity/Inequity. Traupmann and Utne [38] used quite a different strategy for measuring couples' perceptions of what they put into, and what they get out of, their relationship. Traupmann and Utne began by explaining:

> We're interested in the give-and-take that goes on in marriage. We're going to ask you questions about the kinds of things you *put into* your marriage, and the kinds of things you see yourself *getting out* of it.
>
> Now, we know that most people don't ordinarily keep careful track of each contribution they make to their marriage, each contribution their partner makes, and the various benefits and frustrations they both derive from it. Pulling a relationship apart into the separate behaviors that make it up is not something most of us usually do. But in order for us to get some idea of what goes on in early marital relationships, we have to ask you and the other people we're interviewing to *spell out* some of the give-and-take that naturally occurs.
>
> Let me explain two terms we're going to be using. They are *contributions* to marriage and *outcomes* from marriage.
>
> *Contributions.* These are the personal characteristics and behaviors that people *put into* their marriage. Contributions can be *positive* or *negative*. For example, the things that people give in relationships can be very positive like giving understanding or love. But a person's contributions to a relationship also can be negative, like not helping with the household chores, or being too critical.
>
> *Outcomes.* Outcomes are the things people get as a consequence of being married. Just as with contributions, outcomes can be positive or negative,

good or bad. For example, from your marriage you may get a lot of appreciation for your efforts, a good outcome. A bad outcome could be that now that you're married you have less money to spend on things just for you.

It is just these things, contributions and outcomes, that we'll be talking about for the next few minutes.

Assessing Inputs. Then they showed newlyweds a list of twenty-two contributions people can make to a marriage:

PERSONAL CONTRIBUTIONS

Social Grace
  1. Social Graces: Being sociable, friendly, relaxed in social settings.
Intellect
  2. Intelligence: Being an intelligent, informed person.
Appearance
  3. Physical Attractiveness: Being a physically attractive person.
  4. Concern for Physical Appearance and Health: Taking care of your physical appearance and conditioning, through attention to such things as your clothing, cleanliness, exercise, and good eating habits.

EMOTIONAL CONTRIBUTIONS

Liking and Loving
  5. Liking: Liking your partner and showing it.
  6. Love: Feeling and expressing love for your partner.
Understanding and Concern
  7. Understanding and Concern: Knowing your partner's personal concerns and emotional needs and responding to them.
Acceptance
  8. Accepting and Encouraging Role Flexibility: Letting your partner try out different roles occasionally, for example, letting your partner be a "baby" sometimes, a "mother," a colleague or a friend, an aggressive as well as a passive lover, and so on.
Appreciation
  9. Expressions of Appreciation: Openly showing appreciation for your partner's contributions to the relationship—not taking your partner for granted.
Physical Affection
  10. Showing Affection: Being openly affectionate—touching, hugging, kissing.
Sex
  11. Sexual Pleasure: Participating in the sexual aspect of your relationship; working to make it mutually satisfying and fulfilling.
  12. Sexual Fidelity: Living up to or being faithful to your agreements about extra-marital relations.

Security/Freedom

    13. Commitment: Committing yourself to your partner and to the future of your relationship together.

    14. Respecting Partner's Need to be a Free and Independent Person: Allowing your partner to develop as an individual in the way that he/she chooses: for example, allowing your partner freedom to go to school or not; to work at the kind of job or career he/she likes; to pursue outside interests; to do things by him/herself or with his/her friends; to simply be alone sometimes.

DAY-TO-DAY CONTRIBUTIONS

Day-to-Day Maintenance

    15. Day-to-Day Maintenance: Contributing time and effort to household responsibilities such as grocery shopping, making dinner, cleaning and car maintenance.

Finances

    16. Finances: Contributing income to your "joint account."

Sociability

    17. Easy-to-Live With: Being a partner who is easy to live with on a day-to-day basis; that is, being someone with a sense of humor, who isn't too moody, doesn't get drunk too often, and so on.

    18. Companionability: Telling your partner about your day's events and what's on your mind and also being interested in hearing about your partner's concerns and daily activities.

    20. Fitting In: Being compatible with your partner's friends and relatives; they like you and you like them.

Decision-Making

    21. Decision-Making: Taking your fair share of the responsibility for making and carrying out decisions that affect both of you.

Remembering Special Occasions

    22. Remembering Special Occasions: Being thoughtful about sentimental things, such as remembering birthdays, your anniversary, and other special occasions.

After reading each item, the respondent was asked:

How would you describe your contribution in this area?
How would you describe your partner's contribution in this area?

Respondents were asked to make their estimates on the following 8-point scale:

+4. Extremely positive
+3. Very positive

+2. Moderately positive
+1. Slightly positive
−1. Slightly negative
−2. Moderately negative
−3. Very negative
−4. Extremely negative

Assessing Outcomes. Next the interviewers showed couples a list of outcomes consisting of twenty-four of the benefits and frustrations people may encounter in a relationship.

PERSONAL REWARDS

Social Grace
    1. Socially Graceful Partner: Having a partner who is sociable, friendly, relaxed in social settings.
Intellect
    2. Intelligent Partner: Having a partner who is intelligent and informed.
Appearance
    3. Physically Attractive Partner: Having a physically attractive partner.
    4. Physically Fit and Healthy Partner: Having a partner who takes care of appearance and conditioning, who attends to such things as personal cleanliness, dress, exercise, and good eating habits.

EMOTIONAL REWARDS

Liking and Loving
    5. Liking: Being liked by your partner.
    6. Love: Being loved by your partner.
Understanding and Concern
    7. Understanding and Concern: Having your personal concerns and emotional needs understood and responded to.
Acceptance
    8. Acceptance and Encouragement of Role Flexibility: Because of your partner's acceptance and encouragement, being free to try out different roles occasionally; for example, being a "baby" sometimes, a "mother," a colleague or a friend; being an aggressive as well as a passive lover, and so on.
Appreciation
    9. Appreciation: Being appreciated for your contributions to the relationship—not being taken for granted by your partner.
Physical Affection
    10. Affection: Receiving open affection—touching, hugging, kissing.
Sex
    11. Sexual Pleasure: Experiencing a sexually fulfilling and pleasurable relationship with your partner.

12. Sexual Fidelity: Having a partner who is faithful to your agreements about extra-marital relations.

Security

13. Commitment: The security of having your partner's commitment to you and to the future of your relationship together.

Plans and Goals for the Future

14. Plans and Goals for the Future: Planning for and dreaming about your future together.

DAY-TO-DAY REWARDS

Day-to-Day Operations

15. Day-to-Day Operations: Having a smooth operating household, because of the way you two have organized your household responsibilities.

Finances

16. Financial Resources: The amount of income and other financial resources that you may gain through your "joint account."

Sociability

17. Easy-to-Live-With Partner: Having a pleasant living-together situation because your partner is easy to live with on a day-to-day basis.

18. Companionship: Having a partner who is a good companion, who suggests fun things to do and who also goes along with your ideas for what you might do together.

19. Conversation: Knowing your partner is interested in hearing about your day and what's on your mind, and in turn will share concerns and events with you.

20. Fitting In: Having a partner who is compatible with your friends and relatives.

Decision-Making

21. Decision-Making Partner: Having a partner who takes a fair share of the responsibility for making and carrying out decisions that affect both of you.

Remembering Special Occasions

22. Special Occasions Remembered: Having a partner who is thoughtful about sentimental things; who remembers, for example, birthdays, your anniversary, and other special occasions.

OPPORTUNITIES GAINED AND LOST

Opportunities Gained

23. Chance to be Married: Having the opportunity to partake of the many life experiences that depend upon being married; for example, the chance to become a parent and even grandparent, the chance to be

included in "married couple" social events, and finally, having someone to count on in old age.

Opportunities Foregone

24. Opportunities Foregone: Necessarily giving up certain opportunities in order to be in this relationship. The opportunities could have been other possible mates, a career, travel, etc.

After looking over this list of possible outcomes from a marriage the respondent was asked:

How would you describe your outcome in this area?
How would you describe your partner's contribution in this area?

Respondents were asked to make their estimates on the following 8-point scale:

+4. Extremely positive
+3. Very positive
+2. Moderately positive
+1. Slightly positive
−1. Slightly negative
−2. Moderately negative
−3. Very negative
−4. Extremely negative

Assessing Equity/Inequity. Once Traupmann and Utne had assessed a couple's perception of their own and their partner's inputs and outcomes, they could proceed to calculate how men and women rated the equity/inequity of their dating or marital relationship. They simply substituted participants' ratings of their own and their partner's inputs and outcomes into the Equity formula:

Man's perception of equity:

$$\frac{(O_M - I_M)}{(|I_M|)^{k\,M}} - \frac{(O_W - I_W)}{(|I_W|)^{k\,W}}.$$

Woman's perception of Equity:

$$\frac{(O_W - I_W)}{(|I_W|)^{k\,W}} - \frac{(O_M - I_M)}{(|I_M|)^{k\,M}}.$$

As before, the respondent was classified as "Underbenefited" if his Relative Gains fell short of his partner's. He was classified as Equitably

Treated if his Relative Gains were equal to his partner's. He was classified as Overbenefited if his Relative Gains exceeded his partner's.

DOES INEQUITY BREED "DISTRESS"?

5.

PROPOSITION III: When individuals find themselves participating in inequitable relationships, they become distressed. The more inequitable the relationship, the more distress individuals feel.

According to Equity theory, when people are equitably treated, they feel content; when they are inequitably treated, they experience "distress"; i.e., they experience subjective distress accompanied by physiological arousal.

Researchers have devoted considerable effort to devising standard procedures for measuring participants' contentment and distress.

How Have Investigators Measured Distress?

Measuring Subjective Contentment and Distress. Researchers have assessed participants' subjective contentment and distress in two ways:[39]

The Mood Adjective Check List: Some researchers have asked participants to indicate how comfortable they feel *via* the Nowlis and Green (1957) *Mood Adjective Check List (MACL)*.

MOOD ADJECTIVE CHECK LIST (MACL)*

Below is a list of words that describe people's moods and feelings. Indicate how well each word describes the way you feel *right now* by placing a 1, 2, 3, or 4 in the blank before each word.

1 = Not at all   2 = A little   3 = Somewhat   4 = Very much

___ Pleased	___ Friendly
___ Happy	___ Alert
___ Lively	___ Angry
___ Trustful	___ Vulnerable
___ Downhearted	___ Forgiving

This research was sponsored by the Organizational Effectiveness Research Programs (Code 452), Office of Naval Research under contract number 24105, Vincent Nowlis, Principal Investigator. Reprinted by permission.

___ Shocked	___ Cooperative
___ Vigorous	___ Annoyed
___ Sad	___ Upset
___ Guilty	___ Satisfied
___ Startled	___ Joyous
___ Elated	___ Frustrated
___ Fed-up	___ Blue
___ Helpless	___ Hostile
___ Energetic	___ Irritated
___ Active	___ Kindly

The *MACL*'s thirty adjectives represent six dimensions or moods. (The dimensions can roughly be labeled as *elation, activation, social affection, aggression, anxiety,* and *depression.*) The *MACL* is easily scored: the participant's Comfort/Discomfort Index score = Σ (his score on the three positive moods) − Σ (his score on the three negative ones). The more positive the Index, the more contented the participant is; the more negative the score, the more distressed he is. The researchers expect equitably treated people to score higher on the Index than inequitably treated ones.

Mood descriptions: Some researchers have simply asked partipants to describe their current mood via *Mood Description* scales. They are asked how content, how happy, how angry, and how guilty they feel at the moment.

How Content Do You Feel?	How Happy Do You Feel?	How Angry Do You Feel?	How Guilty Do You Feel?
1. Not at all	1. Not at all	1. Not at all	1. Not at all
2. A little	2. A little	2. A little	2. A little
3. Somewhat	3. Somewhat	3. Somewhat	3. Somewhat
4. Very much	4. Very much	4. Very much	4. Very much

The researchers expect equitably treated people to score high on contentment and happiness and low on the anger and quiet scales. They expect inequitably treated people to score low on contentment and happiness; the deprived should score high on anger; the overbenefited should score high on guilt.

Measuring Physiological Arousal.[40] A few researchers have contended that the best way to measure participants' contentment and distress is to measure their physiological arousal by the use of such indicants as the *Galvanic Skin Response (GSR).* Unfortunately, psychophysiological measures are generally unreliable and attempts to measure psychophysiological states are often unsuccessful. There is some evidence, however, that *GSR* level may be a useful indicant of distress.[41]

Austin (1972) attempted to determine whether or not individ-

FIGURE 7.5. "Some Researchers Have Simply Asked Participants to Describe . . . How Comfortable They Feel at the Moment."

uals' reactions to equitable versus inequitable treatment could be detected by *Galvanic Skin Response* measures. Austin began his experiment by assessing participants' *GSR* levels "at rest." Then he asked the participants to participate in an experiment. At a critical point in the experiment, Austin treated them in a fair or a blatantly inequitable way. At this point, unbeknownst to the participants, Austin assessed their *GSR* reactions a second time.

The extent to which the participant's arousal level remained stable (or increased) over time was, of course, Austin's measure of the participant's physiological arousal. As one might expect, participants' treatment, and their subjective reports of comfort and discomfort were found to be weakly correlated with their physiological responses.

Equity and the Prediction of Participants' Contentment and Distress:

Researchers have also devoted considerable effort to testing whether or not Equity theory correctly predicts how contented or distressed individuals will be when they find themselves in equitable/inequitable relationships.

Equity theory proposes that participants will be content when they participate in equitable relations, and will experience distress when they participate in inequitable ones. Theoretically, their distress emanates from two sources:

Internal Sanctions. Since both social norms and individuals' internalized standards of fairness prescribe equitable behavior, individuals who exploit others, or who allow themselves to be exploited, should experience *self-concept distress.*

External Sanctions. Exploiters are generally painfully aware that their victim, or his sympathizers, may retaliate against them. Victims are generally humiliatingly aware that their colleagues may ridicule them, or—now that they have a reputation as "easy marks"—may try to bilk them themselves. Theoretically, then, both those who exploit others and those who allow themselves to be exploited should experience *fear of retaliation distress.*

Reassuringly, we reported a variety of studies in chapters 2 and 3 that provide firm support for Proposition III. The data indicate that people who are equitably treated are far more content than people who are inequitably treated (i.e., persons who are either underrewarded or overrewarded).

Individual Differences in Distress. There should be individual differences in the ways individuals respond emotionally to equity/inequity. For example, individual child-rearing differences should insure that some individuals learn the connection between equity and profit and inequity and punishment much better than others. Individual differences in temperament should insure that some individuals become only mildly disturbed, while others become extremely upset, by the discovery that they have behaved inequitably.

Sad to say, although personality and situational factors should have a substantial effect on participants' responses to equity/inequity, almost no research has been done on individual differences. Let us review the sparse individual difference data that do exist.

Self-concept research: When individuals find themselves behaving equitably, those who have strongly internalized ethical standards and high self-esteem should feel especially content. Their behavior is totally in accord with their ethical and personal standards. On the other hand, when individuals find themselves behaving inequitably, these same individuals with their rigorous moral standards and high self-regard should be most upset. Paradoxically then, after behaving unfairly, the best socialized and most self-confident people should be most distressed and should make the greatest effort to restore equity; either actual or psychological equity.

There is some experimental evidence to support this intriguing derivation. Glass (1964) gave students a series of psychological tests and returned false results to the students. Glass attempted to raise the self-esteem of half of the students by giving them extremely favorable reports. (Their reports said that the test results had revealed that the student was personable, mature, mentally alert, intelligent, and had concern for the feelings of others.) He attempted to lower the self-esteem of the remaining students by giving them extremely unfavorable reports. (The reports said the student had received a poor score on the preceding characteristics.)

After the bogus personality reports had been returned to the now "high" and "low" self-esteem students, Glass led them to voluntarily exploit a fellow student. Students were given no opportunity to compensate him for his suffering; they were, however, given a chance to restore psychological equity. They were given a chance to derogate the victim and justify his suffering. As predicted, Glass found that high self-esteem subjects derogated their hapless victims far more than did low self-esteem subjects.

Other personality variables: Profitable and interesting attempts to identify some of the individual difference variables that may affect a harmdoer's reaction had been made by a variety of other authors.[42] In the future, such studies may be expected to considerably sharpen equity predictions.

DETERMINANTS OF A SCRUTINEER'S MODE
OF EQUITY RESTORATION

6.

> **PROPOSITION IV:** Individuals who discover they are in an inequitable relationship attempt to eliminate their distress by restoring equity. The greater the inequity that exists, the more distress they feel, and the harder they try to restore equity.

Theoretically, individuals who are enmeshed in an inequitable relationship can restore equity in one of two entirely different ways: they can restore actual equity or they can restore psychological equity.

According to Equity theory, two situational variables should be crucial determinants of an exploiter's response: (1) the *adequacy* of possible techniques for restoring equity, and (2) the *cost* of possible techniques for restoring equity. We expect people to prefer techniques that completely restore equity to those that only partially restore it; we expect them to prefer techniques with little material or psychological cost to techniques with greater cost. More precisely, we would expect:

PROPOSITION IV: COROLLARY 1: Other things being equal, the more adequate a participant perceives an available equity-restoring technique to be, the more likely he is to use this technique to restore equity.

PROPOSITION I: COROLLARY 1: Other things being equal, the more costly a participant perceives an available equity-restoring technique to be, the less likely he is to use that technique to restore equity.

This cost/benefit analysis seems logical. Unfortunately, very little research has been done to test its usefulness in predicting which equity-restoring mode subjects will use. Hopefully subsequent researchers will remedy this deficiency.

Summary

In chapter 7, we reviewed the major theoretical issues that Equity theorists confront: When will a scrutineer perceive that participants are in a relationship? How does he go about calculating inputs? Outcomes? Does perceived inequity really generate subjective and physiological distress? What determines how observers and participants try to reduce their distress?

We reviewed the classic theories that provide the glimmerings of an answer to these questions; definitive answers, however, must come from the current generation of researchers.

ENDNOTES

1. Almost any interpersonal attraction text provides a comprehensive review of the factors which motivate individuals to interact with others. For example, see Berscheid and Walster (1969).

2. In Austin and Walster (1973).

3. Additional evidence to support the contention that individuals may strive to maintain equity with the world comes from a fascinating set of studies by Carlsmith and Gross (1969), Darlington and Macker (1966), and Freedman, Wallington, and Bless (1967).

4. See, for example, Anderson et al. (1969), Austin (in press), Berger et al. (1972), Festinger (1954), Homans (1961), Merton (1968), Pritchard (1969), Thorblom (1973), and Zelditch et al. (1970).

5. Reprinted in Ross (1966).

6. See Lerner (1974), Leventhal, Popp, and Sawyer (1973), and Sampson (1969).

7. See Rousseau (1913, p. 232).

8. Reprinted in 1913.

9. See Lane and Messé (1971), Lane, Messé, and Phillips (1971), Leventhal and Lane (1970), Leventhal and Michaels (1969, 1971), Leventhal, Michaels, and Sanford (1972), and Messé and Lichtman (1972).

10. See Garrett (1973), Kahn (1972), Lane and Coon (1972), Lerner (1974), Leventhal, Popp, and Sawyer (1973), Lichtman (1972), Morgan and Sawyer (1967), Pruitt (1972), and Sampson (1969).

11. See Lane and Messé (1971), Leventhal and Lane (1970), and Messé and Lichtman (1972).

12. See Bond and Vinacke (1961), Leventhal and Anderson (1970), Leventhal and Lane (1970), Leventhal, Popp, and Sawyer (1973), Uesugi and Vinacke (1963), Vinacke (1962), and Vinacke and Stanley (1962).

13. Leventhal and Lane (1970) provide support for Leventhal's contention.

14. See Freedland, Thibaut, and Walker (1973), Komorita and Chertkoff (1973), Leventhal and Anderson (1970), Moore and Baron (1973), Ross and McMillen (1973), Shapiro (1972, 1973), and Thibaut et al. (1974).

15. They cite data from Psathas and Stryker (1965) in support of this contention.

16. See Olson (1968) for a sophisticated discussion of this point.

17. In support of this contention, they cite studies by French and Snyder (1959), and Lippitt et al. (1952).

18. In support of the contention, they cite evidence from Harvey and Consalvi (1960), Levinger (1959), and Lippitt et al. (1952).

19. See the research of Caplow (1956), Gamson (1961), Horai and Tedeschi (1969), Komorita and Chertkoff (1973), Michener and Cohen (1973), Patchen (1970), Thibaut and Kelley (1959), and Wolff (1950).

20. See Lerner (1965, 1966, 1970, and 1971a).

21. See, for example, Austin and Walster (1975), Brock and Buss (1962, 1964), Glass (1964), Sykes and Matza (1957), and Walster et al. (1973).

22. See, for example, Michener, Griffith, and Palmer (1971), Michener and Zeller (1972), Murdoch (1967), Murdoch and Rosen (1970), Thibaut and Faucheux (1965), and Thibaut and Guider (1969).

23. See, for example, Deutsch (1974), Mason (1971), or Rousseau (reprinted, 1913).

24. We would predict, for example, that the energy crisis, which will inevitably alter the relative power of the producing versus the consuming nations, will stimulate long-term changes in our definition of international equity.

25. See Anonymous, *Blackwoods Magazine* (1869), Bain (1882), or Stephen (1873).

26. Quoted in Perkins (1909).

27. Reprinted in 1971.

28. For example, the tendency to avoid noxious stimuli.

29. For example, the needs for heat avoidance and cold avoidance together refer to tendency to maintain an equable temperature.

30. For example, the inclination for sensuous gratification.

31. On one point, however, Thibaut and Kelley and Equity theorists would disagree. According to Thibaut and Kelley, one's satisfaction with a relationship is dependent on whether he is getting more or less from it than he has come to expect. If one's outcomes from a relationship fall above one's *CL,* the relationship will be relatively satisfying and attractive; if one's outcomes fall below the *CL,* the relationship will be relatively unsatisfying and unattractive. Equity theorists would, of course, disagree with Thibaud and Kelley's contention that the more a participant receives from a relationship, the more satisfied he will be. Equity theorists would predict that once the individual's outcomes become too high, and he begins to receive more than society, and he, feels he deserves, the individual's satisfaction at his good fortune will be tinged with distress.

32. See chapters 5 and 6 for a review of the experimental literature in support of this contention.

33. For a more comprehensive discussion of these procedures, see Aronson and Carlsmith (1968).

34. Inevitably, future theorists will attempt to develop techniques for making far more precise assessments of equity/inequity. For example, Adams and Freedman (1976) argue that Equity researchers' next step must be to begin to develop psychometric techniques for scaling scrutineers' perceptions of participants' inputs, outcomes, and the equitableness/inequitableness of their relationship. Not until such measurement breakthroughs occur can we really test the mathematical implications of our Equity formula.

35. See Smith (in preparation).

36. Husband's perception of husband's Relative Gains minus wife's Relative Gains.

37. Wife's perception of wife's Relative Gains minus husband's Relative Gains.

38. See Traupmann and Utne (in preparation).

39. See Austin (1972), Austin and Walster (1973), Austin et al. (1973), or Austin and Walster (1974) for a complete description of these scales.

40. See Austin (1972).

41. See Forrest and Dimond (1967), Geer (1966), Sternbach (1966), and Wilson (1967).

42. See Aronfreed (1961), Blumstein and Weinstein (1969), Glass and Wood (1969), Lawler and O'Gara (1967), Tornow (1970), and Weinstein et al. (1969).

CHAPTER
8

The Future of Equity Theory
and Research

We began *Equity: Theory and Research* by observing that every society must be concerned with questions of social justice. Chapters 3–7 documented the critical importance of equity considerations in the lives of our predecessors and ourselves. Let us end this book by looking forward to the future. What, if any, equity concerns will individuals confront in the year 2000? What will *Equity: Theory and Research: Year 2000* be like? No one can forsee the future. Our best guess, however, is that people in the year 2000 will confront even more critical and more formidable equity problems than we now face. What leads us to this conclusion?

Let us begin by trying to envision what the world of Year 2000 will be like. Then we can speculate about the impact these conditions will have on the concerns of future generations.

THE WORLD OF YEAR 2000

An impressive array of futurists have attempted to forecast what Year 2000 will be like. The forecasts of Bell's *Commission on the Year 2000* (in America), de Jouvenel's *Futurable's* project (in France), and Young and Abram's *Committee on the Next Thirty Years* (in Britain) have been widely reported in both the scientific and mass media.[1] If the speculations of such luminaries are correct, what will the world of Year

2000 be like? It will be (1) a world populated by more people, (2) a world populated by somewhat different kinds of people, and (3) a world in which individuals must adjust to great shortages in some areas and enormous abundance in others.

The World of Year 2000: A World Populated by More People

Currently, the world's population is three and a half billion. Most demographers calculate that by Year 2000, the population will rise to from five to seven billion.[2]

Several interlocking scientific advances could send the population soaring even higher. (In Lederberg's terms, things could go "critical.")

For example, for centuries man has replaced diseased or damaged portions of his body with artificial parts. (For example, peg legs were first used in 600 B.C.) By now, technicians have developed a staggering number of replacement parts. Several futurists predict that by Year 2000, routine organ replacements will markedly increase man's life span.[3]

In the long run, an even more staggering possibility exists: man may be able to reproduce an unlimited number of biological carbon copies of himself.

As Toffler (1970) reports:

> Through a process known as "cloning" it will be possible to grow from the nucleus of an adult cell a new organism that has the same genetic characteristics of the person contributing the cell nucleus. . . . Cloning would make it possible for people to see themselves born anew, to fill the world with twins of themselves.* (p. 197)

If such advances *do* occur, the population may well "go critical."

The World of Year 2000: A World Populated by Somewhat Different Kinds of People

The last century was an era of technological innovations that generated enormous changes in the human environment. The coming quarter-century will be an era of biological innovations that may well produce

---

*From *Future Shock*, by Alvin Toffler. Copyright © 1970 by Random House, Inc. Reprinted by permission.

FIGURE 8.1. (From S. Gentile, ed., "Rancor and the Seven Shadows," *Flash Gordon*, 2, June 1969, p. 9. Copyright © 1969 King Features Syndicate Inc. Reprinted by permission.)

enormous changes in the species itself. By Year 2000, the world will probably be populated by somewhat different kinds of people than now exist.

Three types of innovations seem inevitable:

Pharmacological Control of Personality and Behavior. Futurists expect that psycho-pharmacological developments will enable people in the year 2000 to shape personality and behavior in radical ways.[4] Catechol-amines (such as norepinephrine) will alter moods. Pep pills will make people more assertive; tranquilizers will make them more acquiescent. RNA and protein synthesis are essential for learning and memory; their derivatives may well improve the individual's ability to handle information. LSD and its progeny will be used to "expand consciousness" and entertain.

Cyborgs: The Fusion of Man and Machine. Most theorists believe that by Year 2000, man-computer hookups will be common. Toffler (1970) observes:

If we assume that the brain is the seat of consciousness and intelligence ... then it is possible to conceive of a disembodied brain—a brain without arms, legs, spinal cord or other equipment. ... It may then become possible to combine the human brain with a whole set of artificial sensors, receptors and effectors, and to call that tangle of wires and plastic a human being. (p. 209)

He prophesies:

We shall face the novel sensation of trying to determine whether the smiling, assured humanoid behind the airline reservation counter is a pretty girl or a

carefully wired robot . . . the likelihood, of course, is that she will be both.*
(p. 211)

More conservative futurists agree.[5]

To Year 1978 man, the suggestion that humans and computers may merge is shocking. It may be shocking—but it is probably inevitable. Society has already accepted the notion that a person can possess a few artificial parts (a peg leg, a speech-assist device, a Dacron muscle) and still remain human. Where would we draw a line? Only a small conceptual step separates us from the acceptance of "man" attached to a few artificial parts, to the acceptance of "man" (or his brain) attached to a higher proportion of machine components. In any case, most futurists assume that man and machine will merge in the forseeable future.

The Genetic Alteration of Man. Obviously, eugenicists do not have the time to breed a new race of human beings by Year 2000. Geneticists, however, will be engaged in eugenic research and pilot programs. Most futurists agree that by Year 2000, a few geneticists will be absorbed in trying to breed an intellectual elite.[6] Eugenicists in complementary programs will be trying to breed a race that is superior in many respects—a race of people who are more intelligent, more healthy, more handsome, more industrious, more popular, etc., than their fellows.[7] Other geneticists will concentrate on breeding some people to live in space; and others to live in the oceans.

The World of Year 2000: A World of Shortage and Abundance

One can almost predict whether an American futurist will be an optimist or pessimist, if he knows whether the futurists wrote pre-1970 or post-1970.

Before 1970, American futurists were very optimistic. They predicted that by Year 2000, Americans would be incredibly affluent. For example, today the U.S. *per capita* GNP is approximately $3,860 (in 1965 U.S. dollars). Kahn and Weiner (1967) predicted that by Year 2000, the GNP would rise to $4,760 (in 1965 dollars).

Clarke (1958) looked forward to a time when man could possess every material thing he wanted. Clarke argued that "replicators" will be devised which can copy any product. "Leaping lightly across

---

*From *Future Shock*, by Alvin Toffler.

FIGURE 8.2. "Other Geneticists Will Concentrate on Breeding Some People to Live in Space . . . and Others to Live in the Oceans."

some centuries of intensive development and discovery," Clarke provides a compelling description of how such a replicator might operate. The replicator would consist of three parts: store, memory, and organizer. The *store* would contain all necessary raw materials; i.e., the simple elements hydrogen, oxygen, and nitrogen. The *memory* would store an abundance of "blueprints." Any object in the physical world can be completely specified by two factors: its composition and its shape or pattern. The memory's "blueprints" would consist of a complete physical description of the object to be produced. The *organizer* would use the blueprints to transform the basic raw materials into a perfect replication.

Such a replicator could, of course, reproduce any product, organic or inorganic. Clarke observes:

> All material possessions . . . soiled handkerchiefs, diamond tiaras, Mona Lisas totally indistinguishable from the original, once-worn mink stoles, half-consumed bottles of the most superb champagnes . . . would be literally as cheap as dirt. (p. 161)

Futurists became much more pessimistic by the early 1970s, and even the most sheltered Americans began to realize that foreign nations were beginning to claim an ever larger share of the world's resources.[8]

To make things worse, at about the same time, Americans began to notice that some crucial resources were beginning to disappear. Futurists began to observe that heat, earth, and water pollution were destroying much of the natural environment.[9] Taylor (1970) opened his *Doomsday Book* with a haunting quote:

> Put bacteria in a test-tube, with food and oxygen, and they will grow explosively, doubling in number every twenty minutes or so, until they form a solid, visible mass. But finally multiplication will cease as they become poisoned by their own waste products. In the centre of the mass will be a core of dead and dying bacteria, cut off from the food and oxygen of their environment by the solid barrier of their neighbours. The number of living bacteria will fall almost to zero, unless the waste products are washed away.
>
> Mankind today is in a similar position. (p. 1)

Futurists began to observe that some crucial resources would soon disappear.[10] The oil shortages in 1974 and the long lines at Eastern gas pumps brought their arguments home to Americans.

Even today, some futurists argue that in Year 2000, we will still

FIGURE 8.3. (From Li'l Abner by Al Capp. Copyright © by News Syndicate Co. Inc. World rights reserved. Reprinted with permission of the Chicago-Tribune–New York News Syndicate, Inc.)

be riding the crest of affluence; they predict that man's fall will not come until some time thereafter. For example, Boulding (1973) predicts that man will casually continue to use up the world's resources until he is forced to reshape his lifestyle. Shakespeare in *Hamlet,* insisted that man was "in anticipation, like a God;" futurists such as Boulding aren't so sure. *These* modern day "optimists" are, in fact, the most pessimistic futurists of all. They argue that by the time man realizes he must do something, it will be too late.

Regardless of whether one goes with the pre-1970 optimists, or the post-1970 pessimists, however, one thing is clear: man is going to have to adapt to a radically changed, and changing, lifestyle. The best bet is that circa Year 2000, men will begin to experience a confusing mixture of great shortages in some few commodities, while continuing to enjoy an enormous abundance of all others.

Hopefully, the futurists' predictions provide a glimmering of what Year 2000 will be like. Let us now proceed to the question with which we began: What equity concerns, if any, will confront the individual in the year 2000?

THE NATURE OF JUSTICE

As we stated in our introduction, every society is faced with the task of devising some acceptable system for allocating community resources. But some societies have a far easier time of it than others. In a stable world, societies have the time to evolve stable definitions of social justice. Eventually, a society's rules become so hallowed that citizens simply "know" how things should be, and have, in fact, some difficulty really believing that things could ever be otherwise.

Today's world is a relatively stable one; in most societies, citizens do share some basic understanding as to what constitutes social justice and social equity. There is at least rough agreement as to which inputs should entitle a citizen to reward or punishment.

By the year 2000, however, traditional notions of social justice are likely to be severely shaken. Several factors will cause citizens to question traditional standards of equity.

Existing Inequities Will Become Salient

Futurists warn that by Year 2000, the gap between the affluent postindustrial nations and the underdeveloped nations will remain large.

Kahn and Weiner (1967) predict that the GNP of the "haves" (in 1965 U.S. dollars) will be $5,775; the GNP of the "have-nots" will be a lowly $325. de Sola Pool (1967) cautions:

> The growth of communication will certainly make any discrepancy between the well-off and the deprived societies known. Peasants will no longer be unaware of the discrepancies. (p. 675)

As the disparities in incomes, both nationally and internationally, become more salient, both the haves and the have-nots will become intensely concerned with formulating some definition of social justice.

Men Will Have Difficulty Evaluating Novel Characteristics

We have argued that both man and his resources will be markedly different by Year 2000. "Planetarians" will face the difficult problem of deciding how much reward the "new men" are entitled to. Is the man who has been bred to be "genetically superior" entitled to more reward than his fellows? Or less, because life is easier for him? How much does a cyborg deserve? If society is restratified, "who's who"? Who deserves the most rewards? Government officials, who rule by committee? Technocrats, who can commune with their computer but perhaps not with their fellow humans? Professionals, who are advised by computer? The bulk of mankind, who possess no special skills, but do possess the votes? New definitions of value will clearly have to be negotiated. The inevitable conflicts men encounter in negotiations will also make them more concerned with formulating a workable definition of social justice.

Men Will be Motivated to Redefine Equity

As we noted in chapter 7, theorists from a wide variety of historical periods and disciplines have pointed out that social change seems to generate philosophical change.[11] During periods of social upheaval, citizens become motivated to take a close look at their position and to try to figure out ways to improve their lot. In the rapidly changing future, then, selfishness will also motivate men to try to redefine the nature of social justice.

For these and a variety of other reasons in the year 2000, people should become increasingly preoccupied with questions of social justice.[12]

The Long Range Solution: A Move Toward Equality

Futurists agree on one thing: massive social change will continue for the imaginable future. Given this fact, it is probable that citizens will eventually come to the conclusion that it is futile to try to evolve any stable agreement as to who deserves what. Theorists foresee that societies will move increasingly to the *equal* division of material resources. *Within-country differences* are expected to shrink first.[13] Eventually, (well after year 2500) *International differences* are expected to erode.

One of the most gifted of the early futurists was the Marquis de Condorcet. In 1794, while facing death in prison, he wrote *A Sketch for a Historical Picture of the Progress of the Human Mind.* Condorcet expressed a faith in the future progress of mankind:

> Our hopes, as to the future condition of the human species, may be reduced to three points: the destruction of the inequality between different nations; the progress of equality in one and the same nation, and lastly, the real improvement of man. (Quoted in Flechtheim, 1966, p. 265)

According to subsequent futurists, Condorcet's hopes, like his predictions, may well be realized. Men may increasingly come to equate "equity" with "equality" rather than "proportionality."

The Nature of "Reward"

By Year 2000, humans will not only have somewhat different ideas as to who is entitled to reward; they will also have a somewhat broader notion as to what constitutes reward.

Traditionally, society has viewed man through a very restricted lens. When government officials talk about "social progress" what they usually mean is "increased Gross National Product." Today we can detect the first glimmerings of a new and broader perspective.[14] Toffler (1970) reflects this view:

> . . . all modern nations maintain elaborate machinery for measuring economic performance. We know virtually day by day the directions of change with respect to productivity, prices, investment, and similar factors. Through a set of "economic indicators" we gauge the overall health of the economy, the speed at which it is changing, and the overall directions of change. Without these measures, our control of the economy would be far less effective.
>
> By contrast, we have no such measures, no set of comparable "social indicators" to tell us whether the society, as distinct from the economy, is also healthy. We have no measures of the "quality of life." We have no systematic indices to tell us whether men are more or less alienated from one

another; whether education is more effective; whether art, music and litera-ture are flourishing; whether civility, generosity or kindness are increasing. "Gross National Product is our Holy Grail," writes Stewart Udall, former United States Secretary of the Interior, ". . . but we have no environmental index, no census statistics to measure whether the country is more livable from year to year." (pp. 454–455)

In contrast, Year 2000 man will have every reason to consider and reconsider the nature of happiness.

Futurists are uncertain whether to be optimistic or pessimistic about the year 2000; uncertain whether it will be an age of unbounded affluence, or an age in which critical shortages mar the general af-fluence. Regardless of who is right, man in the year 2000 will clearly have a practical reason to rethink what he really wants out of life.

If the optimists are right, and people *do* have more material benefits than they can envision, obviously they will lose interest in acquiring still more economic and material goods. They should become more interested in securing the "psychic" goods, love, services, variety, excitement, education, tranquility, that contribute to happiness.[15]

If the pessimists are right, and Year 2000 men must confront a confusing mixture of shortage and affluence, people will be even more motivated to reconsider their priorities. Do they want to sacrifice to continue to secure the "necessities" of life? Do they want to learn to do without—substituting new satisfactions for old?

In either case, we might expect that, were we able to ask Year 2000 man what things he cares about, we might get answers that we, living in the 1970s, could never have envisioned.

ENDNOTES

1. See, also, the forecasts of Beckwith (1967), Clarke (1958), Gordon (1965), Helmer (1972), Kahn and Wiener (1967), and Toffler (1970, 1972).

2. See Bestushev-Lada (1970) and Helmer (1967).

3. See, for example, Helmer (1967), Kahn and Wiener (1967), and Kenedi (1965).

4. Such as Beckwith (1967) and Quarton (1967).

5. See, for example, Helmer (1967).

6. See Beckwith (1967) and Neyfach (1969).

7. See Kahn and Wiener (1967).

8. See, for example, Heilbroner (1974) or Maynes (1974).

9. See Boulding (1966), Ehrlich (1968), Fuller (1972), Huxley (1972), or Jantsch (1972).

10. See Boulding (in Toffler, 1972).

11. See Mason (1971), Rousseau (1913), and Walster and Walster (1975).

12. See Beckwith (1967), Kahn and Wiener (1967), and Stendahl (1967).

13. For example, Beckwith (1967) predicts that regional and occupational differences will disappear by 2300 at the latest.

14. See, for example, Bradburn (1965), Flax (1972), or Shelly (1970).

15. See Clarke (1958), Gordon (1965), and Toffler (1970).

APPENDIX

I

The Walster et al. (1973)
Equity Formula: A Correction[*]

G. William Walster
University of Wisconsin

Aristotle (translated 1962) was the first theorist reckless enough to propose a formula for calculating whether or not individuals are in an equitable relationship. Adams (1965) utilized the Aristotle formula, i.e., Outcomes$_A$/Inputs$_A$ = Outcomes$_B$/Inputs$_B$, in his now classic research. Unfortunately, the Aristotle/Adams formula only yields meaningful results if A and B's Inputs and Outcomes are entirely positive or entirely negative; in mixed cases the formula yields extremely peculiar results.

In Walster et al. (1973) we proposed an Equity model that transcends this limitation. The rationale behind this formula is as follows:

ASSUMPTIONS

1. One can measure Inputs (I) and Outcomes (O) in the same units; thus $O - I$ can serve as a valid measure of a participant's gain or loss from a relationship.[1]
2. Inputs cannot equal zero.
3. In addition every equity problem is scaled (by multiplying all inputs and outcomes by a positive constant) such that the minimum of $|I_A|$ and $|I_B| \geqslant 1$.

_____
   *This article is reprinted from *Representative Research in Social Psychology*, 6 (1975): 65–67.

CONSTRAINTS

1. If $O = I$ the implication is that, regardless of what A or B's inputs were, he has neither gained nor lost anything in the relationship. It seems reasonable to argue that in an equitable relationship, if person A neither gains nor loses anything, B should also neither gain nor lose. This formulation is in accord with Adams. Graphically (see Figure 1):

2. If $I_A = I_B$, then $O_A - I_A$ should be equal to $O_B - I_B$. If $I_A < I_B$, $O_A - I_A$ should be less than $O_B - I_B$. Conversely, if $I_A > I_B$, $O_A - I_A$ should be greater than $O_B - I_B$.

3a. Suppose $O_A > I_A$ (i.e., as a result of inputting I_A, A enjoys a gain). From (2) it follows that as I_B becomes ever greater than I_A, $O_B - I_B$ should become increasingly positive. But what if $I_B < I_A$? At some point, should B's inputs get so low that $O_B - I_B$ actually becomes negative? We would argue "no." $O_B - I_B$ should remain positive and approach zero as $I_B \rightarrow -\infty$. ($O_B - I_B < 0$ would be inconsistent with 1.) Graphically (see Figure 2):

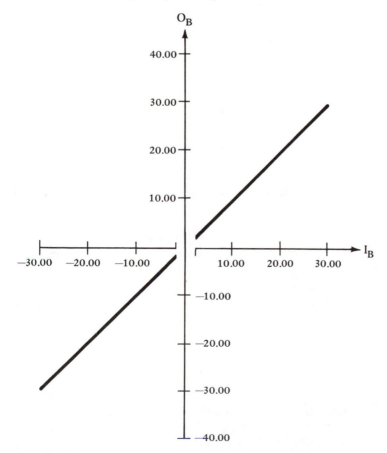

FIGURE 1. *B's Outputs, as a Function of His Inputs, when* $O_A - I_A = 0$.

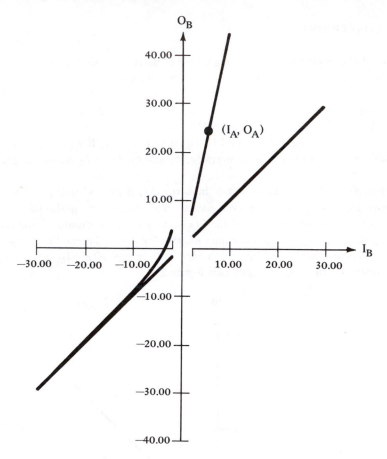

FIGURE 2. *B's* **Outputs, as a Function of His Inputs, when** $O_A - I_A > 0.$

3b. Similarly suppose $O_A < I_A$ (i.e., A suffers a loss as a result of inputting I_A). From (2) it follows that as I_B becomes less than I_A, $O_B - I_B$ should decrease and thus remain negative. But if $I_B > I_A$, $O_B - I_B$ should *remain* negative and approach zero as $I_B \rightarrow + \infty$. (As in 3a, for $O_B - I_B$ to become positive given sufficiently large I_B would be inconsistent with 1.) Graphically (see Figure 3):

4.   2, 3a, and 3b, should hold regardless of the sign of either I_A or I_B.

FORMULA

The following formula satisfies the above constraints:

$$(O_A - I_A)/(|I_A|)^{k_A} = (O_B - I_B)/(|I_B|)^{k_B}$$

where $k_A = \text{sign}(I_A) \times \text{sign}(O_A - I_A)$ and $k_B = \text{sign}(I_B) \times \text{sign}(O_B - I_B)$. Solving

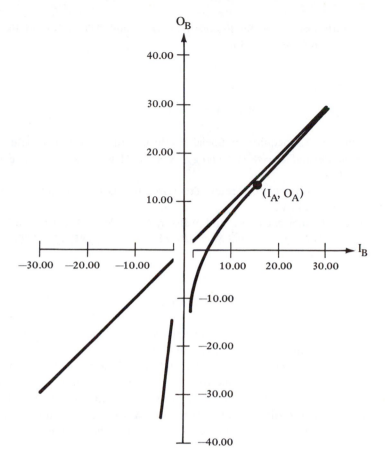

FIGURE 3. *B's* Outputs, as a Function of His Inputs, when $O_A - I_A < 0$.

for O_B we have:

$$O_B = I_B + (|I_B|)^{k_B}(O_A - I_A)/(|I_A|)^{k_A}$$

Note that from 3a and 3b sign $(O_B - I_B)$ = sign $(O_A - I_A)$. Thus in computing k_B, sign $(O_A - I_A)$ can be substituted for sign $(O_B - I_B)$.

This formula—which we cited in Walster et al. (1973)—is the only model existing that enables one to calculate the equitableness of a given relationship, regardless of sign of participants' inputs or outcomes. [NOTE: Two crucial exponents—k_A and k_B—must, of course, be added if the definitional formula reported in Walster et al. (1973) is to yield sensible results.]

At this stage in research, it is likely that our Equity model—or any researcher's model—will quickly be revised by other researchers determined to develop a definition of "equity" that better mirrors subjects' definitions of "equity." However, we are confident that it is a better strategy to propose a precise—albeit an imperfect—definition of Equity than to rely on readers' intuitions. As Aristotle's successor, Sir Francis Bacon, insisted, "Truth is more likely to arise from error than from confusion."

REFERENCES

Adams, J. S. Inequity in Social Exchange. In L. Berkowitz (Ed.), *Advances in Experimental Social Psychology*, Vol. II. New York: Academic Press, 1965, 267–299.

Aristotle. *Nicomachean Ethics.* Translated by Martin Ostwald. New York: Bobbs-Merrill, 1962, Ch. V.

Walster, E., Berscheid, E., and Walster, G. W. New Directions in Equity Research. *Journal of Personality and Social Psychology,* 1973, *25,* 151–176.

ENDNOTE

1. In previous research, subjects have had no difficulty in making such evaluations. For example, in one experiment, we asked subjects to envision a specific setting, and to indicate in dollars and cents how much they thought a variety of possible inputs entitled one to. Then they indicated how much a variety of possible outcomes were worth. By comparing such estimates, we could easily design an experimental setting in which Participant A would get far more outcomes than he deserved, exactly what he deserved, or far less than he deserved.

APPENDIX
II

Problem Sets[1]

Students may gain a more intuitive understanding of the nature of the Equity formula if they work through some sample cases. First, let us consider how one goes about calculating the *Relative Gains* of a single participant (say Person A) in an Equity relationship. Then we can consider how one goes about calculating the equitableness/inequitableness of the relationship between Person A and Person B.

Basically, the first term of the Equity formula:

$$\text{Relative Gains Person } A = \frac{O_A - I_A}{(|I_A|)^{k_A}}$$

takes into account two quantities: (1) Person A's *input value* (I_A), and (2) Person A's *net profit* ($O_A - I_A$) from the AB relationship.[2]

So far, so good. But what is the purpose of exponent (k_A)? The purpose of the exponent is simply to change the way Person A's Relative Gains are computed: sometimes, the signs of both A's input value and his net profit are the same (both are + or both are −). This is the case, for example, whenever A makes a positive contribution to the AB relationship (+), and reaps a profit (+), or when A makes a negative contribution to the relationship (−) and incurs a loss (−). Since k_A = sign (I_A) × sign ($O_A - I_A$), in these cases k_A = +1 × +1 (or −1 × −1) = +1. Thus, in these cases, Person A's Relative Gains are calculated by

$$\frac{O_A - I_A}{|I_A|}.$$

Sometimes, the signs of both A's input value *and* his net profit are different. This is the case, for example, when A contributes positively to the AB relationship (+) but incurs a loss (−) *or* when A makes a negative contribution (−) and reaps a profit (+). Since k_A = sign (I_A) × sign ($O_A - I_A$) = −1, in these cases, Person A's Relative Gains are calculated by ($O_A - I_A$) × $|I_A|$.[3]

When we work through all these operations, we end up with a measure of Person A's Relative Gains; a measure of Person A's relative profit from the AB relationship.

Let us now consider some sample cases. If we classify cases according to the sign of Person A's inputs (+ or −) and the sign of A's net profit (+ or −), we end up with six different cases.

	Inputs	
	+	**−**
+	Case 1	Case 2 Case 3
−	Case 4 Case 5	Case 6

(Net Profit (Outcomes-Inputs))

Let us consider these prototypic cases in greater detail.

$$\text{Person } A\text{'s Relative Gains} = \frac{(O_A - I_A)}{(|I_A|)^{k_A}}$$

k_A = sign (I_A) × sign $(O - I)$. Person A's Relative Gains will be zero if his inputs equal his outcomes. His Relative Gains will be positive if $O > I$, and negative if $O < I$.

Case 1 A's Inputs (+)
A's Outcomes (+)
A's Net Profit (+)

e.g.,

$$\frac{(4) - (2)}{(|2|)^{(+1)(+1)}} = \frac{2}{2^{+1}} = \frac{2}{2} = 1$$

Case 2 A's Inputs (−)
A's Outcomes (+)
A's Net Profit (+)

e.g.,

$$\frac{(5) - (-2)}{(|-2|)^{(-1)(+1)}} = \frac{7}{2^{-1}} = 7 \times 2 = 14$$

Case 3 A's Inputs (−)
A's Outcomes (−)
A's Net Profit (+)

e.g.,

$$\frac{(-4) - (-20)}{(|-20|)^{(-1)(+1)}} = \frac{16}{20^{-1}} = 16 \times 20 = 320$$

Case 4   A's Inputs (+)
          A's Outcomes (+)
          A's Net Profit (−)

e.g.,

$$\frac{(2)-(5)}{(|5|)^{(+1)(-1)}} = \frac{-3}{5^{-1}} = -3 \times 5 = -15$$

Case 5   A's Inputs (+)
          A's Outcomes (−)
          A's Net Profit (−)

e.g.,

$$\frac{(-2)-(3)}{(|3|)^{(+1)(-1)}} = \frac{-5}{3^{-1}} = -5 \times 3 = -15$$

Case 6   A's Inputs (−)
          A's Outcomes (−)
          A's Net Profit (−)

e.g.,

$$\frac{(-9)-(-2)}{(|-2|)^{(-1)(-1)}} = \frac{-7}{2^1} = \frac{-7}{2} = -3.5$$

Now that we have had some practice computing Person A's Relative Gains let us move on to the Person A/Person B relationship. Let us practice calculating the equity/inequity of the AB relationship:

$$\frac{O_A - I_A}{(|I_A|)^{k_A}} = \frac{O_B - I_B}{(|I_B|)^{k_B}}.$$

From Cases 1–6, seven types of equitable/inequitable relationships can be derived.

Type 1 is very simple: Person A and Person B have exactly the same inputs and outcomes.[4]

Type 1			*Case 6*	*versus*	*Case 6*
	Inputs	Outcomes	$\frac{(-9)-(-3)}{(|-3|)^{(-1)(-1)}}$	$=$	$6^3 \frac{(-9)-(-3)}{(|-3|)^{(-1)(-1)}}$
Person A	−3	−9	$\frac{-6}{3^{+1}}$	$=$	$\frac{-6}{3^{+1}}$
Person B	−3	−9	−2	$=$	−2

The next three types of Equity are combinations of Cases 1, 2, and 3; cases in which Person A's and Person B's Relative Gains are positive.

Type 2

Inputs	Outcomes
Person A	−2	2
Person B	2	18

Type 3

Inputs	Outcomes
Person A	−2	4
Person B	−4	−1

Type 4

Inputs	Outcomes
Person A	−2	−1
Person B	2	6

	Case 2	versus	Case 1
	$\dfrac{(2)-(-2)}{(\lvert-2\rvert)^{(-1)(+1)}}$	$=$	$\dfrac{(18)-(2)}{(\lvert2\rvert)^{(+1)(+1)}}$
	$\dfrac{4}{2^{-1}}$	$=$	$\dfrac{16}{2^{+1}}$
	8	$=$	8

	Case 3	versus	Case 1
	$\dfrac{(-1)-(-2)}{(\lvert-2\rvert)^{(-1)(+1)}}$	$=$	$\dfrac{(6)-(2)}{(\lvert2\rvert)^{(+1)(+1)}}$
	$\dfrac{1}{2^{-1}}$	$=$	$\dfrac{4}{2^{+1}}$
	2	$=$	2

	Case 2	versus	Case 3
	$\dfrac{(4)-(-2)}{(\lvert-2\rvert)^{(-1)(+1)}}$	$=$	$\dfrac{(-1)-(-4)}{(\lvert-4\rvert)^{(+1)(-1)}}$
	$\dfrac{6}{2^{-1}}$	$=$	$\dfrac{3}{4^{-1}}$
	12	$=$	12

Finally, the next three types of Equity are combinations of Cases 4, 5, and 6; cases in which Person A's and Person B's Relative Gains are negative.

Type 5

Input	Outcome
Person A	6	2
Person B	4	−2

Type 6

Input	Outcome
Person A	3	1
Person B	−2	−14

	Case 4	versus	Case 5
	$\dfrac{(2)-(6)}{(\lvert6\rvert)^{(+1)(-1)}}$	$=$	$\dfrac{(-2)-(4)}{(\lvert4\rvert)^{(+1)(-1)}}$
	$\dfrac{-4}{6^{-1}}$	$=$	$\dfrac{-6}{4^{-1}}$
	-24	$=$	-24

	Case 4	versus	Case 6
	$\dfrac{(5)-(3)}{(\lvert3\rvert)^{(+1)(-1)}}$	$=$	$\dfrac{(-14)-(-2)}{(\lvert-2\rvert)^{(-1)(-1)}}$
	$\dfrac{-2}{3^{-1}}$	$=$	$\dfrac{-12}{2^{+1}}$
	-6	$=$	-6

Type 7	Input	Outcome
Person *A*	−2	− 10
Person *B*	1	− 3

Case 6 versus *Case 5*

$$\frac{(-10)-(-2)}{(|-2|)(-1)(-1)} = \frac{(-3)-(1)}{(|1|)(+1)(-1)}$$

$$\frac{-8}{2^{+1}} = \frac{-4}{1^{-1}}$$

$$-2.5 = -4$$

ENDNOTES

1. Our thanks to Dr. Arnold Upmeyer, University of Mannheim, for developing these problem sets.

2. Both Person *A*'s input value and his net profit can be either positive or negative.

3. Without the exponent k, the formula would yield meaningless results when $I < O$ and $O - I > O$, or $I > O$ and $O - I < O$.

4. Of course, any of the six cases can be used in the Type 1 Equity relationship.

BIBLIOGRAPHY

Abelson, R. P., and M. J. Rosenberg. "Symbolic Psychologic: A Model of Attitudinal Cognition." *Behavioral Science* 3 (1958): 1–13.

Adams, J. S. "Toward an Understanding of Inequity," *Journal of Abnormal and Social Psychology* 67 (1963): 422–436.

_____. "Inequity in Social Exchange." In *Advances in Experimental Social Psychology.* Vol. 2. Edited by L. Berkowitz, pp. 267–299. New York: Academic Press, 1965.

Adams, J. S., and S. Freedman. "Equity Theory Revisited: Comments and Annotated Bibliography." In *Advances in Experimental Social Psychology.* Vol. 9. Edited by L. Berkowitz and E. Walster, pp. 43–90. New York: Academic Press, 1976.

Adams, J. S., and P. R. Jacobsen. "Effects of Wage Inequities on Work Quality." *Journal of Abnormal and Social Psychology* 69 (1964): 19–25.

Adams, J. S., and W. B. Rosenbaum. "The Relationship of Worker Productivity to Cognitive Dissonance about Wage Inequities." *Journal of Applied Psychology* 46 (1962): 161–164.

Aderman, D.; D. Brehm; and L. B. Katz. "Empathetic Observation of an Innocent Victim: The Just World Revisited." *Journal of Personality and Social Psychology* 29 (1974): 342–347.

Alger, I., and H. Rusk, "The Rejection of Help by Some Disabled People." *Archives of Physical Medicine Rehabilitation* 36 (1955): 277–281.

Alinsky, S. *Rules for Radicals.* New York: Random House, 1971.

Allinsmith, W. "The Learning of Moral Standards." In *Inner Conflict and Defense,* edited by D. R. Miller, and G. E. Swanson, in collaboration with Wesley Allinsmith [and others], pp. 141–176. New York: Holt, Rinehart and Winston, 1960.

Altman, I., and D. A. Taylor. *Social Penetration: The Development of Interpersonal Relationships.* New York: Holt, Rinehart and Winston, 1973.

Anderson, B.; J. Berger; M. Zelditch, Jr.; and B. P. Cohen. "Reactions to Inequity." *Acta Sociologica* 12 (1969): 1–12.

Anderson, B., and R. K. Shelly. "Reactions to Inequity, III: Inequity and Social Influence." *Acta Sociologica* 14 (1971): 236–244.

Andrews, I. R. "Wage Inequity and Job Performance: An Experimental Study." *Journal of Applied Psychology* 51 (1967): 39–45.

Andrews, I. R., and E. R. Valenzi. "Overpay Inequity or Self-Image as a Worker: A Critical Examination of an Experimental Induction Procedure." *Organizational Behavior and Human Performance* 5 (1970): 266–276.

Aristotle. In *Why Revolution? Theories and Analyses,* edited by C. T. Paynton and R. Blackey, p. 11. Cambridge, Mass.: Schenkman Publishing Co., 1971.

Arnold, M. B. *Neurological and Physiological Aspects.* Emotion and Personality, vol. 2. New York: Columbia University Press, 1960.

Aronfreed, J. "The Nature, Variety and Social Patterning of Moral Responses to Transgression." *Journal of Abnormal and Social Psychology* 63 (1961): 223–240.

―――. "The Socialization of Altruistic and Sympathetic Behavior: Some Theoretical and Experimental Analyses." In *Altruism and Helping Behavior,* edited by J. Macaulay and L. Berkowitz, pp. 103–126. New York: Academic Press, 1970.

Aronfreed, J., and V. Paskal. "Altruism, Empathy, and the Conditioning of Positive Affect." Study reported at the American Psychological Association, New York, 1966.

Aronson, E. "Some Antecedents of Interpersonal Attraction." In *Nebraska Symposium on Motivation, 1969,* edited by W. J. Arnold and D. Levine. Lincoln, Neb.: University of Nebraska Press, 1970.

Aronson, E., and J. M. Carlsmith. "Experimentation in Social Psychology." In *The Handbook of Social Psychology.* Vol. 2. Edited by G. Lindzey and E. Aronson, pp. 1–79. Reading, Mass.: Addison-Wesley Publishing Co., 1968.

Arrowood, A. J. "Some Effects on Productivity of Justified and Unjustified Levels of Reward under Public and Private Conditions." Ph.D. dissertation, University of Minnesota, 1961.

Austin, W. "Theoretical and Experimental Explorations in Expectancy Theory." Master's thesis, University of Wisconsin, 1972.

―――. "Equity Theory and Social Comparison Processes." In *Social Comparison Theory: Theoretical and Empirical Perspectives,* edited by J. Suls and R. Miller. Washington, D.C.: Hemisphere Publishing, forthcoming.

Austin, W. G.; N. McGinn; and J. Traupmann. "The Impact of Magnitude of Inequity on Satisfaction." *Psychonomic Bulletin,* submitted.

Austin, W., and M. K. Utne. "The Effect of a Criminal's Suffering on Simulated Jurors' Assignment of Punishment to an Offender." *Journal of Personality and Social Psychology,* in preparation.

Austin, W., and E. Walster. "Reactions to Confirmations and Disconfirmations of Expectancies of Equity and Inequity." *Journal of Personality and Social Psychology* 30 (1974): 208–216.

_____. " 'Equity with the World': An Investigation of the Trans-relational Effects of Equity and Inequity." *Sociometry* 38 (1975): 474–496.

Austin, W.; E. Walster; and M. A. Pate. "The Effect of 'Suffering in the Act' on Liking and Assigned Punishment." Unpublished research report, University of Wisconsin, 1973.

Austin, W.; E. Walster; and M. K. Utne. "Equity and the Law: The Effect of a Harmdoer's 'Suffering in the Act' on Liking and Assigned Punishment." In *Advances in Experimental Social Psychology.* Vol. 9. Edited by L. Berkowitz and E. Walster, pp. 163–190. New York: Academic Press, 1976.

Backman, C. W., and P. F. Secord. "The Effect of Perceived Liking on Interpersonal Attraction." *Human Relations* 12 (1959): 379–384.

Bain, A. *John Stuart Mill: A Criticism, With Personal Recollections.* New York: H. Holt, 1882.

Baker, K. "The Social Segment." Unpublished manuscript, 1973.

_____. "Experimental Analysis of Third-Party Justice Behavior. *Journal of Personality and Social Psychology* 30 (1974): 307–316.

Bakke, E. W. *The Unemployed Worker: A Study of the Task of Making a Living Without a Job.* New Haven, Conn.: Yale University Press, 1940*a*.

_____. *Citizens Without Work.* New Haven, Conn.: Yale University Press, 1940*b*.

Baldwin, J. *Notes of a Native Son.* Boston: Beacon Press, 1955.

_____. *The Fire Next Time.* New York: The Dial Press, 1963.

Bales, R. F. *Interaction Process Analysis.* Reading, Mass.: Addison-Wesley Publishing Co., 1950.

Bandura, A. "Vicarious Processes: A Case of No-Trial Learning." In *Advances in Experimental Social Psychology.* Vol. 2. Edited by L. Berkowitz, pp. 3–48. New York: Academic Press, 1965.

Bandura, L., and T. L. Rosenthal. "Vicarious Classical Conditioning as a Function of Arousal Level." *Journal of Personality and Social Psychology* 3 (1966): 54–62.

Baskett, G. D. "Interview Decisions as Determined by Competency and Attitude Similarity." *Journal of Applied Psychology* 57 (1973): 343–345.

Beckwith, B. P. *The Next 500 Years: Scientific Predictions of Major Social Trends.* New York: Exposition Press, 1967.

Bell, D., ed. *Daedalus: Toward the Year 2000: Work in Progress.* Boston: American Academy of Arts and Sciences, 1967.

Benton, A. A. "Productivity, Distributive Justice, and Bargaining among Children." *Journal of Personality and Social Psychology* 18 (1971): 68–78.

Berger, J.; M. Zelditch, Jr.; B. Anderson; and B. P. Cohen. "Structural Aspects of Distributive Justice: A Status Value Formulation." In *Sociological Theories in Progress.* Vol. 2. Edited by J. Berger, M. Zelditch, Jr., and B. Anderson, pp. 119–146. Boston: Houghton Mifflin Co., 1972.

Berger, S. M. "Conditioning through Vicarious Instigation." *Psychological Review* 29 (1962): 450–456.

Bergler, E. *Divorce Won't Help.* New York: Harper and Brothers, 1948.

Berkowitz, L. *Aggression: A Social Psychological Analysis.* New York: McGraw-Hill Book Co., 1962.

_____. "Responsibility, Reciprocity, and Social Distance in Help-Giving: An Experimental Investigation of English Social Class Differences." *Journal of Experimental Social Psychology* 4 (1968): 46–63.

_____. "Beyond Exchange: Ideals and Other Factors Affecting Helping and Altruism." Unpublished manuscript, University of Wisconsin, Madison, 1972.

Berkowitz, L., and W. H. Connor. "Success, Failure, and Social Responsibility." *Journal of Personality and Social Psychology* 4 (1966): 644–669.

Berkowitz, L., and L. R. Daniels. "Responsibility and Dependency." *Journal of Abnormal and Social Psychology* 66 (1963): 429–436.

Berkowitz, L., and P. Friedman. "Some Social Class Differences in Helping Behavior." *Journal of Personality and Social Psychology* 5 (1967): 217–225.

Bernard, J. "Factors in the Distribution of Success in Marriage." *American Journal of Sociology* 40 (1934): 51.

_____. "The Adjustments of Married Mates." In *Handbook of Marriage and the Family,* edited by H. T. Christensen, pp. 675–739. Chicago: Rand McNally & Co., 1964.

Berscheid, E.; D. Boye; and J. M. Darley. "Effects of Forced Association upon Voluntary Choice to Associate." *Journal of Personality and Social Psychology* 8 (1968): 13–19.

Berscheid, E.; D. Boye; and E. Walster. "Retaliation as a Means of Restoring Equity." *Journal of Personality and Social Psychology* 10 (1968): 370–376.

Berscheid, E.; K. Dion; E. Walster; and G. W. Walster. "Physical Attractiveness and Dating Choice: A Test on the Matching Hypothesis." *Journal of Experimental Social Psychology* 7 (1971): 173–189.

Berscheid, E., and E. Walster. "When Does a Harmdoer Compensate a Victim?" *Journal of Personality and Social Psychology* 6 (1967): 435–441.

_____. *Interpersonal Attraction.* Reading Mass.: Addison-Wesley Publishing Co., 1969.

Berscheid, E.; E. Walster; and A. Barclay, "Effect of Time on Tendency to Compensate a Victim." *Psychological Reports* 25 (1969): 431–436.

Berscheid, E.; E. Walster; and G. Bohrnstedt. "The Body Image Report." *Psychology Today* 7 (1973): 119–131.

Bestushev-Lada, I. "Bourgeois 'Futurology' and the Future of Mankind." *Reprints from the Soviet Press* 10, no. 7 (1970).

Blackwoods Magazine 106 (1869): 320.

Blau, P. M. *The Dynamics of Bureaucracy: A Study of Interpersonal Relations in Two Government Agencies.* rev. ed. Chicago: University of Chicago Press, 1955.

———. *Exchange and Power in Social Life.* New York: John Wiley & Sons, 1964.

———. "Social Exchange." In *International Encyclopedia of the Social Sciences.* Vol. 7. Edited by D. L. Sills, pp. 452–457. New York: Macmillan Publishing Co., 1968.

Blood, R. O. *Marriage.* New York: Free Press, 1962.

Blood, R. O., and D. M. Wolfe. *Husbands and Wives.* New York: Free Press, 1960.

Blumstein, P. W., and E. A. Weinstein. "The Redress of Distributive Injustice." *American Journal of Sociology* 74 (1969): 408–418.

Bohannan, P., ed. *Divorce and After.* Garden City, N.Y.: Doubleday & Co., 1971.

Bond, J. R., and E. Vinacke. "Coalitions in Mixed-Sex Triads." *Sociometry* 24 (1961): 61–75.

Boulding, K. E. "The Economics of the Coming Spaceship Earth." In *Environmental Quality,* edited by H. Jarrett. Baltimore, Md.: Johns Hopkins University Press, 1966.

———. *The Economy of Love and Fear.* Belmont, Calif.: Wadsworth Publishing Co., 1973.

Bradburn, N. M. *The Structure of Psychological Well-Being.* Chicago: Aldine Publishing Co., 1969.

Bramel, B.; B. Taub; and B. Blum. "An Observer's Reaction to the Suffering of His Enemy." *Journal of Personality and Social Psychology* 8 (1968): 384–392.

Bramel, D. "Interpersonal Attraction, Hostility, and Perception." In *Experimental Social Psychology,* edited by J. Mills. Toronto: Macmillan Co., 1969.

Brandt, R. B., ed. *Social Justice.* Englewood Cliffs, N.J.: Prentice-Hall, 1962.

Bredemeier, H. C. "The Socially Handicapped and the Agencies: A Market Analysis." In *Mental Health of the Poor,* edited by F. Reissman, J. Cohen, and A. Pearl, pp. 88–109. New York: The Free Press of Glencoe, 1964.

Brehm, J. W., and A. R. Cohen. *Explorations in Cognitive Dissonance.* New York: John Wiley & Sons, 1962.

Brehm, J. W., and A. H. Cole. "Effect of a Favor Which Reduces Freedom." *Journal of Personality and Social Psychology* 3 (1966): 420–426.

Briar, S. "Welfare from Below: Recipients' Views of the Public Welfare System." *California Law Review* 54 (1966): 370–385.

Brickman, P., and D. T. Campbell. "Hedonic Relativism and Planning the Good Society." In *Adaptation-Level Theory: A Symposium,* edited by M. H. Appley. New York: Academic Press, 1971.

Brislin, R. W., and S. A. Lewis. "Dating and Physical Attractiveness: A Replication." *Psychological Reports* 22 (1968): 976.

Brock, T. C., and L. A. Becker. "Debriefing and Susceptability to Subsequent Experimental Manipulations." *Journal of Experimental Social Psychology* 2 (1966): 314–323.

Brock, T. C., and A. H. Buss. "Dissonance, Aggression, and Evaluation of Pain." *Journal of Abnormal and Social Psychology* 65 (1962): 197–202.

_____. "Effects of Justification for Aggression in Communication with the Victim on Post-Aggression Dissonance." *Journal of Abnormal and Social Psychology* 68 (1964): 403–412.

Broll, L.; A. E. Gross; and I. M. Piliavin. "Effects of Offered and Requested Help on Help Seeking and Reactions to Being Helped." *Journal of Abnormal and Social Psychology*, submitted, 1973.

Brown, B. R. "The Effects of Need to Maintain Face on Interpersonal Bargaining." *Journal of Experimental Social Psychology* 4 (1968): 107–122.

Bryan, J. A., and M. A. Test. "Models and Helping: Naturalistic Studies in Aiding Behavior." *Journal of Personality and Social Psychology* 8 (1968): 377–383.

Burgess, E. W., and L. W. Cottrell. *Predicting Success or Failure in Marriage.* Englewood Cliffs, N.J.: Prentice-Hall, 1939.

Burgess, E. W., and P. Wallin. *Engagement and Marriage.* Philadelphia: J.B. Lippincott Co., 1953.

Burgess, R. L., and J. D. Gregory. "Equity and Inequity in Exchange Relations: An Experimental Re-examination of Distributive Justice." Read at the West Coast Conference for Small Group Research, Honolulu, 1971.

Caldwell, J. C. "Fertility Attitudes in Three Economically Contrasting Rural Regions of Ghana." *Economic Development and Cultural Change* 15 (1967): 217–257.

_____. *Population Growth and Family Change in Africa: The New Urban Elite in Ghana.* Canberra: Australian National University Press, 1968.

Caplow, T. "A Theory of Coalitions in the Triad." *American Sociological Review* 21 (1956): 489–493.

Carlsmith, J. M., and A. E. Gross. "Some Effects of Guilt on Compliance." *Journal of Personality and Social Psychology* 11 (1969): 232–239.

Cartwright, D., and F. Harary. "Structural Balance: A Generalization of Heider's Theory." *Psychological Review* 63 (1956): 277–293.

Cartwright, D., and A. Zander. *Group Dynamics.* Evanston, Ill.: Row Peterson, 1962.

Centers, R., and G. H. Blumberg. "Social and Psychological Factors in Human Procreation: A Survey Approach." *Journal of Social Psychology* 40 (1954): 245–257.

Chaikin, A. L., and J. M. Darley. "Victim or Perpetrator: Defensive Attribution and the Need for Order and Justice." *Journal of Personality and Social Psychology* 25 (1973): 268–276.

Chertkoff, J. M. "Sociopsychological Theories and Research on Coalition Formation." In *The Study of Coalition Behavior,* edited by S. Groennings, E. W. Kelley, and M. Leiserson. New York: Holt, Rinehart and Winston, 1970.

Christensen, H. T. "Children in the Family: Relationship of Number and Spacing to Marital Success." *Journal of Marriage and the Family* 30 (1968): 283–289.

Clare, J. E., and C. V. Kiser. "Preference for Children of Given Sex in Relation to Fertility." In *Social and Psychological Factors Affecting Fertility,* edited by P. K. Whelpton and C. V. Kiser (1946–1958): 621–673. New York: Milbank Memorial Fund, 1951.

Clark, J. V. "A Preliminary Investigation of Some Unconscious Assumptions Affecting Labor Efficiency in Eight Supermarkets." Unpublished Ph.D. dissertation, Harvard University, 1958.

Clarke, A. C. *Profiles of the Future: An Inquiry into the Limits of the Possible.* New York: Harper & Row, Publishers, 1958.

Clausen, J. A., and S. R. Clausen. "The Effects of Family Size on Parents and Children." *Psychological Perspectives on Fertility* 7 (1973): 185–208.

Coles, R. *Children of Crisis: A Study of Courage and Fear.* Boston: Little, Brown and Co., 1967.

Collins, B. E., and H. Guetzkow. *A Social Psychology of Group Processes for Decision Making.* New York: John Wiley & Sons, 1964.

Collins, J. G. "The Role of the Law Enforcement Agency." In *The Battered Child,* edited by R. E. Helfer and C. H. Kempe, pp. 201–210. Chicago: University of Chicago Press, 1968.

Cuthbert, A. W. "The Influence of Authoritarianism, Severity, and Causality on Attribution of Responsibility." Unpublished Ph.D. dissertation, University of California at Berkeley, 1965.

Dansereau, F.; J. Cashman; and G. Green. "Instrumentality Theory and Equity Theory as Complementary Approaches in Predicting the Relationship of Leadership and Turnover Among Managers." *Organizational Behavior and Human Performance* 10 (1973): 184–200.

Darley, J. M., and C. D. Batson. "From Jerusalem to Jericho: A Study of Situational and Dispositional Variables in Helping Behavior." *Journal of Personality and Social Psychology* 27 (1973): 100–108.

Darley, J. M., and B. Latané. "Norms and 'Normative' Behavior: Field Studies of Social Interdependence." Paper presented at Wisconsin Conference in Research of Helping and Altruism, June 1968.

Darlington, R. B., and C. E. Macker. "Displacement of Guilt-Produced Altruistic Behavior." *Journal of Personality and Social Psychology* 4 (1966): 442–443.

Davidson, J. "Cognitive Familiarity and Dissonance Reduction." In *Conflict, Decision, and Dissonance,* edited by L. Festinger, pp. 45–60. Stanford, Calif.: Stanford University Press, 1964.

Davies, J. C. "Toward a Theory of Revolution." *American Sociological Review* 27 (1962): 5–19.

Davis, K. B. *Factors in the Sex Life of Twenty-two Hundred Women.* New York: Harper and Brothers, 1929.

Davis, K. E., and E. E. Jones. "Changes in Interpersonal Perception as a

Means of Reducing Cognitive Dissonance." *Journal of Abnormal and Social Psychology* 61 (1960): 402–410.

Davis, M. S. *Intimate Relations.* New York: The Free Press, 1973.

de Beauvoir, S. *The Second Sex.* New York: Bantam Books, 1952.

de Jong, de Josselin J. P. B. *Levi-Strauss's Theory on Kinship and Marriage.* Leiden, Holland: Brill, 1952.

de Sola Pool, I. "The International System in the Next Half Century." In *Daedalus: Toward the Year 2000: Work in Progress,* pp. 930–935. Boston: American Academy of Arts and Sciences, 1967.

Del Vecchio, G. "The Problem of Penal Justice (Imprisonment or Reparation of Damage)." Translated by Silving. *Revista Juridica de la Universidad de Puerto Rico* 27 (1959).

de Tocqueville, A. *The Old Regime and the French Revolution.* Translated by J. Bonner. New York: Harper and Brothers, 1856.

Deutsch, M. "The Effects of Cooperation and Competition upon Group Processes." In *Group Dynamics,* edited by D. Cartwright and A. Zander, pp. 414–448. Evanston, Ill.: Row Peterson, 1962.

_____. "Awakening the Sense of Injustice." In *Social Injustice in North America,* edited by M. Ross and M. Lerner. Canada: Holt, Rinehart and Winston, 1974.

Dillon, W. S. *Gifts and Nations.* The Hague: Mouton, 1968.

Donnenwerth, G. V., and U. G. Foa. "Effect of Resource Class on Retaliation to Injustice in Interpersonal Exchange." *Journal of Personality and Social Psychology* 29 (1974): 785–793.

Doob, A. Personal communication, 1972.

Dornic, S. "Subjective Distance and Emotional Involvement: A Verification of the Exponent Invariance." Reports from the Psychological Laboratories, University of Stockholm, no. 237 (November 1967).

Douglas, J. W. B., and J. M. Bloomfield. *Children Under Five.* London: Allen and Unwin, 1958.

Douvan, E. "Changing Sex Roles: Some Implications and Constraints." Presented at a symposium, "Women: Resource in a Changing World." The Radcliffe Institute, April 1972.

_____. "Interpersonal Relationships—Some Questions and Observations." Presented at Raush Conference, 1974.

Dow, T. E. "Family Size and Family Planning in Nairobi." *Demography* 4 (1967): 780–797.

Durkheim, E. *The Division of Labor in Society.* Translated by G. Simpson. New York: The Free Press, 1933.

Dyer, E. D. "Parenthood as Crisis: A Re-Study." *Marriage and Family Living* 25 (1963): 196–201.

Ehrlich, P. R. *The Population Bomb.* New York: Ballantine Books, 1968.

Ekman, G., and O. Bratfisch. "Subjective Distance and Emotional Involvement: A Psychological Mechanism." *Acta Psychologica* 24 (1965): 446–453.

Elder, G. H., Jr. "Appearance and Education in Marriage Mobility." *American Sociological Review* 34 (1969): 519–533.

Farber, B., and L. S. Blackman. "Marital Role Tensions and Number and Sex of Children." *American Sociological Review* 21 (1956): 596–601.

Fawcett, J. T., and F. S. Arnold. "The Value of Children: Theory and Method." *Representative Research in Social Psychology* 4 (1973): 23–36.

Feldman, H. Unpublished research cited by R. O. Blood, in *Marriage,* p. 207. New York: Free Press, 1962.

Feldman, R. E. "The Response to Compatriot and Foreigner Who Seek Assistance: Field Experiments in Paris, Athens, and Boston." Unpublished Ph.D. dissertation, Harvard University, March 1967.

Festinger, L. "A Theory of Social Comparison Processes." *Human Relations* 7 (1954): 117–140.

———. *A Theory of Cognitive Dissonance.* Evanston, Ill.: Row Peterson, 1957.

Festinger, L.; S. Schachter; and K. Back. *Social Pressures in Informal Groups: A Study of Human Factors in Housing.* New York: Harper & Row, Publishers, 1950.

Finley, M. I. *The Portable Greek Historians: The Essence of Herodotus.* New York: The Viking Press, 1959.

Finn, R. H., and S. M. Lee. "Salary Equity: Its Determination, Analysis, and Correlates." *Journal of Applied Psychology* 56 (1972): 283–292.

Flax, M. J. *A Study in Comparative Urban Indicators: Conditions in 18 Large Metropolitan Areas.* Washington, D.C.: The Urban Institute, 1972.

Flechtheim, O. K. "Futurology—The New Science of Probability?" In *History and Futurology,* pp. 69–80. Meisenheim am Galn, Germany: Verlag Anton Hain, 1966.

Foa, U. G. "Interpersonal and Economic Resources." *Science* 171 (1971): 345–351.

Foa, U. G., and E. B. Foa. *Societal Structures of the Mind.* Springfield, Ill.: Charles C Thomas, 1974.

Forrest, D. W., and S. J. Dimond. "Association between Galvanic Skin Response and Rorschach Performance." *Psychosomatic Medicine* 29 (1967): 676–682.

Freedman, J. Personal communication.

Freedman, J. L.; S. A. Wallington; and E. Bless. "Compliance without Pressure: The Effect of Guilt." *Journal of Personality and Social Psychology* 7 (1967): 117–124.

Freedman, R.; P. K. Whelpton; and A. A. Campbell. *Family Planning, Sterility, and Population Growth.* New York: McGraw-Hill Book Co., 1959.

French, J. R. P., Jr., and R. Snyder. "Leadership and Interpersonal Power." In *Studies in Social Power,* edited by D. Cartwright, pp. 118–149. Ann Arbor, Mich.: University of Michigan Press, 1959.

Freud, S. *The Problem of Anxiety.* New York: W. W. Norton & Co., 1936.

Friedland, N.; J. Thibaut; and L. Walker. "Some Determinants of the Violation of Rules." *Journal of Applied Social Psychology* 3 (1970); 103–118.

Friedman, A., and P. Goodman. "Wage Inequity, Self-Qualifications, and Productivity." *Organizational Behavior and Human Performance* 2 (1967): 406–417.

Friedman, L. M., and S. Macaulay. *Law and the Behavioral Sciences.* Indianapolis: The Bobbs-Merrill Co., 1969.

Frisch, D. M., and M. S. Greenberg. "Reciprocity and Intentionality in the Giving of Help." Proceedings of the 76th Annual Convention of the *American Psychological Association* 3 (1968): 383–384.

Fromm, E. *The Art of Loving.* New York: Harper & Row, Publishers, 1956.

Fry, M. "Justice for Victims." In *Compensation for Victims of Criminal Violence: A Round Table.* Atlanta, Ga.: Emory University Law School, *Journal of Public Law* 8 (1956): 155–253.

Fuller, R. B. "Technology and the Human Environment." In *The Ecological Conscience,* edited by R. Disch. Englewood Cliffs, N.J.: Prentice-Hall, 1972.

Gamson, W. A. "A Theory of Coalition Formation." *American Sociological Review* 26 (1961): 373–382.

Garrett, J. B. "Effects of Protestant Ethic Endorsement on Equity Behavior." Paper presented at the meeting of the American Psychological Association, Montreal, August 1973.

Garrett, J. B., and W. L. Libby, Jr. "Role of Intentionality in Mediating Responses to Inequity in the Dyad." *Journal of Personality and Social Psychology* 28 (1973): 21–27.

Garrison, R. J; V. E. Aronson; and S. C. Reed. "Assortive Marriage." *Engenics Quarterly* 15 (1968): 113–127.

Geer, J. "Fear and Autonomic Arousal." *Journal of Abnormal Psychology* 71 (1966): 253–255.

Gergen, K. J. *The Psychology of Behavior Exchange.* Reading, Mass.: Addison-Wesley Publishing Co., 1969.

Gergen, K. J., and M. K. Gergen. "International Assistance from a Psychological Perspective." *The Yearbook of International Affairs* 25 (1971): 87–103.

Gergen, K. J.; S. J. Morse; and K. Bode. "Overpaid or Overworked? Cognitive and Behavioral Reactions to Inequitable Rewards." *Journal of Applied Social Psychology* 4 (1974): 259–274.

Gergen, K. J.; M. Seipel; and P. Diebold. "Intentionality and Ability to Reciprocate as Determinants of Reactions to Aid." In preparation.

Gibran, K. *The Forerunner, His Parables and Poems.* London: Heinemann, 1963.

Giles, B. A., and G. V. Barrett. "Utility of Merit Increases." *Journal of Applied Psychology* 55 (1971): 103–109.

Glass, D. C. "Changes in Liking as a Means of Reducing Cognitive Discrepancies between Self-Esteem and Aggression." *Journal of Personality* 32 (1964): 520–549.

Glass, D. C., and J. D. Wood. "The Control of Aggression by Self-Esteem and Dissonance." In *The Cognitive Control of Motivation,* edited by P. G. Zimbardo, pp. 207–228. Glenview, Ill.: Scott, Foresman and Co., 1969.

Goffman, E. "On Cooling the Mark Out: Some Aspects of Adaptation to Failure." *Psychiatry* 15 (1952): 451–463.

Goldin, G. J.; S. L. Perry; R. J. Margolin; and B. A. Stotsky. "Dependency and Its Implications for Rehabilitation." *Northeastern Studies in Vocational Rehabilitation,* Monograph no. 1, 1967.

Goodman, P. S., and A. Friedman. "An Examination of Adams' Theory of Inequity." *Administrative Science Quarterly* 16 (1971): 271–288.

Goranson, R. E., and L. Berkowitz. "Reciprocity and Responsibility Reactions to Prior Help." *Journal of Personality and Social Psychology* 3 (1966): 227–232.

Gordon, J. *The Poor of Harlem: Social Functioning in the Underclass.* New York: Office of the Mayor, 1965. Cited in H. Posman, *Poverty and Social Welfare: Research in Public Assistance.* Proceedings of a conference on research on poverty. Bureau of Social Science Research, Washington, D.C., 1968.

Gottesman, I. I. "Personality and Natural Selection." In *Methods and Goals in Human Behavior Genetics,* edited by S. G. Vandenberg, pp. 63–80. New York: Academic Press, 1965.

Gouldner, A. "The Norm of Reciprocity: A Preliminary Statement." *American Sociological Review* 25 (1960): 161–178.

Greenberg, M. S. "A Preliminary Statement on a Theory of Indebtedness." In *Justice in Social Exchange,* symposium presented at the Western Psychological Association, San Diego, September 1968.

Greenberg, M. S., and D. M. Frisch. "Effect of Intentionality on Willingness to Reciprocate a Favor." *Journal of Experimental Social Psychology* 8 (1972): 99–111.

Greenberg, M. S., and S. P. Shapiro. "Indebtedness: An Adverse Aspect of Asking For and Receiving Help." *Sociometry* 34 (1971): 290–301.

Gross, A. E., and J. G. Latané. "Some Effects of Receiving and Giving Help." Unpublished manuscript, 1973.

Gross, A. E.; I. M. Piliavin; B. S. Wallston; and L. Broll. "When Humanitarianism Is Not Humane: Helping—The Recipient's View." Paper presented at American Psychological Association, Honolulu, September 1972. Unpublished manuscript, revised, 1973.

Gurin, G.; J. Veroff; and S. Feld. *Americans View Their Mental Health.* New York: Basic Books, 1960.

Gurr, T. R. *Why Men Rebel.* Princeton, N.J.: Princeton University Press, 1970.

Guthrie, G. M. "Psychological Factors and Preferred Family Size." *Saint Louis Quarterly* 6 (1968): 391–398.

Hamilton, G. V. *A Research in Marriage.* New York: Lear, 1948.

Harper, R. F. *The Code of Hammurabi: King of Babylon About 2250 B.C.* Chicago: The University of Chicago Press, 1904.

Harvey, O. J., and C. Consalvi. "Status and Conformity to Pressures in Informal Groups." *Journal of Abnormal and Social Psychology* 60 (1960): 182–187.

Hastorf and Regan. Personal communication, 1962.

Heider, F. *The Psychology of Interpersonal Relations.* New York: John Wiley & Sons, 1958.

Heilbroner, R. L. *An Inquiry Into the Human Prospect.* New York: W. W. Norton & Co., 1974.

Heisel, D. F. "Attitudes and Practices of Contraception in Kenya." *Demography* 5 (1968): 632–641.

Helmer, O. "Prospects of Technological Progress." Rand Corporation, August 1967, p. 3643.

Henry, A. F., and J. F. Short, Jr. *Suicide and Homicide: Some Economic, Sociological, and Psychological Aspects of Aggression.* Glencoe, Ill.: Free Press, 1954.

Herter, G. L. *How to Live with a Bitch.* Waseca, Minn.: Herter's, 1972.

Hobbes, T. *Leviathan.* Indianapolis: The Bobbs-Merrill Co., 1958.

_____. In *Leviathan,* edited by Francis B. Randall. New York: Washington Square Press, 1964.

Hoffman, L. W. "The Decision to Work." In *The Employed Mother in America,* edited by F. E. Nye, and L. W. Hoffman, pp. 18–39. Chicago: Rand McNally & Co., 1963.

Holmes, S. J., and C. E. Hatch. "Personal Appearance as Related to Scholastic Records and Marriage Selection in College Women." *Human Biology* 10 (1938): 65–76.

Homans, G. C. "Social Behavior as Exchange." *American Journal of Sociology* 63 (1958): 597–606.

_____. *Social Behavior: Its Elementary Forms.* New York: Harcourt, Brace & World, 1961.

Horai, J., and J. T. Tedeschi. "The Effects of Threat Credibility and Magnitude of Punishment upon Compliance." *Journal of Personality and Social Psychology* 12 (1969): 164–169.

Hornstein, H. A.; E. Fisch; and M. Holmes. "Influence of a Model's Feeling about His Behavior and His Relevance as a Comparison Other on Observers' Helping Behavior." *Journal of Personality and Social Psychology* 10 (1968): 222–226.

Huesmann, L. R., and G. Levinger. "Incremental Exchange Theory: A Formal Model for Progression in Dyadic Social Interaction." In *Advances in Experimental Social Psychology.* Vol. 9. Edited by L. Berkowitz and E. Walster, pp. 192–229. New York: Academic Press, 1976.

Huston, T. L. "Ambiguity of Acceptance, Social Desirability, and Dating Choice." *Journal of Experimental Social Psychology* 9 (1973): 32–42.

Huxley, A. *Brave New World.* New York: Harper & Row, Publishers, 1932.

_____. *Tomorrow and Tomorrow and Tomorrow and Other Essays.* New York: Harper & Row, Publishers, 1972.

Jacoby, A. P. "Transition to Parenthood: A Reassessment." *Journal of Marriage and Family Living,* November 1969, pp. 720–727.

James, W. "What Is an Emotion?" *Mind* 9 (1884): 188–205.

Jantsch, E. "For a Science of Man." In *Can We Survive Our Future?* edited by G. R. Urban and M. Glenny, pp. 103–126. New York: St. Martin's Press, 1972.

Jaques, E. *Measurement of Responsibility.* London: Tavistock, 1956.

———. *Equitable Payment.* New York: John Wiley & Sons, 1961.

Jecker, J., and D. Landy. "Liking a Person as a Function of Doing Him a Favor." *Human Relations* 22 (1969): 371–378.

Joffe, N. F. "Non-Reciprocity Among East European Jews." In *The Study of Culture at a Distance,* edited by M. Mead and R. Metraux, pp. 386–387. Chicago: University of Chicago Press, 1953.

Johnson, D. "The Influence of Age, Education, and Frequency of Purchase of Fabrics on the Amount and Type of Information Desired by the Consumer." Unpublished Master's thesis, University of Wisconsin, 1971.

Jones, A. In Marjorie Palmer, "Marriage and the Formerly Fat: The Effect Weight Loss Has on Your Life Together." *Weight Watchers* 7 (1974).

Jones, H. E. "Homogamy in Intellectual Abilities." *American Journal of Sociology* 35 (1929): 369–382.

Jourard, S. M. *Self-Disclosure.* New York: John Wiley & Sons, 1971.

Julian, J. W., and F. A. Perry. "Cooperation Contrasted with Intra-Group and Inter-Group Competition." *Sociometry* 30 (1967): 79–90.

Kahn, A. "Reactions to Generosity or Stinginess from an Intelligent or Stupid Work Partner: A Test of Equity Theory in a Direct Exchange Relationship." *Journal of Personality and Social Psychology* 21 (1972): 116–123.

Kahn, H., and A. J. Wiener. *The Year 2000: A Framework for Speculation on the Next Thirty-Three Years.* New York: Macmillan Publishing Co., 1967.

Kalish, R. A. "Of Children and Grandfathers: A Speculative Essay on Dependency." *The Gerontologist* 7 (1967): 65–69, 79, 185ff.

Kalven, J., Jr., and H. Zeisel, *The American Jury.* Chicago: University of Chicago Press, 1971.

Karlsson, G. *Adaptability and Communication in Marriage: A Swedish Predictive Study of Marital Satisfaction.* Uppsala, Sweden: Almquist and Wikiells, 1951.

Karsh, B., and R. E. Cole. "Industrialization and the Convergence Hypothesis: Some Aspects of Contemporary Japan." *Journal of Social Issues* 24 (1968): 45–64.

Katz, I.; D. D. Glass; and S. Cohen. "Ambivalence, Guilt, and the Scapegoating of Minority Group Victims." *Journal of Experimental Social Psychology* 9 (1973): 423–436.

Kenedi, R. M. In *The World in 1984,* edited by N. Calder, p. 204. Baltimore, Md.: Penguin, 1965.

Kessler, J. J., and Y. Wiener. "Self-Consistency and Inequity Dissonance as Factors in Undercompensation." *Organizational Behavior and Human Performance* 8 (1972): 456–466.

Kiesler, S., and R. Baral. "The Search for a Romantic Partner: The Effects of Self-Esteem and Physical Attractiveness on Romantic Behavior." In *Personality and Social Behavior,* edited by K. Gergen and D. Marlowe, Reading, Mass.: Addison-Wesley Publishing Co., 1970.

Kipnis, D. "Does Power Corrupt?" *Journal of Personality and Social Psychology* 24 (1972*a*): 33–41.

_____. "The Powerholder." Presented at the Second Albany Symposium on Power and Influence, October 1972*b*.

Kiser, C. V., ed. *Research in Family Planning.* Princeton, N.J.: Princeton University Press, 1962.

_____. "Assortative Mating by Educational Attainment in Relation to Fertility." *Eugenic Quarterly* 15 (1968): 98–112.

Klein, S. M. "Pay Factors as Predictors to Satisfaction: A Comparison of Reinforcement, Equity and Expectancy." *Academy of Management Journal* 16 (1973): 598–610.

Knox, J. B. "The Concept of Exchange in Sociological Theory: 1884 and 1961." *Social Forces* 41 (1963): 341–346.

Komarovsky, M. *Blue-Collar Marriage.* New York: Vintage Books, 1967.

_____. The Unemployed Man and His Family. New York: Octagon Books, 1971.

Komorita, S. S., and J. M. Chertkoff. "A Bargaining Theory of Coalition Formation." *Psychological Review* 80 (1973): 149–162.

Krebs, D. "Altruism—An Examination of the Concept and a Review of the Literature." *Psychological Bulletin* 73 (1970): 258–302.

Krebs, D., and J. Baldwin. Reported in D. Krebs and P. Whitten, "Guilt-Edged Giving—The Shame of It All." *Psychology Today,* January 1972, pp. 50–78.

Ladieu, G.; E. Hanfmann; and T. Dembo. "Studies in Adjustment to Visible Injuries: Evaluation of Help by the Injured." *Journal of Abnormal and Social Psychology* 42 (1947): 169–192.

Lane, I. M., and R. C. Coon. "Reward Allocation in Pre-School Children." *Child Development* 43 (1972): 1382–1389.

Lane, I. M., and L. A. Messé. "Equity and the Distribution of Rewards." *Journal of Personality and Social Psychology* 20 (1971): 1–17.

Lane, I. M.; L. A. Messé; and J. L. Phillips. "Differential Inputs as a Determinant in the Selection of a Distributor of Rewards." *Psychonomic Science* 22 (1971): 228–229.

Lang, R. O. "The Rating of Happiness in Marriage." Unpublished Master's thesis, University of Chicago, 1932.

Latané, B., and J. M. Darley. *The Unresponsive Bystander: Why Doesn't He Help?* New York: Appleton-Century-Crofts, 1970.

Lawler, E. E., III. "Effects of Hourly Overpayment on Productivity and Work Quality." *Journal of Personality and Social Psychology* 10 (1968*a*): 306–313.

_____. "Equity Theory as a Predictor of Productivity and Work Quality." *Psychological Bulletin* 70 (1968*b*): 596–610.

_____. *Pay and Organizational Effectiveness: A Psychological View.* New York: McGraw-Hill Book Co., 1971.

Lawler, E. E., III; C. A. Koplin; T. F. Young; and J. A. Fadem. "Inequity Reduction over Time in an Induced Overpayment Situation." *Organizational Behavior and Human Performance* 3 (1968): 253–268.

Lawler, E. E., and P. W. O'Gara. "The Effects of Inequity Produced by Underpayment on Work Output, Work Quality, and Attitudes Toward the Work." *Journal of Applied Psychology* 51 (1967): 403–410.

Lazarus, R.; E. M. Opton; M. S. Nomikos; and N. O. Rankin. "The Principle of Short-Circuiting of Threat: Further Evidence." *Journal of Personality* 33 (1965): 622–635.

Leeds, R. "Altruism and the Norm of Giving." *Merrill-Palmer Quarterly* 9 (1963): 229–240.

Legant, P. "The Deserving Victim: Effects of Length of Pre-Trial Detention, Crime Severity, and Juror Attitudes on Simulated Jury Decisions." Unpublished Ph.D. dissertation, Yale University, 1973.

Legant, P., and D. R. Mettee. "Turning the Other Cheek vs. Getting Even: Vengeance, Equity and Attraction." *Journal of Personality and Social Psychology* 25 (1973): 243–253.

LeMasters, E. E. "Parenthood as Crisis." *Marriage and Family Living* 19 (1957): 352–355.

Lerner, M. J. "Evaluation of Performance as a Function of Performer's Reward and Attractiveness." *Journal of Personality and Social Psychology* 1 (1965): 355–360.

——. "The Unjust Consequences of the Need to Believe in a Just World." Paper read at the American Psychological Association, New York, September 1966.

——. "Conditions Eliciting Acceptance or Rejection of a 'Martyr'," Unpublished manuscript, University of Kentucky, 1968.

——. "The Desire for Justice and Reactions to Victims." In *Altruism and Helping Behavior,* edited by J. Macaulay and L. Berkowitz, pp. 205–229. New York: Academic Press, 1970.

——. "Deserving vs. Justice: A Contemporary Dilemma." Research Report no. 24. Department of Psychology, University of Waterloo, May 15, 1971a.

——. "Observer's Evaluation of Victim: Justice, Guilt, and Veridical Perception." *Journal of Personality and Social Psychology* 20 (1971b): 127–135.

——. "Justified Self-Interest and the Responsibility for Suffering: A Replication and Extension." *Journal of Human Relations* 19 (1971c): 550–559.

——. "The Justice Motive: 'Equity' and 'Parity' among Children." *Journal of Personality and Social Psychology* 29 (1974): 539–550.

Lerner, M. J., and R. R. Lichtman. "Effects of Perceived Norms on Attitudes and Altruistic Behavior toward a Dependent Other." *Journal of Personality and Social Psychology* 9 (1968): 226–232.

Lerner, M. J., and G. Matthews. "Reactions to the Suffering of Others under Conditions of Indirect Responsibility." *Journal of Personality and Social Psychology* 5 (1967): 319–325.

Lerner, M. J., and C. H. Simmons. "Observer's Reaction to the 'Innocent Victim's: Compassion or Rejection?" *Journal of Personality and Social Psychology* 4 (1966): 203–210.

Leventhal, G. S. "Reward Allocation in Social Relationships." Paper presented at the meeting of the Southeastern Psychological Association, Atlanta, April 1972.

_____. "Reward Allocation by Males and Females." Paper presented at the meeting of the American Psychological Association, Montreal, August 1973.

_____. "The Distribution of Rewards and Resources in Groups and Organizations." In *Advances in Experimental Social Psychology.* Vol. 9. Edited by L. Berkowitz and E. Walster, pp. 91–131. New York: Academic Press, 1976*a*.

_____. "Fairness in Social Relationships." In *Contemporary Topics in Social Psychology,* edited by J. Thibaut, J. T. Spence, and R. Carson. Morristown, N.J.: General Learning Press, 1976*b*.

Leventhal, G. S.; J. Allen; and B. Kemelgor. "Reducing Inequity by Reallocating Rewards." *Psychonomic Sciences* 14 (1969): 295–296.

Leventhal, G. S., and D. Anderson. "Self-Interest and the Maintenance of Equity." *Journal of Personality and Social Psychology* 15 (1970): 57–62.

Leventhal, G. S., and J. T. Bergman. "Self-Depriving Behavior as a Response to Unprofitable Inequity." *Journal of Experimental Social Psychology* 5 (1969): 153–171.

Leventhal, G. S., and D. W. Lane. "Sex, Age, and Equity Behavior." *Journal of Personality and Social Psychology* 15 (1970): 312–316.

Leventhal, G. S., and J. W. Michaels. "Extending the Equity Model: Perception of Inputs and Allocation of Reward as a Function of Duration and Quantity of Performance." *Journal of Personality and Social Psychology* 12 (1969): 303–309.

_____. "Locus of Cause and Equity Motivations as Determinants of Reward Allocation." *Journal of Personality and Social Psychology* 17 (1971): 229–235.

Leventhal, G. S.; J. W. Michaels; and C. Sanford. "Inequity and Interpersonal Conflict: Reward Allocation and Secrecy about Reward as Methods of Preventing Conflict." *Journal of Personality and Social Psychology* 23 (1972): 88–102.

Leventhal, G. S.; A. L. Popp; and L. Sawyer. "Equity or Equality in Children's Allocation of Reward to Other Persons?" *Child Development* 44 (1973): 753–763.

Leventhal, G. S.; E. Reilly; and P. Lehrer. "Change in Reward as a Determinant of Satisfaction and Reward Expectancy." Paper read at Western Psychological Association, Portland, Oregon, 1964.

Leventhal, G. S.; T. Weiss; and R. Buttrick. "Attribution of Value, Equity, and the Prevention of Waste in Reward Allocation." *Journal of Personality and Social Psychology* 27 (1973): 276–286.

Leventhall, G. S.; T. Weiss; and G. Long. "Equity, Reciprocity, and Reallocating the Rewards in the Dyad." *Journal of Personality and Social Psychology* 13 (1969): 300–305.

Levinger, G. "The Development of Perceptions and Behavior in Newly Formed Social Power Relationships." In *Studies in Social Power,* edited by D. Cartwright, pp. 83–98. Ann Arbor, Mich.: University of Michigan Press, 1959.

Levinger, G.; D. J. Senn; and P. W. Jorgensen. "Progress Toward Permanence in Courtship: A Test of the Kerckhoff-Davis Hypotheses." *Sociometry* 33 (1970): 427–443.

Levinger, G., and J. D. Snoek. *Attraction in Relationship: A New Look at Interpersonal Attraction.* Morristown, N.J.: General Learning Press, 1972.

Levi-Strauss, C. "Reciprocity, The Essence of Social Life." In *The Family: Its Structure and Function,* edited by R. Coser, pp. 36–48. New York: St. Martin's Press, 1964.

Lichtman, R. J. "Values and the Distribution of Rewards." Paper presented Southeastern Psychological Association, Atlanta, April 1972.

Lincoln, H., and G. Levinger. "Observers' Evaluations of the Victim and the Attacker in an Aggressive Incident." *Journal of Personality and Social Psychology* 22 (1972): 202–210.

Lipman, A., and R. Sterne. "Aging in the U.S.: Ascription of a Terminal Sick Role." *Sociology and Social Research* 53 (1962): 194–203.

Lippitt, R.; N. Polansky; F. Redl; and S. Rosen. "The Dynamics of Power." *Human Relations* 5 (1952): 37–64.

Locke, H. J. *Predicting Adjustment in Marriage: A Comparison of a Divorced and a Happily-Married Group.* New York: Henry Holt, 1951.

Locke, J. *Two Treatises on Government.* Lonson: Printed for R. Butler, Berkeley Square; W. Reid, Charing-Cross; W. Sharpe, Covent Garden; and J. Bumpas, Holborn Bars, 1821.

Macaulay, S., and E. Walster. "Legal Structures and Restoring Equity." *Journal of Social Issues* 27 (1971): 173–188.

McBride, A. B. *The Growth and Development of Mothers.* New York: Harper & Row, Publishers, 1973.

McCall, M. M. "Courtship as Social Exchange: Some Historical Comparisons." In *Kinship and Family Organization,* edited by B. Farber, pp. 190–200. New York: John Wiley & Sons, 1966.

McDougall, W. *An Introduction to Social Psychology.* London: Methuen, 1908.

McGinn, N. "Justice and Self-Interest in the Allocation of Rewards in a Dyad." Unpublished senior thesis, University of Wisconsin, 1973.

McGuire, W. J. "The Nature of Attitudes and Attitude Change." In *The Handbook of Social Psychology,* 2nd ed. Vol. 3. Edited by G. Lindzey and E. Aronson, pp. 136–314. Reading, Mass.: Addison-Wesley Publishing Co., 1969.

Maher, B. A. *Principles of Psychopathology: An Experimental Approach.* New York: McGraw-Hill Book Co., 1966.

Malinowski. B. *Argonauts of the Western Pacific: An Account of Native Enterprise and Adventure in the Archipelagoes of Melanesian New Guinea.* New York: E. P. Dutton & Co., 1922.

Martin, W. T. "Family Planning Attitudes and Knowledge: A Study of African Families in Nairobi." Unpublished manuscript, 1970.

Marwell, G.; K. Ratcliff; and D. R. Schmitt. "Minimizing Differences in a Maximizing Difference Game." *Journal of Personality and Social Psychology* 12 (1969): 158–163.

Marwell, G.; D. R. Schmitt; and R. Shotola. "Cooperation and Interpersonal Risk." *Journal of Personality and Social Psychology* 18 (1971): 9–32.

Marx, K. *Wage—Labour and Capital.* New York: International Publishers, 1933.

Maslow, A. H. *Motivation and Personality.* 2nd ed. New York: Harper & Row, Publishers, 1970.

Mason, P. *Patterns of Dominance.* New York: Oxford University Press, 1971.

Masters, J. C. "Effects of Social Comparison upon Subsequent Self-Reinforcement Behavior in Children." *Journal of Personality and Social Psychology* 10 (1968): 391–401.

Mauss, M., *The Gift: Forms and Functions of Exchange in Archaic Societies.* Glencoe, Ill.: Free Press, 1954.

Maynes, C., Jr. "Hungry New World vs. American Ethic." *St. Paul Pioneer Press* [Focus], 8 December 1974, pp. 1, 10.

Meade, R. "Assessment of Personal Motivations for Childbearing." Paper presented at the Conference on Psychological Measurement in Family Planning and Population Policy, University of California, Berkeley, February 1971.

Merton, R. K. *Social Theory and Social Structure.* Glencoe, Ill.: The Free Press, 1957.

———. "Contributions to the Theory of Reference Group Behavior." In *Social Theory and Social Structure,* pp. 279–438. New York: The Free Press, 1968.

Messé, L. A. "The Concept of Equity in Bargaining." Paper presented at the Peace Research Society (International), Ann Arbor, Michigan, November 1969.

———. "Equity and Bilateral Bargaining." *Journal of Personality and Social Psychology* 17 (1971): 287–291.

Messé, L. A., and R. J. Lichtman. "Motivation for Money as a Mediator of the Extent to which Quality and Duration of Work Are Inputs Relevant to the Distribution of Rewards." Paper presented at the Southeastern Psychological Association, Atlanta 1972.

Michener, H. A., and E. D. Cohen. "Effects of Punishment Magnitude in the Bilateral Threat Situation: Evidence for the Deterrence Hypothesis." *Journal of Personality and Social Psychology* 26 (1973): 427–438.

Michener, H. A.; J. Griffith; and R. L. Palmer. "Threat Potential and Rule Enforceability as Sources of Normative Emergence in a Bargaining Situation." *Journal of Personality and Social Psychology* 20 (1971): 230–239.

Michener, H. A., and R. A. Zeller. "The Effects of Coalition Strength on the Formation of Contractual Norms." *Sociometry* 35 (1972): 290–304.

Midlarsky, E. "Aiding Responses: An Analysis and Review." *Merrill-Palmer Quarterly* 14 (1968): 229–260.

Mikula, G. "Gewinnaufteilungsverhalten in Gleichgeschlechtlichen Dyaden: Eine Vergleichsstudie Österreichischer und Amerikanischer Studenten." *Psychologie und Praxis* 16 (1972): 97–106.

Mill, J. S. *On the Subjection of Women.* Greenwich, Conn.: Fawcett, 1971.

Mills, J. "Changes in Moral Attitudes Following Temptation." *Journal of Personality* 26 (1958): 517–531.

Milwaukee Journal. 17 October 1973, sec. 1, p. 2.

Moore, L. M., and R. M. Baron. "Effects of Wage Inequities on Work Attitudes and Performance." *Journal of Experimental Social Psychology* 9 (1973): 1–16.

Morgan, W. R., and J. Sawyer. "Bargaining, Expectations, and the Preference for Equality over Equity." *Journal of Personality and Social Psychology* 6 (1967): 139–149.

Morris, S. C., III, and S. Rosen. "Effects of Feld Adequacy and Opportunity to Reciprocate on Help Seeking." *Journal of Experimental Social Psychology* 9 (1973): 265–276.

Morse, S. J.; H. T. Reis; and J. Gruzen. "Hedonism and Equity in Heterosexual Interaction." Paper presented at a symposium on "Exchange Theory and Interpersonal Relationships" at the American Psychological Association, Montreal, Canada, August 1973.

Mueller, E. "Attitudes Toward the Economics of Family Size and Their Relation to Fertility." Unpublished manuscript, University of Michigan, 1970.

Murdock, P. "The Development of Contractual Norms in a Dyad." *Journal of Personality and Social Psychology* 6 (1967): 206–211.

Murdock, P., and D. Rosen. "Norm Foundation in an Interdependent Dyad." *Sociometry* 33 (1970): 264–275.

Murray, H. A. *Explorations in Personality.* New York: Oxford University Press, 1938.

Murstein, B. I. "The Relationship of Mental Health to Marital Choice and Courtship Progress." *Journal of Marriage and the Family* 29 (1967a): 447–451.

_____. "Empirical Tests of Role, Complementary Needs, and Homogamy Theories of Marital Choice." *Journal of Marriage and the Family* 29 (1967b): 689–696.

_____. "Physical Attractiveness and Marital Choice." *Journal of Personality and Social Psychology* 22 (1972): 8–12.

Murstein, B. I.; M. Goyette; and M. Cerreto. "A Theory of the Effect of Exchange Orientation on Marriage and Friendship." Unpublished manuscript, 1974.

Myrdal, A., and V. Klein. *Women's Two Roles: Home and Work.* London: Routledge & Kegan Paul, 1956.

Nemeth, C. "Effects of Free Versus Constrained Behavior on Attraction between People." *Journal of Personality and Social Psychology* 15 (1970): 302–311.

Newton, N. "Pregnancy, Childbirth, and Outcome: A Review of Patterns of Culture and Future Research Needs." In *Childbearing: Its Social and Psychological Aspects,* edited by S. A. Richardson and A. F. Guttmacher, pp. 147–228. Baltimore: Williams and Wilkins, 1967.

Neyfach, A., in V. Zorza (interviewer). "Spectre of a Genetic 'Arms Race'," *Guardian Weekly,* 13 December 1969, p. 6.

Nomikos, M., E. Opton; J. Averill; and R. Lazarus. "Surprise versus Suspense in the Production of Stress Reaction." *Journal of Personality and Social Psychology* 8 (1968): 204–208.

Novicow, J. "The Mechanism and Limits of Human Association: The Foundations of a Sociology of Peace." *American Journal of Sociology* 23 (1917): 289–349.

Nowlis, V., and R. Green. "The Experimental Study of Mood." Technical Report no. 3. Office of Naval Research: Contract no. Nonr-668 (12), 1957.

Oliver, D. L. *A Solomon Island Society.* Boston: Beacon Press, 1967.

Olson, M. *The Logic of Collective Action.* New York: Schocken Books, 1968.

Opsahl, R. L., and M. D. Dunnette. "The Role of Financial Compensation in Industrial Motivation." *Psychological Bulletin* 66 (1966): 99–118.

Pannen, D. E. "Anticipation of Future Interaction and the Estimation of Current Rewards." Unpublished Ph.D. dissertation, University of Minnesota, 1976.

Patchen, M. *The Choice of Wage Comparisons.* Englewood Cliffs, N.J.: Prentice-Hall, 1961.

_____. "Models of Cooperation and Conflict: A Critical Review." *Journal of Conflict Resolution* 3 (1970): 389–407.

Patterson, G. R. *Families: Applications of Social Learning to Family Life.* Champaign, Ill.: Research Press Co., 1971.

Pepitone, A. "The Role of Justice in Interdependent Decision Making." *Journal of Experimental Social Psychology* 7 (1971): 144–156.

Perkins, J. G. *The Life of the Honourable Mrs. Norton.* New York: H. Holt and Co., 1909.

Piliavin, J. A., and I. M. Piliavin. "Distance and Donations." Unpublished manuscript, University of Pennsylvania, 1969.

_____. "Bystander Behavior in Emergencies." Proposal submitted to the National Science Foundation, July 1971.

_____. "The Effect of Blood on Reactions to a Victim." *Journal of Personality and Social Psychology* 23 (1972): 353–361.

_____. "The Good Samaritan: Why Does He Help?" Unpublished manuscript, 1973.

Piliavin, I. M.; J. Rodin; and J. A. Piliavin. "Good Samaritanism: An Underground Phenomenon?" *Journal of Personality and Social Psychology* 13 (1969): 289–299.

Piliavin, J., and E. Walster. "Equity and the Innocent Bystander." *Journal of Social Issues* 28 (1972): 165–189.

Poffenberger, T. "Motivational Aspects of Resistance to Family Planning in an Indian Village." *Demography* 5 (1968): 757–766.

Pohlman, E. *The Psychology of Birth Planning.* Cambridge, Mass.: Schenkman Publishing, 1969.

Pollock, F., and F. W. Maitland, *The History of English Law,* 2nd ed. Vol. 2. Cambridge: The University Press, 1898.

Pondy, L. R., and J. G. Birnberg. "An Experimental Study of the Allocation of Financial Resources within Small Hierarchical Task Groups." *Administrative Science Quarterly* 14 (1969): 192–201.

Porter, L. W., and E. E. Lawler. *Managerial Attitudes and Performance.* Homewood, Ill.: Richard D. Irwin, 1968.

President's Commission on Population Growth and the American Future. New York: New American Library, 1972.

Pritchard, R. D. "Equity Theory: A Review and Critique." *Organizational Behavior and Human Performance* 4 (1969): 176–211.

Pritchard, R. D.; M. D. Dunnette; and D. O. Jorgenson. "Effects of Perceptions of Equity and Inequity on Worker Performance and Satisfaction." *Journal of Applied Psychology Monograph* 56 (1972): 75–94.

Pruitt, D. G. "Reciprocity and Credit Building in a Laboratory Dyad." *Journal of Personality and Social Psychology* 8 (1968): 143–147.

———. "Methods for Resolving Differences of Interest: A Theoretical Analysis." *Journal of Social Issues* 28 (1972): 133–154.

Psathas, G., and S. Stryker. "Bargaining Behavioral Orientation in Coalition Formation." *Sociometry* 28 (1965): 124–144.

Puzo, M. *The Godfather.* New York: G. P. Putnam's Sons, 1969.

Quarton, G. C. "Deliberate Efforts to Control Human Behavior and Modify Personality." In *Daedalus: Toward the Year 2000: Work in Progress,* pp. 837–853. Boston: American Academy of Arts and Sciences, 1967.

Radcliffe, J. M., ed. *The Good Samaritan and the Law.* Garden City, N.Y.: Doubleday & Co., 1966.

Radl, S. L. *Mother's Day is Over.* New York: Charter House, 1973.

Rainwater, L., and K. K. Weinstein. *And The Poor Get Children.* Chicago: Quadrangle, 1960.

Rainwater, L. *Family Design: Marital Sexuality, Family Size, and Family Planning.* Chicago: Aldine Publishing Co., 1965.

Reed, R. B. "Interrelationship of Marital Adjustment, Fertility Control, and Size of Family." In *Social and Psychological Factors Affecting Fertility,* edited by P. K. Whelpton and C. V. Kiser (1946–1958): 259–301. New York: Milbank Memorial Fund, 1947.

Reed, E. W., and S. C. Reed. *Mental Retardation: A Family Study.* Philadelphia: W. B. Saunders, 1965.

Renne, K. S. "Correlates of Dissatisfaction in Marriage." *Journal of Marriage and the Family* 32 (1970): 54–67.

Rose, A. M., and A. F. Prell. "Does the Punishment Fit the Crime?" *The American Journal of Sociology* 61 (1955): 247–259.

Rosenberg, M. J. "An Analysis of Affective Cognitive Consistency." In *Attitude Organization and Change.* Edited by M. J. Rosenberg and C. I. Hovland, pp. 15–64. New Haven, Conn.: Yale University Press, 1960.

Rosenberg, M. J., and L. P. Abelson. "An Analysis of Cognitive Balancing." In *Attitude Organization and Change.* Edited by M. J. Rosenberg and C. I. Hovland. New Haven, Conn.: Yale University Press, 1960.

Rosenthal, R. *Experimenter Effects in Behavioral Research.* New York: Appleton-Century-Crofts, 1966.

Ross, A. S. "Modes of Guilt Reduction." Paper read at Eastern Psychological Association, New York, April 1966.

Ross, M., and M. J. McMillen. "External Referents and Past Outcomes as Determinants of Social Discontent." *Journal of Experimental Social Psychology* 9 (1973): 437–449.

Ross, W. D., ed. *The Works of Aristotle.* Vol. 9. London: Oxford University Press, 1966.

Ross, M.; J. Thibaut; and S. Evenbeck. "Some Determinants of the Intensity of Social Protest." *Journal of Experimental Social Psychology* 7 (1971): 401–418.

Rousseau, J. J. Translated by G. D. H. Cole. *The Social Contract and Discourses.* London: J. M. Denton and Sons, 1913.

Rubin, Z. "The Measurement of Romantic Love." *Journal of Personality and Social Psychology* 16 (1970): 265–273.

———. *Liking and Loving: An Invitation to Social Psychology.* New York: Holt, Rinehart and Winston, 1973.

Sampson, E. E. "Studies of Status Congruence." In *Advances in Experimental Social Psychology.* Vol. 4. Edited by L. Berkowitz, pp. 225–270. New York: Academic Press, 1969.

Sampson, R. V. *The Psychology of Power.* New York: Vintage Books, 1968.

Sarnoff, I. *Personality Dynamics and Development.* New York: John Wiley & Sons, 1962.

Scanzoni, J. *Sexual Bargaining: Power Politics in the American Marriage.* Englewood Cliffs, N.J.: Prentice-Hall, 1972.

Schafer, S. *Restitution to Victims of Crime.* London: Stevens & Son, 1960.

Schelling, T. C. *The Strategy of Conflict.* Cambridge, Mass.: Harvard University Press, 1960.

Schmitt, D. R., and G. Marwell. "Withdrawal and Reward Allocation as Responses to Inequity." *Journal of Experimental Social Psychology* 8 (1972): 207–221.

Schopler, J., and V. D. Thompson. "Role of Attribution Processes in Mediating Amount of Reciprocity for a Favor." *Journal of Personality and Social Psychology* 10 (1968): 243–250.

Schwartz, S. H. "Elicitation of Moral Obligation and Self-Sacrificing Behavior: An Experimental Study of Volunteering to be a Bone Marrow Donor." *Journal of Personality and Social Psychology* 15 (1970): 283–293.

Schwartz, S. H., and A. Ben David. "Focus of Blame, Defense against Responsibility, and Helping in an Emergency." Unpublished manuscript, 1975.

———. "Responsibility and Helping in an Emergency: Effects of Blame, Ability, and Denial of Responsibility." *Sociometry* 39 (1976): 406–415.

Scott, M. B., and S. M. Lyman. "Accounts." *American Sociological Review* 33 (1968): 46–62.

Shapiro, E. G. "Equity and Equality in the Allocation of Rewards in a Dyad." Paper presented at the American Sociological Association, New Orleans, August 1972. Unpublished Ph.D. dissertation, University of Michigan, 1972.

_____. "The Effect of Expectations of Future Interaction on Reward Allocations in Dyads: Equity or Equality." Unpublished manuscript, University of Iowa, 1973.

Sharp, F. C., and M. C. Otto. "Retribution and Deterrence in the Moral Judgments of Common Sense." *International Journal of Ethics* 20 (1910): 428–458.

Shaw, M. E., and J. L. Sulzer. "An Empirical Test of Heider's Levels in Attribution of Responsibility." *Journal of Abnormal and Social Psychology* 69 (1964): 39–47.

Shelly, M. W., ed. *Analyses of Satisfaction.* Vol. 4–5. Lawrence, Kansas: University of Kansas Press, 1970.

Sigall, H., and D. Landy. "Beauty Is Talent: Task Evaluation as a Function of the Performer's Physical Attractiveness." *Journal of Personality and Social Psychology* 29 (1974); 299–304.

Silverman, A., and A. Silverman. *The Case Against Having Children.* New York: David McKay, Co., 1971.

Silverman, I. "Physical Attractiveness and Courtship." *Sexual Behavior* September 1971, pp. 22–25.

Simmel, G. "A Chapter in the Philosophy of Value." *The American Journal of Sociology* 5 (1900): 577–603.

Simon, P. "El Condor Pasa" (English lyrics). Cross Music, 1970.

Smith, A. *The Theory of Moral Sentiments.* London and New York: Cr. Bell and Sons, 1892.

Smith, B. L. "Effects of Overpayment and Underpayment on Reallocation of Rewards." Unpublished Ph.D. dissertation, University of Mississippi, 1970.

Smith, D. "Equity and Newlyweds' Adjustments." Unpublished Master's thesis, University of Wisconsin, 1977.

Smith, R. J., and P. E. Cook. "Leadership in Dyadic Groups as a Function of Cominance and Incentives." *Sociometry* 36 (1973): 561–568.

Solomon, L. "The Influence of Some Types of Power Relationships and Motivational Treatments upon the Development of Interpersonal Trust." New York: Research Center for Human Relations, New York University, January 1957.

Soule, G. *The Coming American Revolution.* New York: The Macmillan Co., 1935.

Spencer, H. *Essays: Moral, Political and Aesthetic.* New York: Appleton and Co., 1874.

Spock, B. *Baby and Child Care.* New York: Pocket Books, 1957.

Spuhler, J. N. "Assortative Mating with Respect to Physical Characteristics." *Eugenics Quarterly* 15 (1968): 128–140.

Steiner, I. D. *Group Process and Productivity.* New York: Academic Press, 1972.

Stendahl, K. "Religion, Mysticisms, and the Institutional Church." In *Daedalus: Toward the Year 2000: Work in Progress,* p. 854–859. Boston: American Academy of Arts and Sciences, 1967.

Stendler, C. B. "Sixty Years of Child Training Practices." *Journal of Pediatrics* 36 (1950): 122–134.

Stephan, J. F. *Liberty, Equality, Fraternity,* 1873. Reprinted Cambridge: Cambridge University Press, 1967.

Stephenson, G. M., and J. H. White. "An Experimental Study of Some Effects of Injustice on Children's Moral Behavior." *Journal of Experimental Social Psychology* 4 (1968): 460–469.

_____. "Privilege, Deprivation, and Children's Moral Behavior: An Experimental Clarification of the Role of Investments." *Journal of Experimental Social Psychology* 6 (1970): 167–176.

Sternbach, R. A. *Principles of Psychophysiology.* New York: Academic Press, 1966.

Storer, N. W. *The Social System of Science.* New York: Holt, Rinehart and Winston, 1966.

Stouffer, S. A.; E. A. Suchman; L. C. DeVinney; S. A. Star; and R. M. Williams, Jr. *The American Soldier: Adjustment During Army Life.* Vol. 1. Princeton, N.J.: Princeton University Press, 1959.

Streib, G. F. "Family Patterns in Retirement." *Journal of Social Issues* 14 (1958): 46–60.

Stroebe, W.; C. A. Insko; V. D. Thompson; and B. D. Layton. "Effects of Physical Attractiveness, Attitude Similarity, and Sex on Various Aspects of Interpersonal Attraction." *Journal of Personality and Social Psychology* 18 (1971): 79–91.

Stycos, J. M. *Family and Fertility in Puerto Rico.* New York: Columbia University Press, 1955.

Sunley, R. "Early Nineteenth-Century American Literature on Child-Rearing." In *Childhood in Contemporary Cultures.* Edited by M. Mead and M. Wolfenstein, pp. 150–167. Chicago: University of Chicago Press, 1955.

Sussman, M. B., and L. Burchinal. "Kin Family Network: Unheralded Structure in Current Conceptualizations of Family Functioning." *Marriage and Family Living* 24 (1962a): 231–240.

_____. "Parental Aid to Married Children: Implications for Family Functioning." *Marriage and Family Living* 24 (1962b): 320.

Sutherland, E. *Principles of Criminology.* Philadelphia: J. B. Lippincott Co., 1966.

Swain, M. D., and C. V. Kiser. "The Interrelation of Fertility, Fertility Planning, and Ego-Centered Interest in Children." In *Social and Psychological Factors Affecting Fertility,* edited by P. K. Whelpton and C. V. Kiser (1946–1958): 801–834. New York: Milbank Memorial Fund, 1953.

Sykes, G. M., and D. Matza. "Techniques of Neutralization: A Theory of Delinquency." *American Sociological Review* 22 (1957): 664–670.

Tawney, R. H. *Equality.* London: Allen and Unwin, 1939.

Taylor, G. R. *Doomsday Book.* London: Thames and Hudson, 1970.

Teichman, M. "Satisfaction from Interpersonal Relationship following Resource Exchange." Unpublished Ph.D. dissertation, University of Missouri at Columbia, 1971.

Terman, L. M. *Psychological Factors in Marital Happiness.* New York: McGraw-Hill Book Co., 1938.

Tesser, A., and M. Brodie. "A Note on the Evaluation of a 'Computer Date'," *Psychonomic Science* 23 (1971): 300.

Thibaut, J. W. "An Experimental Study of the Cohesiveness of Underprivileged Groups." *Human Relations* 3 (1950): 251–278.

Thibaut, J., and C. Faucheux. "The Development of Contractual Norms in a Bargaining Situation under Two Types of Stress." *Journal of Experimental Social Psychology* 1 (1965): 89–102.

Thibaut, J., and C. L. Gruder. "Formation of Contractual Agreements between Parties of Unequal Power." *Journal of Personality and Social Psychology* 11 (1969): 59–65.

Thibaut, J. W., and H. H. Kelley. *The Social Psychology of Groups.* New York: John Wiley & Sons, 1959.

Thibaut, J. W., and H. W. Riecken. "Some Determinants and Consequences of the Perception of Social Causality." *Journal of Personality* 24 (1955): 113–133.

Thibaut, J.; L. Walker; S. LaTour; and P. Houlden. "Procedural Justice as Fairness." *Stanford Law Review* 26 (1974): 1271–1289.

Toffler, A. *Future Shock.* New York: Bantam, 1970.

Toffler, A., ed., *The Futurists.* New York: Random House, 1972.

Törnblom, K. Y. "Distributive Justice: Typology and Propositions." Unpublished manuscript, 1973.

Tornow, W. W. "Differential Perception of Ambiguous Job Characteristics as Inputs or Outcomes Moderating Inequity Reduction." Ph.D. dissertation, University of Minnesota, 1970.

Traupmann, J. "Equity Restoration and Friendship." Unpublished manuscript, University of Wisconsin, 1975.

Trotsky, L. *History of the Russian Revolution.* Ann Arbor, Mich.: University of Michigan Press, 1957.

Turner, J. L.; E. B. Foa; and U. G. Foa. "Interpersonal Reinforcers: Classification in a Relationship and Some Differential Properties." *Journal of Personality and Social Psychology* 19 (1971): 168–180.

Udry, J. R. *The Social Context of Marriage.* Philadelphia: J. B. Lippincott Co., 1971.

Uesugi, T. K., and W. E. Vinacke. "Strategy in a Feminine Game." *Sociometry* 26 (1963): 75–88.

United Nations. *Mysore Population Study* ST/SOA/SER. A/34. New York: Department of Economics and Social Affairs, 1961.

United Press International, 25 September 1973, 2:17 AED.

Utne, M. K., "Functions of Expressions of Liking in Response to Inequity." Master's thesis, University of Wisconsin at Madison, 1974.

Valenzi, E. R., and I. R. Andrews. "Effect of Hourly Overpay and

Underpay Inequity when Tested with a New Induction Procedure." *Journal of Applied Psychology* 55 (1971): 22–27.

Vershure, B. "Employees' Length of Service, Productivity Level, Age, Subjects' Sex, and the Equitable Distribution of Rewards." Unpublished Master's thesis, Wayne State University, 1974.

Vinacke, W. E. "Power, Strategy, and the Formation of Coalitions in Triads under Four Incentive Conditions." Technical Report no. 1, University of Hawaii, October 1962.

_____. "Variables in Experimental Games: Toward a Field Theory." *Psychological Bulletin* 71 (1969): 293–318.

Vinacke, W. E., and S. Stanley. "Strategy in a Masculine Quiz Game." Technical Report no. 2, University of Hawaii, 1962.

Vroom, V. H. *Work and Motivation.* New York: John Wiley & Sons, 1964.

Waller, W. "The Rating and Dating Complex." *American Sociological Review* 2 (1937): 727–734.

Waller, W., revised by R. Hill. *The Family: A Dynamic Interpretation.* New York: Holt, Rinehart and Winston, 1938.

Wallington, S. A. "Consequences of Transgression: Self-Punishment and Depression." *Journal of Personality and Social Psychology* 28 (1973): 1–7.

Walster, E. "Effect of Self-Esteem on Liking for Dates of Various Social Desirabilities." *Journal of Experimental Social Psychology* 6 (1970): 248–253.

_____. *The Walster Global Measures of Participants' Perceptions of Inputs, Outcomes, and Equity/Inequity,* 1977. (Available from author.)

Walster, E.; V. Aronson; D. Abrahams; and L. Rottman. "Importance of Physical Attractiveness in Dating Behavior." *Journal of Personality and Social Psychology* 4 (1966): 508–516.

Walster, E.; E. Berscheid; and A. N. Barclay. "A Determinant of Preference for Modes of Dissonance Reduction." *Journal of Personality and Social Psychology* 7 (1967): 211–215.

Walster, E.; E. Berscheid; and G. W. Walster. "New Directions in Equity Research." *Journal of Personality and Social Psychology* 25 (1973): 151–176.

Walster, E., and J. A. Piliavin. "Equity and the Innocent Bystander." *Journal of Social Issues* 28 (1972): 165–189.

Walster, E., and P. Prestholdt. "The Effect of Misjudging Another: Overcompensation or Dissonance Reduction?" *Journal of Experimental Social Psychology* 2 (1966): 85–97.

Walster, E.; J. Traupmann; and G. W. Walster. "Equity and Extramarital Sex." *The Archives of Sexual Behavior,* submitted.

Walster, E., and G. W. Walster. "Equity and Social Justice: An Essay." *The Journal of Social Issues* 31 (1975): 21–43.

Walster. E.; G. W. Walster; D. Abrahams; and Z. Brown. "The Effect on Liking of Underrating or Overrating Another." *Journal of Experimental Social Psychology* 2 (1966): 70–84.

Walster, E.; G. W. Walster; and S. Traupmann. Equity and Premarital Sex. Unpublished manuscript, 1977.

Weick, K. E. "Reduction of Cognitive Dissonance through Task Enhancement and Effort Expenditure." *Journal of Abnormal and Social Psychology* 68 (1964): 533–539.

Weick, K. E., and B. Nesset. "Preferences among Forms of Equity." *Organizational Behavior and Human Performance* 3 (1968): 400–416.

Weinstein, A. G., and R. L. Holzbach. "Impact of Individual Differences, Reward Distribution, and Task Structure on Productivity in a Simulated Work Environment." *Journal of Applied Psychology* 58 (1973): 296–301.

Weinstein, E. A.; W. L. DeVaughan; and M. G. Wiley. "Obligation and the Flow of Deference in Exchange." *Sociometry* 32 (1969): 1–12.

Weiss, R. F.; J. L. Boyer; J. P. Lombardo; and M. H. Stitch. "Altruistic Drive and Altruistic Reinforcement." *Journal of Personality and Social Psychology* 25 (1973): 390–400.

Whelpton, P. K.; A. A. Campbell; and J. E. Patterson. *Fertility and Family Planning in the United States.* Princeton, N.J.: Princeton University Books, 1966.

Whiting, J. W. M., and I. L. Child. *Child Training and Personality: Cross-Cultural Study.* New Haven, Conn.: Yale University Press, 1953.

Wicker, A. W., and G. Bushweiler. "Perceived Fairness and Pleasantness of Social Exchange Situations." *Journal of Personality and Social Psychology* 15 (1970): 63–75.

Wiegand, E. *Use of Time by Full-Time and Part-Time Homemakers in Relation to Home Management.* Ithaca, N.Y.: Cornell University Agricultural Experiment Station, 1954.

Wilson, G. "GSR Responses to Fear-Related Stimuli." *Perceptual and Motor Skills* 24 (1967): 401–402.

Wilson, M. *Use of Time by Oregon Farm Homemakers.* Corvallis: Oregon State College Agricultural Station, 1929.

Wolfenstein, M. "Trends in Infant Care." *American Journal of Orthopsychiatry* 23 (1953): 120–130.

Wolff, K. H., translator and editor. *The Sociology of Georg Simmel.* Glencoe, Ill.: The Free Press, 1950.

Worthy, M.; A. L. Gary; and G. M. Kahn. "Self-Disclosure as an Exchange Process." *Journal of Personality and Social Psychology* 13 (1969): 63–69.

Yuchtman, E. "Reward Structure, the Quality of Work Environment, and Social Accounting." In *Corporate Social Accounting,* edited by M. Dierkes and R. A. Bauer, pp. 183–190. New York: Praeger Publishers, 1973.

Zajonc, R. B. "The Concepts of Balance, Congruity, and Dissonance." *Public Opinion Quarterly* 24 (1960): 280–286.

Zaleznik, A.; C. R. Christensen; and F. J. Roethlisberger. "The Motivation, Productivity, and Satisfaction of Workers." Cambridge, Mass.: Graduate School of Business Administration, Harvard University, 1958.

Zelditch, M. Jr.; J. Berger; B. Anderson; and B. P. Cohen. "Equitable Comparisons." *Pacific Sociological Review* 13 (1970): 19–26.

Index